The Complete Idiot's Reference Card

20 Important Words and Phrases

1. Please — Sil vous plaît — *see voo pleh*
2. Thank you very much — Merci beaucoup — *mehr-see boo-koo*
3. You're welcome — De rien, Pas de quoi — *duh ryaN, pahd kwah*
4. Excuse me — Pardon, Excusez-moi — *pahr-dohN, ehk-kew-zay mwah*
5. My name is… — Je m'appelle… — *zhuh mah-pehl*
6. I would like… — Je voudrais… — *zhuh voo-dreh*
7. I need… — Il me faut…, J'ai besoin de… — *eel muh foh, zhay buh-zwaN duh*
8. Do you have… — Avez-vous… — *ah-vay voo*
9. Please give me… — Donnez-moi s'il vous plaît… — *doh-nay mwah seel voo pleh*
10. Could you help me please? — Pourriez-vous m'aider s'il vous plaît? — *poor-yay voo meh-day see voo pleh*
11. Do you speak English? — Parlez-vous anglais? — *pahr-lay voo ahn-leh*
12. I speak a little French — Je parle un peu le français — *zhuh pahrl uhN puh luh frahn-seh*
13. I don't understand — Je ne comprends pas — *zhuh nuh kohN-prahN pah*
14. Please repeat — Répétez, s'il vous plaît — *ray-pay-tay seel voo pleh*
15. What did you say? — Qu'est-ce que vous avez dit? — *kehs-kuh voo ah-vay dee*
16. I'm lost — Je me suis égaré(e) — *zhuh muh swee zay-gah-ray*
17. I'm looking for… — Je cherche… — *zhuh shehsh…*
18. Where are the bathrooms? — Où sont les toilettes? — *oo sohN lay twah-leht*
19. Where is the police station? — Où est le commissariat de police? — *oo eh luh koh-mee-sah-ryah duh poh-lees*
20. Where is the American Embassy? — Où est l'ambassade américaine? — *oo eh l'ahN-bah-sahd ah-may-ree-kahN*

alpha books

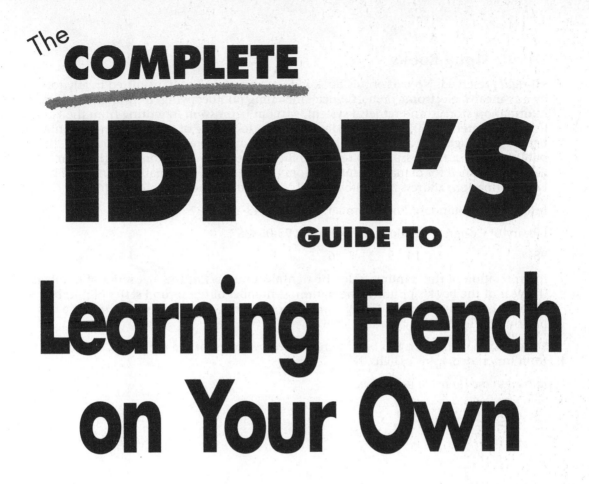

The COMPLETE IDIOT'S GUIDE TO Learning French on Your Own

by Gail Stein

alpha books

A Division of Macmillan General Reference
A Simon & Schuster Macmillan Company
1633 Broadway, 8th Floor, New York, NY 10019

International Standard Book Number: 0-02-861043-1

Library of Congress Catalog Card Number: 95-083357

98   10 9 8 7 6 5

Interpretation of the printing code: the rightmost number of the first series of numbers is the year of the book's printing; the rightmost number of the second series of numbers is the number of the book's printing. For example, a printing of 96-1 shows that the first printing of the book occurred in 1996.

Screen reproductions in this book were created by means of the program Collage Plus from Inner Media, Inc., Hollis, NH.

Printed in the United States of America

Publisher
Theresa Murtha

Editors
Nancy Mikhail
Megan Newman

Copy Editors
Mitzi Foster Gianakos
Anne Owen

Cover Designer
Michael Freeland

Designer
Kim Scott

Illustrators
Jason Hand
Casey Price
Ryan Oldfather

Manufacturing Coordinator
Brook Farling

Production Team Supervisor
Laurie Casey

Indexers
Erika Millen
Carol Sheehan

Production Team
Angela Calvert, Kim Cofer, Tricia Flodder,
Aleata Howard, Christine Tyner, Megan Wade

Contents at a Glance

Contents

17 Let's Eat Out   205

18 Let's Have Fun   227

Foreword

As the eyes are windows to the soul, language provides insight and depth to our understanding of another culture. In fact, knowledge of another language enhances understanding of our own language, and generally it strengthens our ability to communicate more effectively in both.

Images of France and French language have fascinated Americans of all ages throughout our history. Its sound and rhythm are particularly beautiful to the ear and emphasized by a culture that evokes images of fine art, literature, wine, and culinary delights, not to mention romantic love and sex appeal.

It also evokes terror.

Those of us who are perfectionists or can't fathom speaking a French word outside the context of the latest American or British pop tune with a French refrain know what I'm talking about. Those of us who have tried using our high school French on a French waiter know that response that strikes fear in one's heart. You know the one I'm talking about. The one that says in only slightly accented, but perfect English, "I beg your pardon, what did you say you wanted?" Of course, the only thing worse than that is if he actually answers you—in French! Then you have to actually understand his response and pray for the correct reply.

If this troubles you, then hope and salvation are only pages away. Whether you're a beginner or have a few years of French language training under your belt, the *Complete Idiot's Guide to Learning French On Your Own* makes the basics basic and the harder stuff, well, simpler.

It is the primer that will give you the guideposts you'll need to learn this beautiful tongue while reducing your fear of learning it. Whether you fear mastering the accent, or the dreaded subjunctive, there are tips to enlighten you and rules written in a vernacular that any American or English reader can understand.

At the French Institute Alliance Française, New York's French Cultural Center, we immerse our students in French language training, complemented by French films, an electronic learning center, a full French library, and diverse live cultural programs from France and Francophone countries. As the first American Director in over twenty years, my French was more than a little rusty. The first thing I did upon being appointed was to buy a good French-English dictionary. The second thing I would have done—had it been published at the time—would have been to buy the *Complete Idiot's Guide to Learning French On Your Own*—the perfect complement to the uninitiated, the frightened—or the perfectionist who just wants to get it right.

David S. Black
Executive Director
French Institute Alliance Française

Introduction

Years ago, extensive worldwide travel was simply beyond the reach of most of us. Today, modern technology has made the world a smaller place and has put it at our doorstep. It is now up to you to seize every opportunity to discover it and to broaden your horizons, because yesterday's dreams have become today's reality.

Learning French will allow you to open doors to countless opportunities, experiences, and adventures that beckon you at every turn. It will open your eyes, ears, heart, and soul to new cultures, new ideas, new perspectives, and new situations. The bottom line is, you just never know when it will prove to be the handiest, most useful tool you possess. Read the directions, study the language, and learn to use it slowly, carefully, and with love.

This user-friendly book was designed to help you enjoy your learning experience to the fullest. The light, simple, clearcut approach will instill all the confidence you need to be a successful, competent speaker.

Why and How this Book Is Meant for You

The six parts of this book will take you from the very basics to more extensive knowledge of the patterns of the language. Keep in mind that this is not a phrase book, a dictionary, a grammar book, or a tour book. Rather, it is a combination of the four, with an emphasis on teaching you to communicate effectively in everyday situations: to socialize, to give and obtain information, to express your opinions, to persuade friends and family members to follow a course of action and, plainly and simply, to help you get what you want when you want it. Students, tourists, and business people alike will find this book useful, informative, and easy to use. Each chapter is based on a theme that ties together vocabulary, useful phrases, and grammar, and that provides authentic materials and activities that will give you a better understanding of French-speaking people and immerse you in their culture. Here's what the book covers:

Part 1, "The Very Basics," begins by discussing why French should be a part of your life, is followed by a phonetic pronunciation guide designed for the shy and easily intimidated speaker, and then proceeds to show you just how much French you know before you even get started. Idioms, slang, and typical gestures are presented, as well as basic, elementary grammar terms and rules. Almost immediately you will be able to engage in simple conversations and ask and answer easy questions.

Part 2, "Travel," will help you to plan and take a trip. You'll learn how to express greetings and salutations, and introduce, speak about, and describe yourself and your traveling companions. You'll even be able to ask nosy questions. There's a chapter to help you find your way around the airport, and another that will help you get transportation to wherever you are going (even if you are renting a car). You'll find yourself a pro at giving and receiving directions. Finally, this part will ensure that you get the room you want, with all the creature comforts you desire.

Part 3, "Fun and Games," promises that you will have the greatest experience ever. This section presents in detail anything and everything you could possible want to do in a foreign country: sports, concerts, museums, tourist attractions. You will learn how to interpret the weather report, express your opinions and preferences, and make suggestions. More important, the two chapters on food will enable you to understand and expertly order from a menu, and ensure that you dine on the finest dishes that French cuisine has to offer—even if you follow a special diet. Finally, the chapter on shopping will allow you to buy whatever your heart desires, from *haute couture* fashions (don't worry, everything will fit if you use the conversion tables) to souvenirs for your loved ones.

Part 4, "Problems," prepares you for them all. You'll be able to phone home, receive medical attention and assistance, and get your hair done, clothes cleaned, camera fixed, glasses repaired, shoes resoled, prescriptions filled, and mail delivered. You'll even be able to explain what happened in the past.

Part 5, "Let's Get Down to Business," helps you deal with common business transactions. This section includes a mini-dictionary for banking terms. When you're through with this chapter, you'll even be able to buy or rent a piece of property abroad and be able to express your present and future needs.

Part 6, "Answer Key," gives you the answers to all of the exercises in this book.

By the time you have finished this book, you will have studied and practiced skills that will enable you to feel confident in social and business situations where French is required. It is simply a matter of finding the time, being patient, making the effort to test your abilities, and creating your own adventure.

Extras

Besides all the vocabulary lists, useful phrases, and grammatical explanations, this book has lots of useful and interesting information provided here and there in sidebars throughout the text. The following icons set these tidbits apart:

Cultural Tidbits

Cultural Tidbits provide facts about what life is like in France and other French-speaking countries. Should you travel, they will make your trip more rewarding and enjoyable.

Pitfall

A pitfall tells you how to avoid making a mistake.

Tip

A tip tells you how to work with grammar easily, or reminds you of rules you might have forgotten from previous chapters.

Acknowledgments

I would like to acknowledge the contributions, input, support, and interest of the following people:

Natercia Alves, Marie-Claire Antoine, Monika Bergenthal, Vivian Bergenthal, Richard Calcasola of Maximus Hair Salon, Nancy Chu, Trudy Edelman, Richard Edelman, Marc Einsohn, Barbara Gilson, Robert Grandt, François Haas of the Office of the French Treasury, Martin Hyman, Roger Herz of Roger Herz, Inc., Christina Levy, Nancy Lasker of L'Oréal, Max Rechtman, Marie-Madeleine Saphire, and Barbara Shevrin.

This book is dedicated to:

- My wonderfully patient and supportive husband, Douglas
- My incredibly loving and understanding sons, Eric and Michael
- My proud parents, Jack and Sara Bernstein
- My superior consultant and advisor, Roger Herz
- My mentor from the very beginning, Yetta Rosenblum
- The memory of a very special gentleman, Ernest Rothschild—a true professional

Part 1

The Very Basics

Chapter 1

The Top Ten Reasons You Should Study French

In This Chapter

➤ The many virtues of the French language

➤ Where you can use French

➤ Developing a learning strategy

➤ Why you shouldn't be afraid

You've picked up this book, and you're probably wondering, "Should I or shouldn't I?" You're probably asking yourself if it will be difficult, if you'll have the time, if it's going to be worth the effort, and if you'll stick with it. My name may not be Dave, but here are my top ten reasons why you need to study French:

10. You love Colette's romance novels.

9. You'd like to root for the Montréal Canadiens in French.

8. You loved *Les Misérables* so much that you decided to read the original version in its entirety—all 600 plus pages.

7. You want to avoid ordering francs with mustard and sauerkraut.

6. You never know when you're going to run into Catherine Deneuve.

5. You want to impress your date at a French restaurant.

4. You love French movies but find the subtitles too distracting.

3. They won't let you onto the topless beach in Martinique without it.

2. Two words: French Fries.

And finally, the best reason of all:

1. You want to meet St. Exupéry's "Little Prince."

Are you totally convinced that French is the language for you? Now that I have your undivided attention, let's look at some more down-to-earth, realistic reasons you should study French.

What's Your Fancy?

The following are some serious reasons why you might want to study French:

10. **You're a musician, and France is a country where culture is taken seriously.** You long to go to *L'Opéra* and admire its sculptured façade, its magnificent marble staircase, and its elegant foyer. You really like classical music (although you'd never admit it to your friends) and would like to enjoy the operas you love in their native language: *Carmen* by Bizet, *Faust* by Gounod, *Manon* by Massenet, *Samson et Dalila* by Saint-Saëns. Yes, you want to take your studies further.

9. **You're an artist.** Your dream is to sit in the Place du Tertre in Montmartre and paint watercolor scenes of Paris or do charcoal portraits of the tourists who stop by your easel to admire your work. You're pulled to Paris by its many museums: the Musée du Louvre with its *Mona Lisa* and *Venus de Milo*; the Musée d'Orsay with its impressionist collection; the Centre Georges-Pompidou with its fabulous modern art museum; the well-hidden Musée Picasso; and many more. You long to have a picnic lunch at the Musée Rodin while you sit and admire *Le Penseur* (*The Thinker*) or *Le Baiser* (*The Kiss*). Art is your life, and you want to study in a place where it is respected and loved.

8. **You love French movies and long to understand the actors without the distraction of poorly translated subtitles.**

7. **You're not greedy, but you do want to make more money.** France, a leading nation in the European Economic Community, has the fourth largest economy in the world, and you'd like to take advantage of that. *Haute couture* (high fashion), perfume, leather goods, precision instruments, automobiles, chemical and pharmaceutical products, and jewelry are all thriving French industries—France is a European leader.

6. **You want to prove you're smart.** The French language has the reputation of being difficult. This dates back to a time when only the smartest junior-high-school students were offered French. Of course, anyone who's ever studied French knows that it really isn't any more difficult than any other foreign language.

5. **You want to live in a French-speaking country.** You love the language, you love the people, or maybe you've been relocated by your company. Whatever the reason, if you're going to be staying in a French-speaking country for an extended period of time, you've got to learn the language.

4. **You love to cook and have a special passion for fabulous dishes and desserts.** You want to go to original sources and to understand all the food terms and culinary techniques. If you decide to take a cooking course in France, you want to know what's going on.

3. **You love to eat.** Do you consider yourself a gourmet? If so, then a basic knowledge of French, especially the culinary terms, is a must. Whether you prefer *nouvelle, haute,* or traditional cuisine, Cajun specialties, regional or native dishes, French cooking is truly considered the world's greatest. Whether you eat in Paris or New Orleans, Algeria or Port-au-Prince, the city or the country, you can be sure that the food you are served is fresh and appetizing, and that it has been expertly and lovingly prepared by a chef who takes great pride in his or her work. And a good French wine accompanying your meal is a tribute to the prestige and excellence of this industry in France.

2. **You want to be totally irresistible, and you truly believe that speaking French will attract that special someone.** You're probably right. French, more than any other language, has the reputation of being "the language of love." It doesn't even matter what you say. Just whisper any of the beautiful, flowing, songlike phrases in someone's ear to "Wow!" them and to make their heart beat faster. It's practically foolproof.

1. **You love to travel.** In addition to France, there are more than 40 French-speaking countries in the world, where more than 100 million people speak French on a daily basis. Whether you travel for business or pleasure, romance or adventure, excitement or relaxation, your choices include: sensuous tropical islands with white, sandy beaches; lush rain forests with luxuriant, native vegetation; tempting snow-covered mountains perfect for winter sports; sweaty, sultry jungles where special thrills lurk everywhere; fortified ancient villages where history comes to life or bustling, modern cities where the future rapidly unfolds. You don't have to go far: Louisiana, Maine, New Hampshire, Vermont, Massachusetts, Canada, or you could find yourself across the globe in distant, exotic lands in Africa or Asia. Perhaps you will simply be one of the more than 60 million tourists who visit France each year. The possibilities and opportunities are endless.

Full Speed Ahead

The best way to become proficient in something is to plunge right in. Immerse yourself in anything and everything that is French. Have a love affair with the language and the culture. Follow these suggestions to ensure a long-lasting and fulfilling relationship:

➤ Examine your goals, honestly evaluate your linguistic abilities, and pace yourself accordingly. Take your time, don't rush, and set aside special time each day that you devote only to French.

➤ Invest in or borrow a good bilingual dictionary. Pocket varieties (usually running between $6 and $10) may suit the needs of some learners but prove somewhat deficient for others. Carefully peruse what is available in your local bookstore or library before making a decision on what is best for you. Current popular dictionaries that are easy to use and that provide a comprehensive listing of current, colloquial vocabulary words are:

Collins-Robert (approximately $25)

Larousse (approximately $50)

➤ Take advantage of all opportunities to listen to the language. Rent French movies and try not to read the English subtitles. If broadcast in your area, listen to public service radio or television stations that provide French programs. Search bookstores and public or college libraries for language tapes that will help you hear and master the French sound system. Create your own tapes and use them to perfect your accent. Ask to use language laboratories and computer programs that are available in many high schools and universities.

➤ Read everything you can get your hands on: fairy tales, children's books, comic books (*Astérix* is my personal favorite), newspapers: *Le Monde, France-Soir, Le Figaro, Libération, Le Dauphiné Libéré*, magazines: *Paris Match, Elle, L'Express, Marie-Claire*. If you're not too bashful, read aloud and practice your pronunciation and comprehension at the same time.

Create *un coin français* (a French corner) in a convenient spot in your home. Decorate it with posters or articles. Label items whose names you want to learn and display them for easy viewing. Keep all your materials together and organized in this special French spot.

There's Nothing to Fear

Some people are truly afraid to study a foreign language. They think that it'll be too much work, too hard, too time-consuming. In reality, if you take it slow and don't allow yourself to become overly concerned with grammar and pronunciation, you will manage very well. To help you feel more at ease, try to remember the following:

➤ **Don't be intimidated by the grammar.** Everyone makes mistakes—even native speakers. And besides, usually only one or two correct words (especially verbs) will enable you to be understood.

➤ **Don't be intimidated by the pronunciation.** Put on your best French accent, don't be shy, and speak, speak, speak. In any country, there are many different regional accents. Certainly yours will fit in somewhere!

➤ **Don't be intimidated by the French.** They are perfectly lovely people and accept anyone who makes a sincere attempt to communicate.

➤ **Don't be intimidated by the reputation French has for being difficult.** As you will see, almost immediately, French is easy and fun.

Bonne chance! (*Buhn shahNs!*) Good luck! Let's begin *tout de suite* (*toot sweet*) (immediately)!

The Least You Need to Know

➤ Everyone, from every walk of life, can find a reason to study French.

➤ French is a very useful language to know because it is spoken throughout the world.

➤ You can get by even if your grammar and pronunciation are less than perfect.

➤ There's nothing to fear. Learning French really isn't that difficult.

➤ To become a *francophone* (French speaker), you must first be a *francophile* (lover of French).

ENUNCIATE!

Chapter 2

Pronounce It Properly

In This Chapter

➤ The stress of it all

➤ Finding fluidity

➤ Getting the accent

➤ Phonetically yours

When you speak French, you want to sound like they do in the movies: irresistible, romantic, sexy, sophisticated, chic. It's only natural. So lose your inhibitions, put on your best French accent, and repeat and practice the sounds of the language. Although different from English, these sounds are not too difficult to master. Just follow the rules, learn the proper pronunciation of the phonetic symbols, be patient, and you're on your way!

This is a *work* chapter. It's not terribly exciting, it's not particularly fun, and it's not especially amusing—but don't be reluctant to see it through. Just like anything you might have to learn (a sport, a hobby, a trade or profession), there's work involved, and you must be committed to putting in a certain amount of effort. Think of learning a language as a mental fitness routine. Start slowly and carefully work up to a pace that suits you. Remember, you don't want to burn yourself out at the first workout. So give it your best shot and practice, practice, practice.

Do You Have Stress?

In French, each syllable of a word has just about equal stress, so when speaking, try to pronounce each syllable of a word with equal emphasis. When you remember, place a slightly stronger emphasis on the last syllable of a group of words. Speak smoothly, speak musically, and speak evenly. My best advice: For maximum results, stay on an even keel.

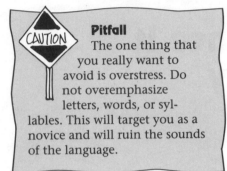

Pitfall
The one thing that you really want to avoid is overstress. Do not overemphasize letters, words, or syllables. This will target you as a novice and will ruin the sounds of the language.

Shall We Have a Liaison? Or Would You Prefer an Elision?

Liaison (linking) and *elision* (sliding) are two linguistic elements of the French language that give it its fluidity and melodious beauty.

Liaison

Liaison refers to the linking of the final consonant of one word with the beginning vowel of the next word. There are many rules in French explaining when a liaison is mandatory, optional, and forbidden. I could go on for pages boring you with rules you'll probably never remember. For that reason, simply follow the pronunciation guide provided in this chapter and the phonetic keys for words and phrases throughout the book. Make a liaison when you see that the pronunciation of the last consonant sound of one word precedes the beginning vowel of the next word. Look at the first example to get a better idea. The first word is *vous*, pronounced *voo*. Its final *s* (pronounced *z*) is linked to the beginning of the next word, *arrivez*. The pronunciation of this word is now *zah-ree-vay*, and the necessary liaison has been painlessly achieved. When in doubt, follow the guide.

As a Rule
Keep the following in mind:

> *H* and *Y* are considered vowels in French.

An *N* in the pronunciation guide refers to nasal sounds, which are explained in more detail later in this chapter.

Words	Liaison
Vous arrivez	*voo zah-ree-vay*
mon ami	*mohN nah-mee*

Elision

Elision occurs when there are two pronounced vowel sounds: one at the end of a word, and the other at the beginning of the next word. The first vowel is dropped and replaced by an apostrophe. To pronounce the words, simply slide them together. If you try to say them separately, the vowel sounds will clash, and you will probably feel like you have a word stuck in your throat. Elision is a very natural device and gives the language fluidity. The following is an example of elision:

Words	Elision	Pronunciation
Je arrive	J'arrive	*zah-reev*
le hôtel	l'hôtel	*lo-tehl*

Accentuate the Positive

If this is your first experience with a foreign language, you'll probably be mystified by accent marks. Just think of them as pronunciation guideposts that will help you speak like an old pro.

Your Own Personal Accent

For some, French pronunciation is a breeze. If you are lucky enough to have been born with a "good ear," chances are you can carry a tune or play a musical instrument. You'll imitate the lilt, intonation, and stress without a problem.

For most of us, however, pronunciation is not without problems. If this is you, you're in good company. Consider my former college French literature teacher, a Rhodes scholar from Oxford University, who later went on to become chairman of the Romance Language Department. He was charming, interesting, sweet, very, very intellectual, well-read, and knowledgeable. He also had the worst French accent I have ever heard. He pronounced every word, every syllable, every letter so harshly and with such stress and emphasis that the students would sit in class squinting in pain. He butchered the pronunciation so much that it was memorable.

In my more naïve days, I often wondered why he would teach a language he obviously had so much trouble speaking. When I think back, I realize that it really didn't matter at all. Why? Because we all understood him despite his terrible pronunciation. And that, *débutant(e)s*, is a very valuable lesson for us all. No matter what you sound like (and you couldn't sound any worse than this teacher), if you use the correct vocabulary words, you will be able to make yourself understood. That should be your goal. Nobody is going to laugh at you; they might just say "Pardon" more than usual. In the end, your level of competence in pronunciation is no big deal. So relax, try your best, and, above all, don't be discouraged.

Accent Marks

There are five different accent marks in French that may be used to change the sounds of letters (é versus è, a versus â, and so on), to differentiate between the meanings of two words whose spellings are otherwise the same (a *has* and à *to, at*, ou *or* and où *where*, and so on) or to replace an *s* that was part of the word many centuries ago in old French.

An *accent aigu* (´) is seen only on an *e* (´).

é produces the sound (*ay*), as in *day*.

An *accent grave* (`) is used with *a* (à), *e* (è), and *u* (ù).

On an *e*, an accent grave produces the sound of (*eh*) as the *e* in the English word *met*.

It doesn't change the sound of the a (à) or u (ù).

An accent *circonflexe* may be used on all vowels: â, ê, î, ô, û. The vowel sounds are longer for â and ô, are slightly longer for ê, and are imperceptible on î and û.

A *cédille* (ç) is used only on a *c* (ç). When the *c* comes before *a*, *o*, or *u*, it means that you pronounce the letter as a soft *c* (the sound of *s*).

A *tréma* (¨) occurs on a second vowel in a series. This accent indicates that the two vowels are pronounced separately, each having its own distinct sound: Haïti (*ay-ee-tee*), Noël (*noh-ehl*).

As a Rule
The *é* may replace an *s* that used to exist in the word in old French. Adding a mental *s* immediately after é may enable you to easily determine the meaning of a word. See if the meaning jumps out at you:

éponge (as in *sponge*)

étranger (as in *stranger*)

As a Rule
This circumflex also often replaces an *s* from old French. Simply stick a mental *s* in the word to see if the meaning jumps out at you: *arrêter* (as in *arrest*), *fête* (as in *feast, festival*).

There Sure Are a Lot of Vowel Sounds!

French vowels are a bit complicated. Why? In general, each vowel has a number of different sounds, and there are specific rules and accent marks that help you determine how a vowel is to be pronounced. I've included some practice exercises to help you. Some of the sentences are pretty silly, but they will help you learn how to pronounce the vowel sounds.

> **As a Rule**
> Remember: The accent grave over the *a* (*à*) doesn't change the pronunciation, while the (*â*) is given a longer sound.

French Letter	Symbol	Pronunciation Guide
a, à, â	ah	Say *a* as in *spa*

Open wide (but not too wide) and say *ahhh*....

ça la	ma	sa	ta	va	papa	Canada
sah lah	*mah*	*sah*	*tah*	*vah*	*pah-pah*	*kah-nah-dah*

French Letter	Symbol	Pronunciation Guide
é final *er* and *ez*; *es* in some one-syllable words; a few *ai*, *et* combinations	ay	Say *ay* as in *day*

é, final *er*, and *ez* are always pronounced *ay*. Instead of driving yourself crazy trying to remember the rules (which are vague), just look at the following guide.

bébé	télé	météo	été	René
bay-bay	*tay-lay*	*may-tay-o*	*ay-tay*	*ruh-nay*
danser	arriver	désirer	parler	tourner
dahN-say	*ah-ree-vay*	*day-zee-ray*	*pahr-lay*	*toor-nay*
chez	nez	allez	passez	assez
shay	*nay*	*ah-lay*	*pah-say*	*ah-say*

continues

des	les	mes	tes	ces
day	*lay*	*may*	*tay*	*say*
ai	gai			
ay	*gay*			
et				
ay				

As a Rule

et (meaning *and*) and *ai* (used with *j'* meaning *I have*) will obviously crop up a lot. Because of their high frequency, it's best to learn them as soon as possible. You'll be glad you did.

French Letter	Symbol	Pronunciation Guide
e in one-syllable words or in the middle of a word followed by a single consonant	uh	Say *e* as in *the*

Again, this is another rule that requires too much thought for simple conversational French. Consult the pronunciation guide until the rule becomes second nature.

ce	je	le	ne	de
suh	*zhuh*	*luh*	*nuh*	*duh*
regarder	demander	prenons	venir	repasser
ruh-gahr-day	*duh-mahN-day*	*pruh-nohN*	*vuh-neer*	*ruh-pah-say*

French Letter	Symbol	Pronunciation Guide
è, ê, and *e* (plus two consonants or a final pronounced consonant) *et, ei, ai*	eh	Say *e* as in *met*

At this point, don't overwhelm yourself with rules. When in doubt, let the guide do the work for you. With practice, you'll get the hang of it.

très	mère	père	achète	bibliothèque
treh	*mehr*	*pehr*	*ah-sheht*	*bee-blee-oh-tehk*

fête	tête	être	même	prêter
feht	*teht*	*ehtr*	*mehm*	*preh-tay*
est	sept	rester	concert	Suzette
eh	*seht*	*reh-stay*	*kohN-sehr*	*sew-zeht*
quel	sel	chef	cher	cette
kehl	*sehl*	*shehf*	*shehr*	*seht*
ballet	bonnet	jouet	complet	cabinet
bah-leh	*bohN-neh*	*zhoo-eh*	*kohN-pleh*	*kah-bee-neh*
seize	treize	Seine	peine	pleine
sehz	*trehz*	*sehn*	*pehn*	*plehn*
aider	jamais	chaise	mais	américaine
eh-day	*zhah-meh*	*shehz*	*meh*	*ah-may-ree-kehn*

French Letter	Symbol	Pronunciation Guide
i, î, y, ui	ee	Say *i* as in *magazine*

Smile and show your teeth when you say *ee*.

il	ici	midi	timide	visiter
eel	*ee-see*	*mee-dee*	*tee-meed*	*vee-zee-tay*
Sylvie	lycée	mystère	dîne	île
seel-vee	*lee-say*	*mee-stehr*	*deen*	*eel*
huit	nuit	qui	guide	bruit
weet	*nwee*	*kee*	*geed*	*brwee*

French Letter	Symbol	Pronunciation Guide
i + ll il when preceded by a vowel	y	Say *y* as in *your*

For the *ill, ail,* or *eil* combinations, remember to keep the *l* silent.

fille	famille	gentille	billet
fee-y	*fah-mee-y*	*zhahN-tee-y*	*bee-yeh*
travail	soleil	oeil	détail
trah-vahy	*soh-lehy*	*uhy*	*day-tahy*

French Letter	Symbol	Pronunciation Guide
i + ll in these words only	eel	Say the word *eel*

Every rule has an exception; or in this case, because there aren't too many, the words might be worth memorizing—especially because they're used frequently.

ville	village	mille	million	tranquille
veel	*vee-lahzh*	*meel*	*mee-lyohN*	*trahN-keel*

French Letter	Symbol	Pronunciation Guide
o (before *se*), *o* (last pronounced sound of word), *ô*, *au*, *eau*	o	Say *o* as in *no*

Keep your lips rounded to pronounce this very open *o* sound. Once again, for *o*, there are many letter combinations you will have to learn eventually. For the time being, follow the pronunciation guide.

radio	trop	mot	stylo	vélo
rah-dyo	*tro*	*mo*	*stee-lo*	*vay-lo*
hôtel	allô	tôt	bientôt	hôpital
o-tehl	*ah-lo*	*to*	*byaN-to*	*o-pee-tahl*
au	aussi	jaune	autre	auteur
o	*o-see*	*zhon*	*otr*	*o-tuhr*
eau	beau	cadeau	gâteau	manteau
o	*bo*	*kah-do*	*gah-to*	*mahN-to*

French Letter	Symbol	Pronunciation Guide
o when followed by a pronounced consonant other than *s*	oh	*o* as in *love*

This *o* sound is not nearly as rounded and open as the one before. It may take some practice to distinguish between the two. If you can't, don't worry—chances are no one is listening that closely anyway. As you practice, try to hear the difference.

notre	pomme	donner	téléphone	octobre
nohtr	*pohm*	*doh-nay*	*tay-lay-fohn*	*ohk-tohbr*

French Letter	Symbol	Pronunciation Guide
ou, où, oû	oo	*Say oo as in tooth*

Round your lips to say *oo*.

toujours	écouter	douze	doux	beaucoup	où	goût
too-zhoor	*ay-koo-tay*	*dooz*	*doo*	*bo-koo*	*oo*	*goo*

French Letter	Symbol	Pronunciation Guide
oy, oi	wah	Say *w* as in *watch*

moi	trois	soir	froid	voiture	pourquoi
mwah	*trwah*	*swahr*	*frwah*	*vwah-tewr*	*poor-kwah*
voyage	voyez				
vwah-yahzh	*vwah-yay*				

French Letter	Symbol	Pronunciation Guide
u, û	ew	No equivalent

There really is no English sound that is equivalent to the French *u* sound. Try the following for best results: Say the sound *oo* as in *Sue* while trying to say *ee* as in *see*. As you try to make the sound, concentrate on puckering your lips as if you just ate a very sour pickle. That's about as close as you can get. If you say *oo*, don't worry, you'll be understood. This is a foreign sound that requires concentration and practice.

Pitfall
You may be tempted to pronounce *oi* like *oy*, as the sound heard at the beginning of the word *oyster*. Avoid the pitfall. Practice the correct *wa* sound until you get it down pat.

super	sur	tu	du	une	salut
scw-pchr	*sewr*	*tew*	*dew*	*ewn*	*sah-lew*

So That's Why I Have a Nose

You must use your nose and your mouth to produce a French nasal sound. Here's how it's done. Hold your nose, then use your mouth to say the vowel sound. It's that simple. Of

Pitfall
Be careful: There is no nasal sound in the following combinations:

vowel + MM,
vowel + M + vowel

vowel + NN, vowel + N + vowel

Word	Pronunciation
homme	uhm
bonne	bohn

course you're not going to walk around with your hand on your nose. That's just a technique to get you started and to make you aware of what a nasal sound should sound like. We are so accustomed to taking English pronunciation for granted that we never stop to consider how we produce certain sounds. When learning a foreign language, it's sometimes necessary to pause and think about the sounds we want to make.

Nasal sounds will occur when a vowel is followed by a single *N* or *M* in the same syllable. In the pronunciation guide, you will see a vowel sound followed by *N*. This indicates that you must make a nasal sound.

French Nasal	Symbol	Pronunciation Guide
an (am), en (em)	ahN	Similar to *on* with little emphasis on *n*

Now hold your nose, say *on,* and you'll quickly get the hang of it. Watch for the *N* indicating the vowel sound.

français	dans	anglais	grand
frahN-seh	*dahN*	*ahN-gleh*	*grahN*
lampe	maman	ambiance	ambition
lahNp	*mah-mahN*	*ahN-byahNs*	*ahN-bee-syohN*
en	encore	souvent	attendre
ahN	*ahN-kohr*	*soo-vahN*	*ah-tahNdr*
décembre	temps	sembler	employé
day-sahNbr	*tahN*	*sahN-blay*	*ahN-plwah-yay*

French Nasal	Symbol	Pronunciation Guide
in (im), ain (aim)	aN	Similar to *an* with little emphasis on *n*

Hold your nose again and practice the sounds:

cinq	Martin	cousin	demain	américain
saNk	*mahr-taN*	*koo-zaN*	*duh-maN*	*ah-may-ree-kaN*
simple	important	impossible	impatient	faim
saNpl	*aN-pohr-tahN*	*aN-poh-seebl*	*aN-pah-syahN*	*faN*

French Nasal	Symbol	Pronunciation Guide
oin	waN	Similar to *wa* of *wag*

You should be getting the hang of nasals by now. Try these:

loin	coin	moins	point	soin
lwaN	*kwaN*	*mwaN*	*pwaN*	*swaN*

French Nasal	Symbol	Pronunciation Guide
ien	yaN	Similar to *yan* of *Yankee*

Try these sounds:

bien	rien	vient	italien	Lucien
byaN	*ryaN*	*vyaN*	*ee-tahl-yaN*	*lew-syaN*

French Nasal	Symbol	Pronunciation Guide
on (om)	ohN	Similar to *on* as in *long*

Here are some more to try:

on	bon	sont	non	onze	pardon
ohN	*bohN*	*sohN*	*nohN*	*ohNz*	*pahr-dohN*
tomber	bombe	comprendre	compter	combien	
tohN-bay	*bohNb*	*kohN-prahNdr*	*kohN-tay*	*kohN-byaN*	

French Nasal	Symbol	Pronunciation Guide
un (um)	uhN	Similar to *un* as in *under*

Be patient for the last of the nasal sounds:

un	brun	lundi	parfum	emprunter
uhN	*bruhN*	*luhN-dee*	*pahr-fuhN*	*ahN-pruhN-tay*

Continuing with Consonants

Most final consonants are not pronounced except for final *c, r, f,* and *l* (think of the word *careful*). Final *s* is not pronounced in French, so avoid the temptation. Doing so will quickly unveil your amateur status.

Éric	Luc	avec	parc
ay-reek	*lewk*	*ah-vehk*	*pahrk*
amour	bonjour	tour	cour
ah-moor	*bohN-zhoor*	*toor*	*koor*
neuf	sauf	chef	actif
nuhf	*sof*	*shehf*	*ahk-teef*
il	Michel	journal	cheval
eel	*mee-shehl*	*zhoor-nahl*	*shuh-vahl*

BUT

salut	dessert	beaucoup	minutes
sah-lew	*duh-sehr*	*bo-koo*	*mee-newt*

French Letter	Symbol	Pronunciation Guide
b, d, f, k, l, m, n, p, s, t, v, z	The same	Same as English

These letters are all so easy because they are pronounced exactly the same in French and in English. You will, however, have to follow the rules for the pronunciation of other consonants.

French Letter	Symbol	Pronunciation Guide
c (hard sound before *a, o, u,* or consonant) *qu,* final *q*	k	Say *c* as in *card*

carte	court	document	classe	
kahrt	*koor*	*doh-kew-mahN*	*klahs*	
qui	quoi	quatre	pourquoi	cinq
kee	*kwah*	*kahtr*	*poor-kwah*	*saNk*

French Letter	Symbol	Pronunciation Guide
c (soft sound before *e, i, y*), *ç, s* at beginning of word, *s* next to a consonant, *tion* (*t*), *x* (only in the words given)	s	*cent*

As you can see, there are lots of ways to get the *s* sound. Practice them all:

ce	cinéma	Nancy	ça
suh	*see-nay-mah*	*nahN-see*	*sah*
nation	attention	invitation	action
nah-syohN	*ah-tahN-syohN*	*aN-vee-tah-syohNn*	*ahk-syohN*
six	dix	soixante	
sees	*dees*	*swah-sahNt*	

French Letter	Symbol	Pronunciation Guide
ch	sh	Say the *ch* in *machine*

We've all had practice with this sound—especially those of us with children. *Shhh.*

chanter	chocolat	sandwich	toucher
shahN-tay	*shoh-koh-lah*	*sahNd-weesh*	*too-shay*

French Letter	Symbol	Pronunciation Guide
g (hard sound before *a, o, u*, or consonant), *gu* (before *i, e, y*)	g	Say the *g* in *good*

These words should present no problem:

garçon	goûter	glace	légume
gahr-sohN	*goo-tay*	*glahs*	*lay-gewm*
Guy	bague	fatigué	guide
gee	*bahg*	*fah-tee-gay*	*geed*

French Letter	Symbol	Pronunciation Guide
g (soft sound before *e, i, y*), ge (soft before *a, o*), *j*	zh	Say the *s* as in *pleasure*

This might take a little practice before you get used to it:

garage	girafe	Gisèle	Égypte
gah-razh	*zhee-rahf*	*zhee-zehl*	*ay-zheept*

âge	orange	manger	voyageons
ahzh	*oh-rahNzh*	*mahN-zhay*	*vwah-yah-zhohN*

je	jour	jaune	jupe
zhuh	*zhoor*	*zhon*	*zhewp*

French Letter	Symbol	Pronunciation Guide
gn	ny	Say the *n* as in *union*

This sound will take some practice, too. Be careful not to overemphasize it:

montagne	Espagne	gagner	accompagner
mohN-tah-nyuh	*ehs-pah-nyuh*	*gah-nyay*	*ah-kohN-pah-nyay*

French Letter	Symbol	Pronunciation Guide
h		Always silent

We've come to the easiest letter of all. *H* is always silent. Most of the time, it is used as a vowel and, therefore, requires elision with a vowel that might precede it: *l'homme* (*the man*). In other instances, *h* is used as a consonant and does not require elision with the preceding vowel: *le héros*. To tell how *h* is being used, you must look in a dictionary, where the consonant *h* is usually indicated with an *.

huit	hôtel	heure	homme
weet	*o-tehl*	*uhr*	*ohm*

French Letter	Symbol	Pronunciation Guide
r	r	No equivalent

The French *r* requires the participation of your throat. First, drop your tongue to the bottom of your mouth and rest it against your teeth. Keep it out pressed there, out of your way. Now clear your throat or gargle and say "r" at the back of your throat at the same time. That's it—you've got the French *r*. A few words of advice: Do not roll your *r*; that's what they do in Spanish. Do not roll your tongue; that's what we do in English. This will require a fair amount of practice on your part until you get it down pat.

merci	au revoir	parler	rentrer
mehr-see	*o ruh-vwahr*	*pahr-lay*	*rahN-tray*

French Letter	Symbol	Pronunciation Guide
s (between vowels), *sion*	z	Say *z* as in *zero*

This sound is easy:

musée	musique	cousin	télévision
mew-zay	*mew-zeek*	*koo-zaN*	*tay-lay-vee-zyohN*

French Letter	Symbol	Pronunciation Guide
th	t	Say *t* as in *to*

There is no **th** sound in French. Native French speakers have a tremendous amount of difficulty with our words *the*, *this*, and *there* because they pronounce *th* as *t*. You, of course, will want to say *th*. Don't. Your nationality will be showing again.

Catherine	thé	théâtre	sympathique
kah-treen	*tay*	*tay-ahtr*	*saN-pah-teek*

French Letter	Symbol	Pronunciation Guide
x	ks	Say *xc* as in *excel*

This last sound (that's right, we've finally reached the end) is a little tricky. Practice it well:

extra	mixte	excellent	exprimer
ehks-trah	*meekst*	*ehk-seh-lahN*	*ehks-pree-may*

Practice Makes Perfect

Now that you are an expert, put on your best accent and practice pronouncing these names that were taken from a Parisian phone book:

You will notice that many French family names begin with *Le* and *La* and are taken from elements in nature. It really does lend an extra beauty to the language when the people are named for beautiful things. In number 14, however, I am sure that Jean Lavache (*John the Cow*) would probably have been happier had his ancestors been associated with something different.

1. Éric Le Parc
2. Colette Lapierre
3. Michel Lechien
4. Alain Lechat
5. Agnès Leloup
6. Roland Lamouche
7. Patrick Leboeuf
8. Solange Laforêt
9. Philippe Lebec
10. Florence Lavigne
11. Monique Le Pont
12. Dominique Lafontaine
13. Daniel La Tour
14. Jean Levache
15. Jeanne Larivière
16. Hubert La Fleur

The Least You Need to Know

➤ Perfect your pronunciation by losing your inhibitions and by reading aloud French newspapers, magazines, and literature.

➤ It's best to allow yourself to slip and slide the sounds together while speaking the language.

➤ If your accent is poor, you'll still be understood.

➤ Practice and devotion will help improve your accent.

➤ Remember that some French accents change the sound of the letter on which they appear.

➤ Use your nose wisely for the correct pronunciation of French nasal sounds.

Chapter 3

You Know More Than You Think

> ### In This Chapter
>
> ➤ Cognates help you understand French
>
> ➤ Tricks to help you understand even more
>
> ➤ French words in the English language
>
> ➤ Pitfalls and traps to avoid

Café, restaurant, amateur, boutique, bureau—the list of French words that you already know is surprisingly extensive. You see, you really do know a lot of French. You don't realize it yet, but your vocabulary is filled with French words and phrases. And there are plenty of French words and expressions that you will find very easy to use and understand with a minimal amount of effort. By the end of this chapter, you will be well on your way to producing intelligent but simple sentences that will allow you to express feelings, thoughts, and opinions.

What You Already Know

There is absolutely nothing on television. After watching the news in French on a local cable station, my husband (who has no French blood coursing through his veins) takes off for the local video rental store to choose some entertainment for the evening. An hour later he returns with a wide grin on his face and cheerfully exclaims: "Oiseau ([wah-zo] that's French for bird, his term of endearment for me), I've got a surprise for you." I wait in eager anticipation to hear that he rented a hot, new release fresh from the theater. Instead, he informs me that he picked out the latest French film.

As a Rule

All French nouns are preceded by a definite article, "the," which indicates gender and number. This will probably seem awkward at first. For the time being, keep in mind that to express "I love chocolate mousse," you must say, "J'adore *la* mousse au chocolat."

le is for masculine singular nouns

la is for feminine singular nouns

l' is for any singular noun that begins with a vowel

Nouns and their definite articles are explained in greater detail in Chapter 6.

As a francophile, I should be jumping for joy, but he can read the disappointment on my face. Truth be told, I find French movies lacking in adventure, and I don't love character studies. The subtitles are extremely distracting. He, on the other hand, can't wait to get the film into the VCR, and I can't understand why. It's true that he had two years of college French, but that was over 30 years ago, and I did all his homework. The Cs he passed with were certainly not an indication of a love affair with the language. So why French films? He likes exotic movies, he loves to hear the language, and, believe it or not, he can understand what the actors and actresses are saying. How can that be? He never listened as a student. How does the man do it?

The simple answer is *cognates*. What are they? Quite simply, a *cognate* is a word that is spelled exactly the same, or almost the same, as a word in English and that has the same meaning. Sometimes we've actually borrowed the word from the French, letter for letter, and have incorporated it into our own vocabulary. Sure, the cognates are pronounced differently in each language, but the meaning of the French word is quite obvious to anyone who speaks English.

Perfect Cognates

Table 3.1 is a list of some cognates that are exactly the same in both French and English. Take your time pronouncing the French words and compare them to their English equivalents. Your goal is to sound French.

Table 3.1 Perfect Cognates

Adjectives	Nouns		
	Le	*La*	*L'*
blond *blohN*	ballet *bah-leh*	blouse *blooz*	accident *ahk-see-dahN*
capable *kah-pahbl*	bureau *bew-ro*	boutique *boo-teek*	accord *ah-kohr*
certain *sehr-taN*	chef *shehf*	date *daht*	ambulance *ahN-bew-lahNs*
content *kohN-tahN*	client *klee-yahN*	dispute *dees-pewt*	animal *ah-nee-mahl*
grave *grahv*	guide *geed*	note *noht*	olive *oh-leev*
horrible *oh-reebl*	hamburger *ahm-bewr-gehr*	permission *pehr-mee-syohN*	omelette *ohm-leht*
immense *ee-mahNs*	journal *zhoor-nahl*	photo *foh-to*	orange *oh-rahnzh*
orange *oh-rahnzh*	sandwich *sahNd-weesh*	route *root*	
permanent *pehr-mah-nahN*	service *sehr-vees*	signification *see-nyee-fee-kah-syohN*	
possible *poh-seebl*	soda *soh-dah*	table *tahbl*	

The rules governing the agreement of adjectives with the nouns they modify will be discussed in detail in Chapter 9.

How Much Do You Understand Already?

I'd venture to guess that, by now, you're in the same league as my husband. The sentences below should be a snap to understand, and the pronunciation should present no problem if you patiently follow the key. Don't be shy! Give it your best effort.

Read the following sentences in French. What are you saying? (*Est* expresses *is* in French.)

1. La blouse est orange.
   lah blooz eh toh-rahNzh

2. Le service est horrible.
   luh sehr-vees eh toh-reebl

3. L'excursion est impossible.
   lehk-skewr-zyohN eh taN-poh-seebl

4. Le guide est capable.
   luh geed eh kah-pahbl

5. Le client est certain.
   luh klee-yahN eh sehr-taN

Near Cognates

Table 3.2 lists the cognates that are nearly the same in both French and English. Take your time pronouncing the French words and compare them to their English equivalents. Remember: Your goal is to sound French.

Table 3.2 Near Cognates

Adjectives	Nouns		
	Le	*La*	*L'*
actif *ahk-teef*	balcon *bahl-kohN*	banane *bah-nahn*	acteur *ahk-tuhr*
aimable *eh-mahbl*	bébé *bay-bay*	banque *bahNk*	adresse *ah-drehs*
ambitieux *ahN-bee-syuh*	café *kah-fay*	bicyclette *bee-see-kleht*	affaire *ah-fehr*
américain *ah-may-ree-kaN*	cinéma *see-nay-mah*	carotte *kah-roht*	âge *ahzh*
amusant *ah-mew-zahN*	coton *koh-tohN*	cathédrale *kah-tay-drahl*	agence *ah-zhahNs*
ancien *ahN-syaN*	dictionnaire *deek-syoh-nehr*	chambre *shahNbr*	anniversaire *ah-nee-vehr-sehr*
bleu *bluh*	dîner *dee-nay*	couleur *koo-luhr*	appartement *ah-pahr-tuh-mahN*
confortable *kohN-fohr-tahbl*	directeur *dee-rehk-tuhr*	enveloppe *ahN-vlohp*	artiste *ahr-teest*
curieux *kew-ryuh*	docteur *dohk-tuhr*	famille *fah-mee-y*	éléphant *ay-lay-fahN*
délicieux *day-lee-syuh*	jardin *zhahr-daN*	fontaine *fohN-tehn*	employé *ahN-plwah-yay*
différent *dee-fay-rahN*	juge *zhewzh*	guitare *gee-tahr*	enfant *ahN-fahN*

Adjectives	Nouns		
	Le	*La*	*L'*
difficile *dee-fee-seel*	légume *lay-gewm*	lampe *lahNp*	exemple *ehks-zahNpl*
élégant *ay-lay-gahN*	mécanicien *may-kah-nee-syaN*	lettre *lehtr*	hôtel *o-tehl*
enchanté *ahN-shahN-tay*	moteur *moh-tuhr*	liste *leest*	océan *oh-say-yahN*
fatigué *fah-tee-gay*	papier *pah-pyay*	maladie *mah-lah-dee*	oncle *ohNkl*
grillé *gree-yay*	parc *pahrk*	marchandise *mahr-shahN-deez*	opéra *oh-pay-rah*
intéressant *aN-tay-reh-sahN*	parfum *pahr-fuhN*	musique *mew-zeek*	opticien *ohp-tee-syaN*
magnifique *mah-nyee-feek*	porc *pohr*	nationalité *nah-syoh-nah-lee-tay*	orchestre *ohr-kehstr*
nécessaire *nay-seh-sehr*	président *pray-zee-dahN*	paire *pehr*	université *ew-nee-vehr-see-tay*
occupé *oh-kew-pay*	professeur *proh-feh-suhr*	personne *pehr-sohn*	
populaire *poh-pew-lehr*	programme *proh-grahm*	pharmacie *fahr-mah-see*	
rapide *rah-peed*	serveur *sehr-vuhr*	région *ray-zhohN*	
riche *reesh*	supermarché *sew-pehr-mahr-shay*	salade *sah-lahd*	
sérieux *say-ryuh*	téléphone *tay-lay-fohn*	soupe *soop*	
sincère *saN-sehr*	théâtre *tay-ahtr*	télévision *tay-lay-vee-zyohN*	
splendide *splahN-deed*	touriste *too-reest*	tente *tahNt*	
superbe *sew-pehrb*	vendeur *vahN-duhr*	tomate *toh-maht*	

Verb Cognates

There are many French verbs (words that show action or a state of being) that are so similar to their English counterparts that you will recognize their meaning almost immediately. The majority of French verbs fall into one of three families: the *er* family, the *ir* family, and the *re* family. This concept is foreign to us, since English has borrowed so much from so many different languages that no "verb families" exist. For now, you will see that the largest French family, by far, is the *er* family. Any verbs belonging to a family are considered *regular*, while those that do not belong to a family are designated as *irregular*. Each family has its own set of rules, which will be explained in Chapter 7. All irregular verbs must be memorized. Look at the three major families and see if you can determine the meanings of the verbs presented in Table 3.3:

Table 3.3 Verb Families

The ER Family

accompagner	*ah-kohN-pah-nyay*	inviter	*aN-vee-tay*
adorer	*ah-doh-ray*	marcher	*mahr-shay*
aider	*eh-day*	modifier	*moh-dee-fyay*
blâmer	*blah-may*	observer	*ohb-sehr-vay*
changer	*shahN-zhay*	pardonner	*pahr-doh-nay*
chanter	*shahN-tay*	passer	*pah-say*
commander	*koh-mahN-day*	payer	*peh-yay*
commencer	*koh-mahN-say*	persuader	*pehr-swah-day*
danser	*dahN-say*	porter	*pohr-tay*
décider	*day-see-day*	préférer	*pray-fay-ray*
déclarer	*day-klah-ray*	préparer	*pray-pah-ray*
demander	*duh-mahN-day*	présenter	*pray-zahN-tay*
désirer	*day-zee-ray*	prouver	*proo-vay*
dîner	*dee-nay*	recommander	*ruh-koh-mahN-day*
échanger	*ay-shahN-zhay*	refuser	*ruh-few-zay*
embrasser	*ahN-brah-say*	regarder	*ruh-gahr-day*
entrer	*ahN-tray*	regretter	*ruh-greh-tay*
envelopper	*ahN-vloh-pay*	remarquer	*ruh-mahr-kay*
hésiter	*ay-zee-tay*	réparer	*ray-pah-ray*
ignorer	*ee-nyoh-ray*	réserver	*ray-zehr-vay*

| signer | *see-nyay* | vérifier | *vay-ree-fyay* |
| tourner | *toor-nay* | | |

The IR Family		**The RE Family**	
accomplir	*ah-kohN-pleer*	défendre	*day-fahNdr*
applaudir	*ah-plo-deer*	répondre	*ray-pohNdr*
finir	*fee-neer*	vendre	*vahNdr*

This Is Easy

As a matter of fact, this is so easy that you can easily read and understand these sentences without any problem at all:

1. Le serveur aide le touriste.
   luh sehr-vuhr ehd luh too-reest

2. Maman prépare de la soupe et de la salade.
   mah-mahN pray-pahr duh lah soop ay duh lah sah-lahd

3. Le mécanicien répare le moteur.
   luh may-kah-nee-syaN ray-pahr luh moh-tuhr

4. Le bébé regarde la télévision.
   luh bay-bay ruh-gahrd lah tay-lay-vee-zyohN

5. Le touriste réserve la chambre.
   luh too-reest ray-sehrv lah shahNbr

6. Le guide recommande le café.
   luh geed ruh-koh-mahNd luh kah-fay

7. L'employé vend la marchandise.
   l'ahN-plwah-yay vahN lah mahr-shahN-deez

8. L'enfant adore la musique moderne.
   lahN-fahN ah-dohr lah mew-zeek moh-dehrn

9. L'acteur préfère l'opéra italien.
   lahk-tuhr pray-fehr l'oh-pay-rah ee-tah-lyaN

10. La famille désire l'hôtel confortable.
    lah fah-mee-y day-zeer lo-tehl kohN-fohr-tahbl

Give Your Opinions

Imagine that you are a tourist in a French-speaking country. Use what you've learned to express these opinions to a fellow tourist:

1. The garden is splendid.

2. The fountain is superb.

3. The artist is popular.

4. The music is splendid.

5. The restaurant is elegant.

6. The theater is old.

7. The cathedral is magnificent.

8. The actor is tired.

9. The hotel is elegant.

10. The opera is amusing.

Some special tricks on pronunciation have already been mentioned in chapter 2. When you look at Table 3.4, you will see how adding an *s* after an accent circonflexe (^) and how substituting an *s* for an *é* or adding one after it will help you figure out the meanings of many words.

Table 3.4 Special Tricks

accent (^)	English	é	English
arrêter *(ah-ruh-tay)*	to arrest	écarlate *(ay-kahr-laht)*	scarlet
bête *(beht)*	beast	échapper *(ay-shah-pay)*	to escape
conquête *(kohN-keht)*	conquest	école *(ay-kohl)*	school
coûter *(koo-tay)*	to cost	épars *(ay-pahr)*	sparse
croûte *(kroot)*	crust	épellation *(ay-puh-lah-syohN)*	spelling
fête *(feht)*	feast	épice *(ay-pees)*	spice
forêt *(foh-reh)*	forest	épier *(ay-pyay)*	to spy
hôpital *(o-pee-tahl)*	hospital	éponge *(ay-pohNzh)*	sponge
hôte *(ot)*	host	épouser *(ay-poo-zay)*	to espouse

False Friends

Just when you think you know it all, exceptions pop up to prevent you from becoming overly confident. *Faux amis* or *false friends* are words spelled exactly the same or almost the same in both French and English, but which have very different meanings in each language and might even be different parts of speech. Don't fall into the trap of thinking that every French word that looks like an English one is automatically a cognate. It's not quite that simple. Beware of the *faux amis* listed in Table 3.5.

Table 3.5   False Friends

English	Part of speech	French	Part of speech	Meaning
attend	verb	attendre *(ah-tahNdr)*	verb	to wait
bless	verb	blesser *(bleh-say)*	verb	to wound
comment	noun	comment *(koh-mahN)*	adverb	how
figure	noun	la figure *(lah fee-gewr)*	noun	face
library	noun	la librairie *(lah lee-breh-ree)*	noun	bookstore
liver	noun	le livre *(luh leevr)*	noun	book
occasion	noun	l'occasion *(loh-kah-zyohN)*	noun	opportunity
prune	noun	la prune *(lah prewn)*	noun	plum
raisin	noun	le raisin *(luh reh-zaN)*	noun	grape
rest	verb	rester *(rehs-tay)*	verb	to remain
sale	noun	sale *(sahl)*	adjective	dirty
sang	verb	le sang *(luh sahN)*	noun	blood
sensible	adjective	sensible *(sahN-seebl)*	adjective	sensitive
stage	noun	le stage *(luh stahzh)*	noun	training course
store	noun	le store *(luh stohr)*	noun	shade
travel	verb	travailler *(trah-vah-yay)*	verb	to work

Are You Well Read?

The famous French literary titles listed here all contain cognates. Give their English equivalents:

Anouilh—*Le Sauvage*

Balzac—*La Comédie humaine*

Baudelaire—*Les Paradis artificiels*

Camus—*L'Étranger*

Cocteau—*La Machine Infernale*

Cocteau—*Les Enfants terribles*

Colette—*La Vagabonde*

Flaubert—*L'Éducation sentimentale*

Gide—*La Symphonic pastorale*

Hugo—*Les Misérables*

Laclos—*Les Liaisons dangereuses*

Malraux—*La Condition humaine*

Molière—*Le Malade imaginaire*

Prévert—*Spectacle*

Rousseau—*Confessions*

Sartre—*La Nausée*

Voltaire—*Lettres Philosophiques*

Zola—*La Joie de Vivre*

The Least You Need to Know

➤ By using cognates you can express yourself in French with a minimal amount of effort.

➤ Many French words and expressions are in use every day in English.

➤ Beware of false friends. Don't let them trap you into mistakes.

"idiom. n. A FORM OF EXPRESSION HAVING A MEANING THAT IS NOT READILY UNDERSTOOD FROM THE MEANING OF ITS COMPONENT WORDS..."

WHAT?

Chapter 4

Are Idioms for Idiots?

In This Chapter

➤ What are idioms?

➤ Idioms vs. slang

➤ Using gestures to express your feelings

Idioms are very important to a complete and correct understanding of the language. Imagine a beautiful young woman walking along the Champs-Élysées, an elegant, tree-lined avenue in Paris. Two men approach from the opposite direction and look her up and down. She hears one man casually say to the other "Oh là là. Elle a du chien." The young lady, having taken a year or two of French in school hears *elle* (she) and *chien* (dog). She immediately puts two and two together and thinks these men have called her a "dog." If she is extraordinarily brazen, perhaps she even smacks one across the face. She has just made a terrible mistake. What she doesn't understand is the idiomatic expression *avoir du chien,* which in English means *to be alluring, sexy.* The English equivalent of what the men said was really: "Boy, is she attractive."

What's an Idiom?

So what exactly is an idiom? In any language, an idiom is a particular word or expression whose meaning cannot be readily understood by either its grammar or the words used. Examples of some common English idioms are:

To look on the bright side.   To fall head over heels.

On the other hand.   To be down and out.

Slinging Slang

What's the difference between an idiom and slang? Slang refers to colorful, popular words or phrases that are not part of the standard vocabulary of a language. Slang is considered unconventional. Many of these words evolved as needed to describe particular things or situations. Here are some examples of English slang:

Give me a break!   Get real!

Tough luck!   Get a life!

What's the Difference Anyway?

Idioms are acceptable in oral and written phrases, whereas slang, although freely used in informal conversations, is generally considered substandard in formal writing or speaking. Much slang is, at best, x-rated.

What Is It?

Take a look at some of these popular expressions used in sentences. I'm sure that you will immediately realize that it would be impossible to translate them into French. Certainly they couldn't be translated word for word. Which are they, idioms or slang?

You drive me crazy!   Keep your shirt on!

Don't jump the gun!   I'm always on the go.

You'll have to pay through the nose.   He likes to play the field.

It's raining cats and dogs!   We'll just have to kill some time.

I'm going to call your bluff.   Can you buy some time?

She got angry and she lost it.   He's on his way up.

Get a head start on the project.   Did you fall for it?

Did you recognize that these are idiomatic expressions that we use in English all the time? Good for you. Now compare those sentences with the ones below:

Shucks!	What a cop out!
She just flipped out!	Don't dis my friend.
My son is a computer geek.	That's tacky!

Did you notice how these slang sentences differed from the idiomatic ones? Excellent! You probably won't be using much French slang, but the idioms sure will come in handy.

There are a great many idioms in French. In this chapter we will look at six categories of idioms that you might find helpful: travel and transportation, time, location and direction, expressing opinions, physical conditions, and weather conditions. Other idiomatic expressions will appear in their appropriate chapters.

And You're Off

Let's say you are taking a trip. We might ask: "Are you going on a plane or on a boat?" In French the word for *on* is *sur* (sewr). If you said: "Je vais sur l'avion" that would imply that you were flying on the exterior of the plane. And, as we all know, that is truly impossible. It pays to know the French idioms to avoid this type of confusion. It is well worth your time to learn the idiomatic expressions covered in Table 4.1.

Table 4.1 Idioms for Travel and Transportation

Idiom	Pronunciation	Meaning
à bicyclette	*ah bee-see-kleht*	by bicycle
à cheval	*ah shuh-vahl*	on horseback
à moto	*ah moh-to*	by scooter
à pied	*ah pyeh*	on foot
en automobile	*ahN no-toh-moh-beel*	by car
en avion	*ahN nah-vyohN*	by plane
en bateau	*ahN bah-to*	by boat
en bus	*ahN bews*	by bus
en métro	*ahN may-tro*	by subway
en taxi	*ahN tahk-see*	by taxi
en train	*ahN traN*	by train
en voiture	*ahN vwah-tewr*	by car

Putting Your Idioms to Use I (or You're Off and Running)

Tell how you would get to the following places:

Example: the drugstore   à pied

1. Your place of business or school	6. The park
2. The movies	7. A tropical island
3. Your doctor	8. A fishing trip
4. The nearest hospital	9. A museum
5. Europe	10. The library

As a Rule

The preposition *en* is usually used when you are traveling inside of something, such as a subway. Use *à* when you expect to feel your hair blowing in the breeze.

It's Time to...

For some travelers time is of the essence and they make sure they get that wake-up call bright and early in the morning. They want to be on the go as soon as possible. For others, its not important at all. They don't even wear a watch. They're on vacation and time is simply unimportant. Whether you're time-conscious or not, the idioms in Table 4.2 will serve you well.

Table 4.2   Time Expressions

Idiom	Pronunciation	Meaning
à bientôt	*ah byaN-to*	see you soon
à ce soir	*ah suh swahr*	until this evening
à demain	*ah duh-maN*	until tomorrow
à l'heure	*ah luhr*	on time
à la fois	*ah lah fois*	at the same time
à samedi	*ah sahm-dee*	until Saturday
à temps	*ah tahN*	on time
à tout à l'heure	*ah too tah luhr*	see you later
au bout de	*o boo duh*	at the end of
au revoir	*o ruh-vwahr*	good-bye
de bonne heure	*duh boh nuhr*	early
de jour en jour	*duh zhoor ahN zhoor*	from day to day

Idiom	Pronunciation	Meaning
de temps à autre	*duh tahN zah o-truh*	from time to time
de temps en temps	*duh tahN zahN tahN*	from time to time
du matin au soir	*dew mah-taN o swahr*	from morning until evening
en même temps	*ahN mehm tahN*	at the same time
en retard	*ahN ruh-tahr*	late
il y a (+ time)	*eel yah*	ago (+ time)
par jour (semaine, mois)	*pahr zhoor (suh-mehn, mwah)*	by day, week, month
tout à l'heure	*too tah luhr*	in a while
tout de suite	*toot sweet*	immediately

Putting Your Idioms to Use II (or What Time Is It?)

What French idioms of time would you use in the following situations?

1. When you leave a friend for the day you would say:

2. If your boss wants something done right away, he wants it done:

3. If you have an interview at 9 a.m. and you arrive at 10 a.m. you arrive:

4. If you have an interview at 9 a.m. and you arrive at 8 a.m. you arrive:

5. If you are going to see a friend later today, you will see him/her:

6. If you go to the movies every once in a while, you go:

7. If you work all day long, you work:

8. If you are leaving a friend for today, but know that you will see him/her tomorrow, you would say:

Go to Your Left, Your Right, Your Left

Probably among the most useful idioms are those telling you how to get where you want to go. Most men, of course, would never dream of asking for directions. They have to prove that they can find it themselves. So when my husband and I find ourselves off the beaten path, I'm the one who goes into the nearest gas station. I like to know exactly where I'm going and, if I get lost, I want precise directions. The idioms of location and direction in Table 4.3 are quite important for any traveler, don't you think? (This list is for men, too.)

Table 4.3   Idioms Showing Location and Direction

Idiom	Pronunciation	Meaning
à côté (de)	*ah ko-tay (duh)*	next to, beside
à droite (de)	*ah drawht (duh)*	to the right (of)
à gauche (de)	*ah gosh (duh)*	to the left (of)
à l'étranger	*ah lay-trahN-zhay*	abroad
à la campagne	*ah lah kahN-pahN-nyuh*	in the country
à la maison	*ah lah meh-zohN*	at home
à part	*ah pahr*	aside
à travers	*ah trah-vehr*	across, through
au loin	*o lwaN*	in the distance
au milieu (de)	*o mee-lyuh (duh)*	in the middle (of)
au-dessous de	*o duh-soo duh*	beneath, below
au-dessus de	*o duh-sew duh*	above, over
de l'autre côté (de)	*duh lohtr ko-tay (duh)*	on the other side (of)
du côté de	*dew ko-tay duh*	in the direction of, toward
en bas (de)	*ahN bah duh*	at the bottom of
en face (de)	*ahN fahs (duh)*	opposite, facing
en haut (de)	*ahN o (duh)*	at the top of
en plein air	*ahN pleh nehr*	in the open air, outdoors
en ville	*ahN veel*	downtown
le long de	*luh lohN duh*	along
par ici (là)	*pahr ee-see (lah)*	this way (that way)
tout droit	*too drwah*	straight ahead
tout près	*too preh*	nearby

Putting Your Idioms to Use III (or Getting There in One Piece)

You can get there. Below is a small map of a city street. There are six buildings to identify:

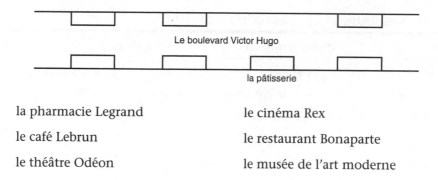

la pharmacie Legrand   le cinéma Rex

le café Lebrun   le restaurant Bonaparte

le théâtre Odéon   le musée de l'art moderne

Read the directions and label the buildings on le boulevard Victor Hugo:

À gauche de la pâtisserie il y a le théâtre Odéon. Et à côté du théâtre il y a le café Lebrun. En face du café se trouve le restaurant Bonaparte. À droite de la pâtisserie, il y a la pharmacie Legrand. De l'autre côté du boulevard, en face, est le cinéma Rex. À gauche du cinéma et tout droit devant le théâtre se trouve le musée de l'art moderne.

So, What Do You Think?

Everyone, at one time or another, has an opinion about something. Some people are certainly more expressive than others. Whether you're talking about your flight, the food you ate, the movie you watched, the people you met, or life in general, you will need to know how to properly express your feelings. Table 4.4 below should help.

Table 4.4 Expressing Your Opinions with Idioms

Idiom	Pronunciation	Meaning
à mon avis	*ah mohN nah-vee*	in my opinion
à vrai dire	*ah vreh deer*	to tell the truth
au contraire	*o kohN-trehr*	on the contrary
bien entendu	*byaN nahN-tahN-dew*	of course
bien sûr	*byaN sewr*	of course
bon marché	*bohN mahr-shay*	cheap
c'est-à-dire	*seh-tah-deer*	that is to say
cela m'est égal	*suh-lah meh tay-gahl*	that's all the same to me (I don't care.)
cela ne fait rien	*suh-lah nuh feh ryaN*	that doesn't matter
d'accord	*dah-kohr*	agreed, O.K.

continues

Table 4.4 Continued

Idiom	Pronunciation	Meaning
de mon côté	*duh mohN ko-tay*	as for me, for my part
jamais de la vie	*zhah-meh duh lah vee*	never, out of the question
n'importe	*nahN-pohrt*	it doesn't matter
ressembler à	*ruh-sahN-blay ah*	to resemble
sans doute	*sahN doot*	without a doubt
tant mieux	*tahN myuh*	so much the better
tant pis	*tahN pee*	too bad
tout à fait	*too tah feh*	entirely
tout de même	*too dmehm*	all the same

Putting Your Idioms to Use IV (or What's Your Opinion?)

Your friend has proposed some afternoon activities. Indicate a willingness to go along with his/her suggestions. Show that you are unwilling to go along with him/her.

How Do You Feel?

Let's say you are freezing cold. So you say to your French host: "Je suis froid," and he cracks up laughing. Why? In English we use adjectives to describe how we are feeling, thus you've chosen (so you think): "I am cold." The French say: "I have cold" (which doesn't mean that they are sick and have a cold). Your French host would literally interpret what you said as that you are cold to the touch of a hand. Of course this sounds very strange and silly to us. Just remember, our idioms sound very off-beat to others.

As a Rule
Always use the verb *avoir* to express your physical conditions.

You will notice that all the idioms below begin with the verb *avoir*, which means *to have*. Of course, it will be necessary to conjugate *avoir* as the subject of the sentence changes, but that will be discussed further in Chapter 9. For now, concentrate on how you feel—*J'ai* (zhay, I have)—using the expressions for physical conditions in Table 4.5.

Table 4.5 Idiomatic Physical Conditions

Idiom	Pronunciation	Meaning
avoir besoin (de)	*ah-vwahr buh-zwaN duh*	to need
avoir chaud	*ah-vwahr sho*	to be hot (person)
avoir envie (de)	*ah-vwahr ahN-vee (duh)*	to need

Idiom	Pronunciation	Meaning
avoir faim	*ah-vwahr faN*	to be hungry
avoir froid	*ah-vwahr frwah*	to be cold (person)
avoir honte (de)	*ah-vwahr ohNt (duh)*	to be ashamed (of)
avoir l'air (+ adj.)	*ah-vwahr lehr*	to seem, look
avoir l'air de (+ inf.)	*ah-vwahr lehr duh*	to seem to, look as if
avoir mal à	*ah-vwahr mahl ah*	to have an ache in
avoir peur (de)	*ah-vwahr puhr (duh)*	to be afraid (of)
avoir quelque chose	*ah-vwahr kehl-kuh shohz*	to have something wrong
avoir raison	*ah-vwahr reh-sohN*	to be right
avoir soif	*ah-vwahr swahf*	to be thirsty
avoir sommeil	*ah-vwahr soh-mehy*	to be sleepy
avoir tort	*ah-vwahr tohr*	to be wrong
avoir…ans	*ah-vwahr…ahN*	to be ___ years old

Putting Your Idioms to Use V (or What's Up?)

Express how you feel, using idioms.

1. sleepy
2. hot
3. hungry
4. thirsty
5. being wrong
6. on your 30th birthday
7. being correct
8. cold

Baby It's Cold Outside

Travelers tend to be obsessed with weather, which makes sense given that many plans are contingent on it. The French way of discussing weather differs from ours. If you said to your French host: "Il est chaud." He or she would assume that you were speaking about something that was warm to the touch. The French use the verb *faire* (to make, to do) to describe most weather conditions. We wouldn't use the verbs *make* and *do* to express ourselves in English. We'd be laughed at. But in France, do as the French do as you study Table 4.6.

As a Rule
Weather conditions are always expressed impersonally with the expression *il fait…* (it's…). *Faire* can be used with other subject nouns and pronouns, but not when discussing the weather.

Table 4.6   Idiomatic Weather Expressions

Idiom	Pronunciation	Meaning
faire beau	*fehr bo*	to be nice weather
faire chaud	*fehr cho*	to be hot weather
faire des éclairs	*fehr day zay-klehr*	to be lightning
faire doux	*fehr doo*	to be mild
faire du soleil	*fehr dew soh-lehy*	to be sunny
faire du tonnerre	*fehr dew toh-nehr*	to be thundering
faire du vent	*fehr dew vahN*	to be windy
faire frais	*fehr freh*	to be cool
faire froid	*fehr frwah*	to be cold
faire jour	*fehr zhoor*	to be daytime, light
faire mauvais	*fehr mo-veh*	to be bad weather
faire nuit	*fehr nwee*	to be night, dark
Quel temps fait-il?	*kehl tahN feh-teel*	What is the weather?

Putting Your Idioms to Use VI (or How's the Weather?)

Look at the weather map of France for the day. Tell what the weather will be in each of the cities listed below:

1. À Paris il fait _____.

2. À Nice il fait _____.

3. À Bordeaux il fait _____.

4. À Strasbourg il fait _____.

5. À Toulouse il fait _____.

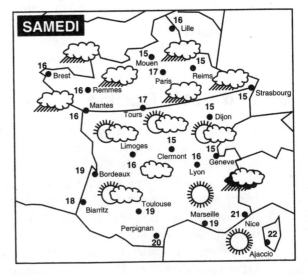

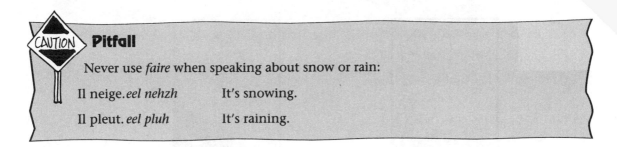

Pitfall

Never use *faire* when speaking about snow or rain:

Il neige. *eel nehzh*   It's snowing.

Il pleut. *eel pluh*   It's raining.

As a Rule

The weather in France is very similar to the weather in the north-eastern United States. So expect a warm, rainy spring, a hot summer, a cool autumn, and a cold winter, and dress appropriately.

It's In Your Hands

The French are very expressive people and tend to speak a lot with their hands. Facial expressions and body language are also an important part of communicating feelings and emotions. Many gestures perfectly convey certain French slang expressions without the use of words. These gestures play an important role in the French language:

1. Mon oeil.
   (mohN nuhy)
   My eye. You can't fool me.

2. J'en ai par-dessus la tête.
   (zhahN nay pahr-duh-sew lah teht)
   I've had it up to here.

3. Au poil!
 (o pwahl)
 Perfect!

4. Extra!
 (ehks-trah)
 Super!

5. C'est la barbe!
 (seh lah bahrb)
 It's boring!

6. Qu'est-ce que tu veux que j'y fasse?
 (kehs-kuh tew vuh kuh zhee fahs)
 What do you want me to do about it?

The Least You Need to Know

➤ Every language has its own peculiar idioms that can't be translated word for word.

➤ Idioms, not slang, will help you speak the language the way it should be spoken.

➤ Proper gestures can help you convey your feelings.

Chapter 5

Good Grief, It's Grammar!

In This Chapter

➤ An overview of very basic grammar

➤ How to use a bilingual dictionary

Today's approach to learning a foreign language is certainly much different than it was in the past. There's been a de-emphasis on grammatical rules and an emphasis on communication. So if you really want to speak like a Frenchman/woman, you will be happy to know that speaking a foreign language doesn't mean you'll mentally have to translate word for word from one language to the other or concentrate on memorizing endless pages of rules. Sure, that's how they tried to teach you in school way back when (and it was pure drudgery). But the powers that be have finally come to realize that communicating doesn't mean walking around with a dictionary under your arm. On the contrary, it means learning to use the language and its patterns the way a native speaker does. To do this, you need to know basic grammar as well as the idioms and colloquialisms used by native speakers.

Groping at Grammar

When you hear the word *grammar*, do you get a sinking feeling in the pit of your stomach like when someone mentions *math?* Did you ever have the pleasure of diagramming a sentence? I still have very vivid memories of many seemingly useless grammatical terms. You don't have to be an expert grammarian to learn a foreign language. All you really need is a basic understanding of four simple parts of speech: nouns, verbs, adjectives, and adverbs. Now don't get all nervous. You'll see how simple it really is.

Naming with Nouns

Nouns refer to people, places, things, or ideas. Just like in English, nouns can be replaced by pronouns (he, she, it, they). Unlike English, however, all nouns in French have a gender. That means that all nouns have a SEX. That ought to grab your attention momentarily. Sorry to disappoint you, but in this case *SEX* refers to the masculine or feminine designation of the noun. In French, all nouns also have a number (singular or plural). Little articles (words that stand for "the" or "a") serve as noun markers and usually help to indicate gender and number. But even if you can't figure out the gender of a noun, you will still be understood, as long as you use the correct word. You will learn more about gender in Chapter 6.

Versatile Verbs

Verbs are words that show action or a state of being. In both English and French, we conjugate verbs. That word "conjugate" sounds a lot scarier than it really is. In English, conjugating is so automatic (because we've been doing it practically since birth) that we don't even realize that we are doing it. I had a friend who took four years of high school French and never understood the concept of verb conjugation (she was absent that day). I explained it to her, and she realized that it's really quite simple. *Conjugating* means giving the correct form of the verb so that it agrees with the subject. For example: In English, we say *I am* but *you are*, *he is*, and so on; *I look* but *she looks*. It just doesn't work to mix and match the subjects and verb forms whether you are speaking English or French. Imagine how silly it would sound to you if a French person said, "I are." You will have to strive to give the form of the verb that matches the subject. But don't despair. Even if you use the wrong verb form, you will be understood. Surely you would understand a foreigner who said, "You is very nice."

That's enough for now. Verb conjugation will be explained in greater depth in Chapter 7.

Appropriate Adjectives

Adjectives help to describe nouns. Unlike English, in French all adjectives agree in number and gender (sex) with the nouns they modify. In other words, in a French sentence, all the words have to match. If the noun is singular, then its adjective must also be singular. If the noun is feminine, then you must be sure to give the correct feminine form of the adjective you are using.

In English, adjectives are generally placed before the nouns they modify: for example, *the blue house*. In French, most adjectives come after the nouns they describe: for example, *la maison bleue*. Don't get nervous. If you make a mistake, you will still be understood. You will find out more about adjectives in Chapter 9.

Active Adverbs

Adverbs are words that describe verbs, adjectives, or other adverbs. In English, most adverbs end in *ly*: for example, *He dances slowly*. In French, they end in *ment*: *Il danse lentement*. Adverbs will probably pose few problems as you learn the language. Adverbs are discussed in greater detail in Chapter 18.

I'm Not an Idiot—I Know How to Use a Dictionary

Sure you know how to use an *English* dictionary. Even if you don't know how to spell the word you're looking up, you usually stumble across it eventually. But using a bilingual dictionary requires a certain, albeit minimal, amount of grammatical expertise. Believe it or not, an open-book dictionary test is probably harder than any test you would have to study for. To use a bilingual dictionary successfully, you must know and be aware of the differences between the various parts of speech.

Putting Your Dictionary to Work

The very first thing you should do is open to the front of your dictionary and find the list of abbreviations. Generally, there is a rather long, comprehensive list. There are only a few abbreviations that are truly essential and that need attention. They are:

➤ *adj.*—adjective.

➤ *adv.*—adverb.

➤ *f.*—indicates a *feminine* noun. The gender of nouns will be explained in Chapter 6.

➤ *n.*—noun (sometimes an *s* is used). The *n.* designation is generally used only if the noun can be either masculine or feminine.

➤ *m.*—indicates a *masculine* noun.

➤ *pl.*—indicates a *plural* noun. More on noun plurals in Chapter 6.

➤ *p.p.*—indicates the *past participle* of a verb. A past participle is necessary when a verb is used in the past tense. An explanation follows in Chapter 21.

➤ *v.i.*—indicates an *intransitive* verb, which can stand alone: *I eat.*

➤ *v.t.*—indicates a *transitive* verb that may be followed by a direct object: *He removes his hat* (*removes* may not stand alone) or may be used in the passive, where the subject is acted upon: *I was seen.*

➤ *v.r.*—indicates a *reflexive* verb, where the subject acts upon itself: *I brush my teeth.* Reflexive verbs will be treated in Chapter 20.

Now, let's see how well you can do with your bilingual French-English, English-French dictionary. We'll start with the English word *mean.* Consider the following sentences and how the meaning of the word *mean* changes:

That man is **mean.** (adjective)

What can that **mean**? (verb)

What is the **mean** (average)? (noun)

If you change *mean* to the plural, its meaning changes:

What is the **means** of transportation? (noun)

Look up the work *mean,* and you see:

mean [min] *vt* signifier; *adj* (miserly) radin, (nasty) méchant, (vicious) sauvage; *n* (math) moyenne *f*; (method) moyen; *m* means ressources *fpl*

Now try completing the following sentences with the correct form of the word *mean:*

1. *That man is **mean.*** Determine the part of speech. Did you choose an adjective? Good! Now complete the French sentence: *Cet homme est _____.* The correct choice is *méchant.*

2. *What can that **mean?*** In this sentence, did you select *mean* as a verb? You got it! The French sentence would read: *Qu'est-ce que ça peut _____.* I hope you chose *signifier.*

3. *What is the **mean?*** This term refers to the *average* of two numbers. Because the correct word is feminine, you will have to use the article *la* before the noun you choose. Articles will be discussed in Chapter 6. The French is: *Quelle est la _____.* The answer is *moyenne.*

4. *What is the **means** of transportation?* ***Means*** is plural in English but masculine, singular in French. Use *le* before the noun you choose. The French is: *Quel est _____ de transport.* The answer is *le moyen.*

As you can see, to successfully look up the meanings of the word you want to use, you must do three things:

1. Check to make sure that you are using the correct part of speech: noun, verb, adjective, or adverb.

2. Check your work by looking up the French word you have chosen and by verifying that the English meaning given is the one you want.

3. Check that you are using the correct form of the word: the right number (singular or plural) and the right gender (masculine or feminine).

A Proper Workout with Your Dictionary

Use a bilingual dictionary to see if you can find the correct word to complete each of the following French sentences. For now, I've supplied the proper articles. *Write all verbs in the infinitive form.* We'll move on to conjugation later, in Chapter 7.

1. Look at the **fire**!   Regarde le _____.

2. The boss is going **to fire** the employee.   Le patron va _____ l'employeé.

3. I see the **light**.   Je vois la _____.

4. I am going **to light** the barbecue. Je vais _____ le barbecue.

5. There is water in **the well**.   Il y a de l'eau dans le _____.

6. He sings **well**.   Il chante _____.

The Least You Need to Know

➤ Nouns refer to people, places, things, and ideas.

➤ Verbs indicate an action or state of being.

➤ Adjectives describe nouns.

➤ Adverbs describe verbs, adjectives, and other adverbs.

➤ You must use both sides of a bilingual dictionary to obtain the proper definition of a word.

REALLY?

Chapter 6

Everthing You Wanted to Know about Sex

In This Chapter

➤ How to determine gender

➤ Sex changes

➤ Producing plurals

You're really not going to find out *everything* you wanted to know about sex in this chapter, but you will get a better understanding of how the French view *gender* (a polite way of saying *sex*). Unlike English where girls are girls, and boys are boys, and everything else is neuter, every single noun (person, place, thing, or idea) in French is designated as *masculine* or *feminine*, *singular* or *plural*. How is this determination made? Sometimes it's obvious, sometimes there are clues, and sometimes it's just downright tricky. This chapter will teach you to make the right connections.

Is It a Girl or a Boy?

If you're speaking about a man or a woman, gender is obvious. But what if you want to talk about a lovely boutique you passed by the other day? There is no obvious clue to you as yet, telling you the gender of the word *boutique*. Do you assume that it's feminine because women like to go to boutiques? In this day and age, that's a dangerous thing to do. There are, however, tricks for determining gender that you will learn as you read and study the chapter.

As a Rule
The word *boutique* ends in *que*—most French words with this ending are feminine.

Suppose that you want to purchase a tie that you saw in the boutique. It would be normal to assume that *cravate* is masculine because men wear ties more often than women do. But you would be wrong in your assumption. In fact, *cravate* is a feminine word. "Why?" you're probably asking yourself. "That really doesn't make any sense." You're right. It doesn't. And unfortunately, there are no clues and no tricks to help you with this word and many others like it. So what do you do? You learn which endings are usually masculine and which are feminine, and for the others, you try to learn the word with its *noun marker* (le [un] or la [une]). If you forget the noun marker, you can always resort to a good French dictionary. Just remember, even if you make a gender mistake, as long as you have the correct vocabulary word, you'll be understood.

As a Rule
Only singular noun markers show the gender of the noun.

Noun Markers

Noun markers are articles or adjectives that tell you whether a noun is *masculine* (m.) or *feminine* (f.), *singular* (sing.) or *plural* (pl.). The most common markers, shown in Table 6.1, are *definite articles* expressing "the" and *indefinite articles* expressing "a," "an," "one," or "some."

Table 6.1 Singular Noun Markers

	Masculine	Feminine
the	le (l') (*luh*)	la (l') (*lah*)
a, an, one	un (*uhN*)	une (*ewn*)

For words beginning with a vowel or vowel sound (*h, y*), the definite articles *le* and *la* become *l'*. The masculine or feminine gender of the noun, so easily determined when the masculine *le* or the feminine *la* is used, remains a mystery when *l'* (masculine or feminine) is used. Therefore, you need to learn the indefinite article *un* or *une* for any word that begins with a vowel.

As a Rule
The *e* is never dropped from the indefinite article *une*. The final *e* does, however, change the sound of the word *un* (uhN) to *une* (ewn).

Singular Nouns

The nouns in Table 6.2 are very easy to mark because they obviously refer to males or females:

Table 6.2 Gender-Obvious Nouns

Masculine Noun	Pronunciation	English	Feminine Noun	Pronunciation	English
le père	*luh pehr*	father	la mère	*lah mehr*	mother
le grand-père	*luh grahN-pehr*	grand-father	la grand-mère	*lah grahN-mehr*	grand-mother
le garçon	*luh gahr-sohN*	boy	la fille	*la fee-y*	girl
l'ami	*lah-mee*	friend(m.)	l'amie	*lah-mee*	friend(f.)
un homme	*uhN nohm*	man	une femme	*ewn fahm*	woman
un oncle	*uhN nohN-kluh*	uncle	une tante	*ewn tahNt*	aunt
un cousin	*uhN koo-zaN*	cousin(m.)	une cousine	*ewn koo-zeen*	cousin(f.)
un ami	*uhN nah-mee*	friend(m.)	une amie	*ewn nah-mee*	friend(f.)

Some nouns can be either masculine or feminine. To indicate whether you are speaking about a male or female, simply change the marker to suit the identity of the person, as listed in Table 6.3:

Example:

Le touriste (male) prend (is taking) des photos.

La touriste (female) aussi prend des photos.

Table 6.3 Nouns for Both Sexes

Word	Pronunciation	Meaning
artiste	*ahr-teest*	artist
camarade	*kah-mah-rahd*	friend

continues

Table 6.3 Continued

Word	Pronunciation	Meaning
concierge	*kohN-syehrzh*	concierge
élève	*ay-lehv*	student
enfant	*ahN-fahN*	child
malade	*mah-lahd*	sick person
secrétaire	*seh-kray-tehr*	secretary
touriste	*too-reest*	tourist

As a Rule
When you come across these words in a dictionary, you will not see a simple *m.* or *f.* Some dictionaries will designate them with an *n.* for noun or *s.* for substantive (which stands for noun) or will simply show *m./f.*

This means that you must choose the correct marker according to the person you are speaking about.

Let's take a look at an interesting sentence:

Jacques Cousteau est une personne importante.

Did you notice the use of the feminine indefinite article *une?* Are you perplexed? After all, Jacques Cousteau is a man. Shouldn't the indefinite article reflect this? Not really. The answer is simple, although somewhat unsatisfactory for men and women alike.

Whether we agree or not, some nouns are always masculine or feminine no matter what the sex of the person to whom you are referring. Notice that the "Always Masculine" list, which generally refers to professions, is much longer than the "Always Feminine" list.

Always Masculine	Always Feminine
agent de police (*ah-zhahN duh poh-lees*)/ police officer	connaissance/acquaintance (*koh-neh-sahNs*)
artisan (*ahr-tee-zahN*)/artisan	personne/person (*pehr-sohn*)
bébé (*bay-bay*)/baby	star (*stahr*)/star
chef (*shehf*)/chef, head	vedette (*vuh-deht*)/star
dentiste (*dahN-teest*)/dentist	victime (*veek-teem*)/victim
écrivain (*ay-kree-vaN*)/writer	
ingénieur (*aN-zhay-nyuhr*)/engineer	
libraire (*lee-brehr*)/bookstore clerk	
mannequin (*mahn-kaN*)/model	
médecin (*mayd-saN*)/doctor	

Always Masculine	Always Feminine
pompier (*pohN-pyeh*)/firefighter	
peintre (*paNtr*)/painter	
professeur (*proh-feh-suhr*)/teacher	

The endings in Table 6.4 can be helpful in determining the gender of the noun and can make marking easier. This will require some memorization and practice on your part.

Table 6.4 Masculine and Feminine Endings

Masculine Endings	Example	Feminine Endings	Example
-acle	spectacle (*spehk-tahkl*)	-ade	limonade (*lee-moh-nahd*)
-age*	garage (*gah-rahzh*)	-ale	cathédrale (*kah-tay-drahl*)
-al	animal (*ah-nee-mahl*)	-ance	chance (*shahNs*)
-eau**	château (*shah-to*)	-ence	essence (*eh-sahNs*)
-et	ticket (*tee-keh*)	-ette	chaînette (*sheh-neht*)
-ier	papier (*pah-pyay*)	-ie	magie (*mah-zhee*)
-isme	cyclisme (*see-kleez-muh*)	-ique	boutique (*boo-teek*)
-ment	changement (*shahNzh-mahN*)	-oire	histoire (*ees-twahr*)
		-sion	expression (*ehks-preh-syohN*)
		-tion	addition (*ah-dee-syohN*)
		-ure	coiffure (*kwah-fewr*)

* except page (pahzh) (f.); plage (plahzh) (f.) beach

** except eau (o) (f.) water; peau (po) (f.) skin

Marking some nouns is as easy as adding an *e* to the masculine form to get the corresponding feminine form. When you do this, there will be a change in the pronunciation of any feminine noun ending in a *consonant*. For the masculine noun, the final consonant is not pronounced. When the *e* is added to form the feminine, the consonant must then be pronounced. Another change is that the final nasal sound of a masculine *in* ending (aN) loses its nasality when the feminine ending becomes *ine* (een). Observe these changes in Table 6.5.

Table 6.5 Sex Changes

Le (L'), Un	La (L'), Une
ami (*ah-mee*)/friend	amie (*ah-mee*)/friend
avocat (*ah-vo-kah*)/lawyer	avocate (*ah-vo-kaht*)/lawyer
client (*klee-yahN*)/client	cliente (*klee-yahNt*)/client
cousin (*koo-zaN*)/cousin	cousine (*koo-zeen*)/cousin
employé (*ahN-plwah-yay*)/employee	employée (*ahN-plwah-yay*)/employee
étudiant (*ay-tew-dyahN*)/student	étudiante (*ay-tew-dyahNt*)/student
voisin (*vwah-zaN*)/neighbor	voisine (*vwah-zeen*)/neighbor

As a Rule
The masculine nouns in Table 6.6 that end in a nasal sound will have corresponding feminine forms where there is no nasal sound.

Some masculine noun endings (usually referring to professions) very conveniently have a corresponding feminine ending. Most of the feminine endings sound different, as you will notice in Table 6.6.

Table 6.6 More Sex Changes

Masculine Ending		Feminine Ending	
-an	paysan (*peh-ee-zahN*)/peasant	-anne	paysanne (*peh-ee-zahn*)/peasant
-el	contractuel (*kohN-trahk-tew-ehl*)/ traffic enforcer	-elle	contractuelle (*koh-trahk-tew-ehl*)/ traffic enforcer
-er	pâstissier (*pah-tee-syay*)/ pastry chef	-ère	pâtissière (*pah-tee-syehr*)/ pastry chef
-eur	vendeur(*vahN-duhr*)/ salesman	-euse	vendeuse/ (*vahN-duhz*) saleswoman
-ien	mécanicien/mechanic (*may-kah-nee-syaN*)	-ienne	mécanicienne (*may-kah-nee-syehn*)/ mechanic
-on	patron (*pah-trohN*)/boss	-onne	patronne (*pah-trohn*)/boss
-teur	spectateur (*spehk-tah-tuhr*)/ spectator	-trice	spectatrice (*spehk-tah-trees*)/ spectator

He Is/She Is

Review what you've learned so far and then complete the list with the missing professions. Be very careful before you choose an ending. Remember, some nouns do not change.

Il est	Elle est	Il est	Elle est
avocat	_____	infirmier	_____
_____	dentiste	pompier	_____
coiffeur	_____	_____	patronne
_____	factrice	mannequin	_____
boucher	_____	_____	pâtissière
_____	étudiante	médecin	_____
_____	chef	_____	ouvrière
électricien	_____		

If you did well with this exercise, then it's time to continue. The good news is: There are no more rules. However, because most nouns in French do not follow any specific set of rules, you should learn them with their markers. You'll see that you'll get the hang of it in no time. And if you make a gender mistake, it's really not that serious—as long as you've chosen the correct noun, you'll be understood.

Pitfall
Beware of trying to use your common sense to guess gender: make-up, stockings, and pocketbook are masculine, while car, shirt, and fishing are feminine.

When There's More Than One Noun

When a French noun refers to more than one person, place, thing, or idea, just like in English, it must be made plural. But it is not enough to simply change the noun—the marker must be made plural, as well. As you study Table 6.7, you will see that in the plural, the masculine and feminine noun markers for *the* and *some* are exactly the same.

Table 6.7 Plural Noun Markers

	Masculine	Feminine
the	les	les
some	des	des

What does this mean? Because *le, la,* and *l'* all become *les* in the plural, and *un* and *une* become *des*, using a plural noun marker does not enable you to determine the gender of any noun. Plural noun markers indicate only that the speaker is referring to more than one noun. This means that you must learn each noun with its singular noun marker.

Plural Nouns

Forming the plural of most nouns in French is really quite easy. All you have to do is add an *unpronounced s* to the singular form:

le garçon (*luh gahr-sohN*), un garçon (*uhN gahr-sohN*)	les garçons (*lay gahr-sohN*), des garçons (*day gahr-sohN*)
la fille (*lah fee-y*), une fille (*ewn fee-y*)	les filles (*lay fee-y*), des filles (*day fee-y*)
l'enfant* (*lahN-fahN*), un enfant** (*uhN nahN-fahN*)	les enfants** (*lay zahN-fahN*) des enfants** (*day zahN-fahN*)

The letters *s, x,* and *z* are all letters that are used to make plurals in French. So what happens if you have a French noun that ends in one of these letters? Absolutely nothing!

le prix (*luh pree*)/ the price, prize	les prix (*lay pree*)
le fils (*luh fees*)/ the son	les fils (*lay fees*)
le nez (*luh nay*)/the nose	les nez (*lay nay*)

As a Rule
Remember *elision and **liaison? Use the pronunciation guide and *slide the sounds joined by the apostrophe: *l'homme* (*lohm*) and *j'écoute* (*zhay-koot*), and **link the sound of the final consonant with the beginning vowel: *les hôtels* (*lay zo-tehl*) and *nous arrivons* (*noo zah-ree-vohN*). Don't pronounce the final *s* if you want your French to sound authentic.

Common words that end in *s:*

l'ananas (*lah-nah-nah*)/ pineapple	le héros (*luh ay-ro*)*/hero
l'autobus (*lo-toh-bews*)/ bus	le mois (*luh mwah*)/month
le bas (*luh bah*)/stocking	le jus (*luh zhew*)/juice
le bras (*luh brah*)/arm	le palais (*luh pah-leh*)/palace
le colis (*luh koh-lee*)/ package	le pardessus (*luh pahr-duh-sew*)/ overcoat
le corps (*luh kohr*)/ body	le pays (*luh pay-ee*)/ country
le dos (*luh do*)/back	le repas (*luh ruh-pah*)/ meal

la fois (*lah fwah*)/time   le tapis (*luh tah-pee*)/rug

Common words that end in *x:*

la croix (*lah krwah*)/cross   la voix (*lah vwah*)/voice

Now There's More Than One

Chances are that when you travel, you're going to see more than one château, museum, church, etc. If you choose to discuss or describe these things, you'll want to make sure that you've got your plurals down pat. Practice makes perfect, so try to express that you see more than one of the things in the following list.

Example: héros/hero

Je vois (*zhuh v waht I see*) des héros.

boutique	automobile
croix/cross	tapis
restaurant	magazine
palais/palace	autobus

As a Rule
There is no elision or liaison with *h as indicated in the dictionary: *le homard (luh oh-mard)* and *les hors-d'oeuvre (lay ohr-duhvr)*.

Other Plurals

The letter *x* is used in French to make plurals.

➤ For nouns ending in *eau:*

le bateau (*luh bah-to*)/boat	les bateaux
le bureau (*luh bew-ro*)/office, desk	les bureaux
le cadeau (*luh kah-do*)/gift	les cadeaux
le chapeau (*luh shah-po*)/hat	les chapeaux
le château (*luh shah-to*)/castle	les chateaux
le couteau (*luh koo-to*)/knife	les couteaux
l'eau (*lo*) (f.)/water	les eaux
le gâteau (*luh gah-to*)/cake	les gateaux
le manteau (*luh mahN-to*)/coat	les manteaux

61

le morceau (*luh mohr-so*)/piece | les morceaux
l'oiseau (*lwah-zo*)/bird | les oiseaux
le rideau (*luh ree-do*)/curtain | les rideaux
le tableau (*luh tah-blo*)/picture, chalkboard | les tableaux

➤ For nouns ending in *eu*, except *le pneu* (*luh pnuh*)/tire: *les pneus:*

l'animal (*lah nee mahl*)/animal | les animaux
le cheveu (*luh shuh vuh*)/hair | les cheveux
le jeu (*luh zhuh*)/game | les jeux
le lieu (*luh lyuh*)/place | les lieux
le neveu (*luh nuh-vuh*)/nephew | les neveux

➤ For nouns ending in *al*, change *al* to *aux* except for *le bal* (*luh bahl*)/ball: *bals*; *le festival* (*luh fehs-tee-vahl*)/festival: *festivals*.

le cheval (*luh shuh-vahl*)/horse | les chevaux
l'hôpital (*lo-pee-tahl*)/hospital | les hôpitaux
le journal (*luh zhoor-nahl*)/newspaper | les journaux

➤ For some nouns ending in *ou,* add *x* to form the plural:

le bijou (*luh bee-zhoo*)/jewel | les bijoux
le caillou (*luh kah-yoo*)/pebble | les cailloux
le genou (*luh zhuh-noo*)/knee | les genoux
le joujou (*luh zhoo-zhoo*)/toy | les joujoux

➤ Just as we have some words in English that are always plural (*pants, sunglasses, shorts, news*), so do the French. Here are some nouns that might prove useful to you:

les ciseaux (m.) (*lay see-zo*)/scissors | les lunettes (f.) (*lay lew-neht*)/eyeglasses
les gens (m.) (*lay zhahN*)/people | les vacances (f.) (*lay vah-kahNs*)/vacation

Learning a foreign language wouldn't be a challenge if there weren't some irregularities. Here are some irregular plurals you might find useful:

l'oeil (m.) (*luhy*)/eye | les yeux (*lay zyuh*)
le travail (*luh trah-vahy*)/work | les travaux (*lay trah-vo*)
madame (*mah-dahm*)/Mrs. | mesdames (*may-dahm*)

mademoiselle (*mahd-mwah-zehl*)/Miss   mesdemoiselles (*mayd-mwah-zehl*)

monsieur (*muh-syuh*)/Mr.   messieurs (*meh-syuh*)

Some compound nouns (nouns made up of two nouns usually joined by a hyphen) do not change in the plural—only their markers do:

> le gratte-ciel (*luh graht-syehl*)
> les gratte-ciel/skyscrapers
>
> le hors d'oeuvre *(*luh ohr-duhvr*)
> les hors d'oeuvre/appetizers (*lay ohr-duhvr*)
>
> le rendez-vous (*luh rahN-day-voo*)
> les rendez-vous/appointments

As a Rule
Although you can refer to one hair in French as *un cheveu*, (for example, if there were a hair in your food), *hair*, in general, is always plural and is referred to as *les cheveux*.

Practice Those Plurals

If you're anything like me, you're always looking for something because you're either (a) very absent-minded or (b) totally lacking a sense of direction. Try your luck at telling someone what you are looking for:

Example: boats

Je cherche (*zhuh shehrsh*/I am looking for) les bateaux.

1. castles
2. eyeglasses
3. people
4. newspapers
5. packages
6. palaces
7. scissors
8. toys

What Have You Learned about Gender?

Read the following employment ads that were taken from an actual French newspaper and check whether the employer is looking for a male or female employee:

The Least You Need to Know

➤ You can change some nouns from masculine to feminine by adding an *e* or by changing the ending of the word.

➤ You must memorize the gender of most nouns.

➤ Most plurals end in *s* or *x*.

➤ Singular and plural nouns sound the same—only the markers change in pronunciation.

Chapter 7

Let's Plan a Trip

In This Chapter

➤ Subject pronouns

➤ Verb families and conjugation

➤ What to do to ask a question

➤ Common verbs from all the families

In the last chapter, you learned about nouns: how to determine their gender and how to make them plural. Nouns and the pronouns used to replace them are very important because you can use them as the subject of a sentence. In this chapter, you will see how you can communicate your thoughts in French by using nouns or pronouns and the verbs that convey the actions that are being performed.

To accomplish this, let's do something exciting. Let's plan a trip. Planning and taking an imaginary trip to a French-speaking country will teach you how to get along in most everyday situations where you would need French. Picture the places you could go: the bustling cities, the sandy beaches, the medieval towns. Imagine the sites you could see: the museums, the cathedrals, the parks, the gardens; and the people you could meet: French, Canadians, Haitians, Africans. The possibilities are endless. Let's start with the basics.

What's the Subject?

You're on a group tour and everyone involved seems to have his or her own agenda. *You* would like to take pictures of the beautiful stained-glass windows of Notre Dame. The woman next to you, *she* insists on the Eiffel Tower. The couple to your right, *they* would prefer to spend the day shopping. And the tour guide, well, *he*'s just disgusted at this point. In order to express the things people do, you need to learn about verbs. Verbs require a *subject*, whether it is stated, as in

> *I* would like to go to the Louvre.

> *The guide* is waiting for us.

or understood, as in a command:

> *Go* to the Pompidou Center. (The subject is understood to be *you*.)

A subject can be a noun or a pronoun that replaces the noun:

> *The artist* is painting a landscape.

> *He (she)* is painting a landscape.

Subject Pronouns

Just as in English, the French subject pronouns in Table 7.1 are given a person and a number (singular or plural):

Table 7.1 Subject Pronouns

Person	Singular		Plural	
first	je* (*zhuh*)	I	nous (*noo*)	we
second	tu** (*tew*)	you	vous** (*voo*)	you
third	il (*eel*)	he	ils***(*eel*)	they
	elle (*ehl*)	she	elles (*ehl*)	they
	on (*ohN*)	one, you, we, they		

The subject pronoun je requires elision and becomes j' before a vowel or vowel sound (h, y).
**The subject pronoun tu is used when speaking to a single (one) friend, relative, child, or pet. Tu is called the familiar form. The u from tu is never dropped for elision: tu arrives.*
**The subject pronoun vous is used in the singular to show respect to an older person or when speaking to someone you don't know very well. Vous is always used when speaking to more than one person, regardless of familiarity. Vous is referred to as the polite form.*
***The subject pronoun ils is used to refer to more than one male or a combined group of males and females.*

Tu versus Vous

Would you use *tu* or *vous* when speaking to the following people? A doctor? Your cousin? Your friend? A salesman? A woman waiting in line for a bus? Two friends? A policeman from whom you are asking directions? Your friends?

Cultural Tidbits

Tu is used by the French when speaking to their pets because they are considered family members. Pets are held in very high regard in France. It is not unusual at all to see a family accompanied by its dog in a French restaurant. No, the dog doesn't sit at the table. It eats on the floor, as usual, out of its own bowl. And, believe it or not, there are special take-out restaurants catering strictly to the family canine.

Pronouns are very useful because they allow you to speak fluidly without having to constantly repeat the noun. Imagine how tedious it would be to hear: Luc is French; Luc is from Paris; Luc would make a wonderful guide. A better version would be: Luc is French; *he*'s from Paris, and *he*'d make a wonderful guide. Use pronouns to replace *proper nouns* (the name of a person or persons), as follows:

Noun	Pronoun
Lucien	Il
Martine	Elle
Philippe et Claude	Ils
Marie et Anne	Elles
Paul et Georgette	Ils

You can also use pronouns to replace the name of a common noun referring to a person, place, thing, or idea, as follows:

Noun	Pronoun
le restaurant	il
la boutique	elle
le restaurant et le café	ils
la boutique et la poste	elles
le restaurant et la boutique	ils

Il, Ils, Elle, Elles?

Are you like me, an incurable gossip? Imagine that you've just attended a fabulous party and now you're driving your best friend home. Of course, the two of you can't wait to talke about all the *invités* (guests). Which pronoun would you use when speaking about: Charles? Lucie et Sylvie? Berthe? Pierre? Luc et Henri? Robert et Suzette? Janine, Charolotte, Michèle, et Roger? Paul, Roland, et Annick?

And which pronoun would you substitute for these nouns, subjects which came up in your conversation about the festivities? La fête? Le bal costumé? La musique et le décor? Les vêtements? Le travail et le coût? La cuisine et la nourriture? L'ambiance? L'hôte et l'hôtesse?

Verbs in Motion

Do you like to bungee jump? Participate in ballroom dancing competitions? Skydive? Or are you a couch potato attracted to more mundane activities like reading a book or watching T.V.? No matter what your preferences, you'll have to learn to use verbs to express any action, motion, or state of being. Verbs are referred to as *regular* if they follow a set pattern of rules and *irregular* if they don't. This chapter will look at regular verbs only.

Regular Verbs

Verbs are generally shown in the infinitive, the basic "to" form of the verb: to live, to laugh, to love. An infinitive, whether in French or English, is the form of the verb before it has been conjugated. We conjugate verbs all the time in English without even paying attention to the fact that we're doing it. *Conjugation* refers to changing the ending of a regular verb so that it agrees with the subject. For example, think of the verb *dance*. The infinitive is *to dance*, and it is conjugated as follows:

I dance	We dance
You dance	You dance
He/she dances	They dance

With irregular verbs, such as the verb *to be*, the entire form changes:

I am	We are
You are	You are
He/she is	They are

Regular verbs in French belong to one of three large families: verbs whose infinitives end in *er*, *ir*, or *re*. The verbs within each family are all conjugated in exactly the same manner, so after you've learned the pattern for one family, you know them all. The *er* family is, by far, the largest.

In order to plan your imaginary trip, you'll need to do the following, as in Table 7.2:

Table 7.2 Regular Verbs in Families

trouver une agence de voyages	*troo-vay ewn nah-zhahNs duh vwah-yahzh*	to find a travel agency
contacter un agent	*kohN-tahk-tay uhN nah-zhahN*	to contact an agent
parler du voyage	*pahr-lay dew vwah-yahzh*	to speak about the trip
préparer une liste de questions	*pray-pah-ray ewn leest duh kehs-tyohN*	to prepare a list of questions
poser des questions	*po-zay day kehs-tyohN*	to ask questions
donner des coups de téléphone	*doh-nay day koo duh-tay-lay-fohn*	to make phone calls
étudier les brochures	*ay-tew-dyay lay broh-shewr*	to study the brochures
décider où aller	*day-see-day oo ah-lay*	to decide where to go
réfléchir avant d'agir	*ray-flay-sheer ah-vahN dah-zheer*	to think before acting
choisir un hôtel	*shwah-zeer uhN no-tehl*	to choose a hotel
établir un itinéraire	*ay-tah-bleer uhN nee-tee-nay-rehr*	to establish an itinerary
remplir les documents nécessaires	*rahN-pleer lay dohk-kew-mahN nay-seh-sehr*	to fill out the necessary documents
attendre le passeport	*ah-tahNdr luh pahs-pohr*	to wait for the passport
répondre à des questions	*ray-pohNdr ah day kehs-tyohN*	to answer questions
rendre les papiers nécessaires	*rahNdr lay pah-pyay nay-seh-sehr*	to return the necessary papers

The verbs in the preceding table are written in the infinitive form. If you want to express what someone is doing, you must choose a subject pronoun and then learn the conjugations, as in Table 7.3:

Table 7.3 Family Conjugations

trouver (to find)	choisir (to choose)	attendre (to wait for)
je trouve *zhuh troov*	je choisis *zhuh shwah-zee*	j'attends *zhah-tahN*
tu trouves *tew troov*	tu choisis *tew shwah-zee*	tu attends *tew ah-tahN*
il, elle, on trouve *eel, ehl, ohN troov*	il, elle, on choisit *eel, ehl, ohN shwah-zee*	il, elle, on attend *eel, ehl, ohN nah-tahN*
nous trouv**ons** *noo troo-vohN*	nous chois**issons** *noo shwah-zee-sohN*	nous attend**ons** *noo zah-tahN-dohN*
vous trouv**ez** *voo troo-vay*	vous chois**issez** *voo shwah-zee-say*	vous attend**ez** *voo zah-tahN-day*
ils, elles trouv**ent** *eel, ehl troov*	ils, elles chois**issent** *eel, ehl shwah-zees*	ils, elles attend**ent** *eel, ehl zah-tahN*

The er Verb Family

Let's start with the biggest and easiest family. This will give you an introduction to conjugation that will put you at ease right from the start. To conjugate *er* verbs, drop *er* from the infinitive and then add the following endings:

je	*e*	nous	*ons*
tu	*es*	vous	*ez*
il, elle, on	*e*	ils, elles	*ent*

Now you can conjugate any *er* verb that belongs to the family. So, if you want to brag about your accomplishments to impress a member of the opposite sex, the sky's the limit.

Je gagne beaucoup d'argent.	I earn a lot of money.
Je joue très bien aux sports.	I play sports very well.
Je dîne dans les restaurants les plus élégant.	I dine in the finest restaurants.

See how easy it is?

Conjugation 101

Use the correct form of the verb to express what each individual is doing on vacation:

For example, (*regarder*): Je *regarde* le spectacle.

1. (traverser) Il _____ la rue.

2. (demander) Elles _____ l'adresse.

3. (chercher) Nous _____ le musée.

4. (accompagner) J'_____ ma famille.

5. (louer) Vous _____ un appartement.

6. (présenter) Sylvie et Luc_____ leurs amis à leurs parents.

The ir Verb Family

To conjugate *ir* verbs, drop *ir* from the infinitive and then add these endings:

je	*is*	nous	*issons*
tu	*is*	vous	*issez*
il, elle, on	*it*	ils, elles	*issent*

Conjugation 102

It's time to see if you're up to the challenge. Be careful with infinitives like *choisir* and *réussir* that already have *i*'s and *s*'s in them. By the time you're finished conjugating them they may look a little strange (Nous réussissons, Tu choisis), but they are correct. Be confident and give the correct form of the verb and express what each tourist does:

1. Nous/finir _____ à huit heures.

2. On/réfléchir _____.

3. Ils/jouir _____ de tout.

4. Tu/applaudir _____ au théâtre.

5. Elle/réussir _____ à parler français.

6. Je/choisir _____ un bon tour.

7. Vous/agir _____ bien.

8. Alice et Berthe/remplir _____ les formulaires.

The re Verb Family

As a Rule
You're in luck. Sometimes things are easier than they appear. There is no ending for the third person singular form (*il, elle, on*) of *re* verbs: Il (*Elle, On*) répond/He, She, One answers. So, in this case, there's no need to be concerned about memorizing anything.

This family is, by far, the smallest. The verbs *attendre* (to wait for), *entendre* (to hear), and *vendre* (to sell) are high-frequency verbs that you'll be using and hearing on a regular basis. So, it will be necessary to commit this conjugation to memory. To conjugate *re* verbs, drop *re* from the infinitive and then add these endings:

je	*s*
tu	*s*
il, elle, on	
nous	*ons*
vous	*ez*
ils, elles	*ent*

Conjugation 103

People on vacation do all sorts of different things. Use your knowledge of *re* verbs to describe their actions. In the following, choose the verb that best completes the sentence. Then, provide the correct verb form to explain what each tourist is doing:

attendre (to wait for)	perdre (to lose)	descendre (to go down)
rendre (to return)	entendre (to hear)	répondre (to answer)

1. Tu _____ le métro.

2. Elles _____ en ville.

3. Nous _____ notre plan de la ville.

4. Vous _____ à des questions.

5. Il _____ les nouvelles (the news).

6. Je _____ les documents.

Ask Me Anything

When planning your trip, you'll find lots of questions that you'll want to ask. Let's concentrate on the easy ones—those that require a simple yes or no answer.

There are four ways to show that you're asking a question. You can use:

1. intonation

2. the tag *n'est-ce pas* (isn't that so?)

3. *Est-ce que* at the beginning of your phrase

4. inversion.

Intonation

The easiest way to show that you're asking a question is to simply change your intonation and raise your voice at the end of the sentence. To do this, place an imaginary question mark at the end of your statement and speak with a rising inflection.

> Tu penses au voyage?　　　Are you thinking about the trip?
> (*tew pahNs o vwah-yahzh*)

Notice how your voice starts out lower and gradually keeps rising until the end of the sentence.

> Tu penses au voyage.　　　You are thinking about the trip.

When using the same sentence as a statement of fact, notice how your voice rises and then lowers by the end of the sentence.

N'est-ce pas?

Another simple way to ask a question is to add the tag *n'est-ce pas* (*nehs pas*/isn't that so) at the end of the sentence.

> Tu penses au voyage, n'est-ce pas?

Est-ce que

Yet another way to ask the same question is to put *Est-ce que* (*ehs-kuh*) at the beginning of the sentence. *Est-ce que* is not translated but does indicate that a question follows:

> Est-ce que tu penses au voyage?

As a Rule

If a subject is followed by two verbs, conjugate only the first verb. The second verb remains in the infinitive:

Je désire danser.
I want to dance.

Il aime jouer au tennis.
He loves to play tennis.

Inversion

The last way to form a question is by *inversion,* which is used far more frequently in writing than in conversation. *Inversion* means reversing the word order of the *subject pronoun* and the *conjugated verb form*. Several rules govern inversion, which can get tricky—but don't despair. If you feel more comfortable using one of the other three methods mentioned, by all means, use them. You will still be speaking perfectly correct French, you will be understood, and your question will be answered. For those who are up to the challenge, the rules are as follows:

As a Rule

Est-ce que becomes *Est-ce qu'* before a vowel or vowel sound (*h, y*): *Est-ce qu'il pense au voyage?*

➤ **Avoid inverting with *je*.** It's awkward and is very rarely used.

➤ **You can ONLY invert subject pronouns with conjugated verbs. DO NOT INVERT with nouns!** Look at some examples to see how inversion works with the subject pronouns:

Tu penses au voyage.	Penses-tu au voyage?
Nous expliquons bien.	Expliquons-nous bien?
Vous parlez français.	Parlez-vous français?
Ils commandent du vin.	Commandent-ils du vin?
Elles habitent à Paris.	Habitent-elles à Paris?

➤ **A -*t*- must be added with *il* and *elle* to avoid having two vowels together.** This usually happens only with verbs in the *er* family. For the *ir* and *re* families, the *il* and *elle* verb forms end in a consonant:

Il travaille aujourd'hui.	Travaille-**t**-il aujourd'hui?
Elle contacte l'agent.	Contacte-**t**-elle l'agent?
Il finit son dessert.	Finit-il son dessert?
Elle attend le bus.	Attend-elle le bus?

➤ **When you have a noun subject and you want to use inversion, you MUST replace the noun with the appropriate pronoun.** You may retain the noun at the beginning of the question, but then you must invert the corresponding pronoun with the conjugated verb form. For example:

Le chanteur **est-il** français? The pronoun *il* was chosen because *le chanteur* (the singer) is a singular, masculine noun. No -*t*- was necessary because the verb ends in a consonant.

La robe **est-elle** trop petite? The pronoun *elle* was chosen because *la robe* (the dress) is a feminine, singular noun. Again, no *-t-* was necessary because the verb ends in a consonant.

Le docteur et le dentiste **travaillent-ils** aujourd'hui? The pronoun *ils* was chosen because we are referring to more than one male noun.

Les brochures **sont-elles** à notre disposition? The pronoun *elles* was chosen because we are referring to a feminine, plural noun.

Le gâteau et la mousse **sont-ils** excellents? The pronoun *ils* was chosen because when referring to two nouns of different genders, the male noun is *always* given precedence.

Remember that whether you are using intonation, *est-ce que*, *n'est-ce pas*, or inversion, you are asking for exactly the same information: a yes/*oui* (*wee*) or no/*non* (*nohN*) answer:

Tu poses des questions intelligentes?

Est-ce que tu poses des questions intelligentes?

Tu poses des questions intelligentes, n'est-ce pas?

Poses-tu des questions intelligentes?

Ask Me if You Can

Imagine that you're sitting on a bus with your tour group. Unfortunately, you're stuck in horrible traffic on the autoroute and you and your fellow travelers are bored beyond belief. To keep yourselves occupied, you decide to ask questions about everyone on board, including yourselves. Using the subjects and actions listed, write questions in as many ways as you can.

1. nous/parler trop
2. il/descendre souvent en ville
3. vous/accomplir beaucoup
4. Marie/téléphoner toujours à sa famille
5. tu/attendre toujours les autres
6. les garçons/jouer au tennis
7. elles/écouter le guide
8. Luc et Anne/sembler heureux

And the Answer Is...

If you're an upbeat person who enjoys doing lots of things, you'll surely want to know how to answer "yes." To answer affirmatively (yes), use *oui* (*wee*) and then give your statement:

Vous dansez?   Oui, je danse.

To answer yes to a negative quesion, use *si*.

Tu ne danses pas bien?   Si, je danse bien.

Perhaps you're in a foul mood and everyone and everything is getting on your nerves. Or maybe "no" is just an honest answer. To answer negatively (no), use *non* (*nohN*) and then add *ne* and *pas* (not), respectively, before and after the conjugated verb form. Remember, if there are two verbs, only the first is conjugated:

Vous fumez?   Non, je ne fume pas.   Non, je ne désire pas fumer.

You can easily vary your negative answers by putting the following negative phrases before and after the conjugated verb:

ne…jamais (*nuh…zhah-meh*)   never

Je ne fume jamais.   I never smoke.

ne…plus (*nuh…plew*)   no longer

Je ne fume plus.   I no longer smoke. (I don't smoke anymore.)

ne…rien (*nuh…ryaN*)   nothing, anything

Je ne fume rien.   I'm not smoking anything.

If you want to increase your vocabulary quickly, you'll need to have as many verbs as possible on the tip of your tongue. Tables 7.4, 7.5, and 7.6 provide you with practical lists of the most frequently used *er, ir,* and *re* verbs—these are the ones that you'll need the most in any given situation.

Verb Tables

Table 7.4 Common er Verbs

aider	*eh-day*	to help
annoncer	*ah-nohN-say*	to announce
bavarder	*bah-vahr-day*	to chat
changer	*shahN-zhay*	to change
chercher	*shehr-shay*	to look for
commencer	*koh-mahN-say*	to begin
danser	*dahN-say*	to dance
demander	*duh-mahN-day*	to ask

dépenser	*day-pahN-say*	to spend (money)
donner	*doh-nay*	to give
écouter	*ay-koo-tay*	to listen (to)
étudier	*ay-tew-dyay*	to study
expliquer	*eks-plee-kay*	to explain
exprimer	*eks-pree-may*	to express
fermer	*fehr-may*	to close
fonctionner	*fohNk-syohN-nay*	to function
garder	*gahr-day*	to keep, watch
habiter	*ah-bee-tay*	to live (in)
indiquer	*aN-dee-kay*	to indicate
jouer	*zhoo-ay*	to play
laver	*lah-vay*	to wash
manger	*mahN-zhay*	to eat
marcher	*mahr-shay*	to walk
nager	*nah-zhay*	to swim
oublier	*oo-blee-yay*	to forget
parler	*pahr-lay*	to speak
penser	*pahN-say*	to think
préparer	*pray-pah-ray*	to prepare
présenter	*pray-zahN-tay*	to present, introduce
quitter	*kee-tay*	to leave, remove
regarder	*ruh-gahr-day*	to look at, watch
regretter	*ruh-gruh-tay*	to regret
rencontrer	*rahN-kohN-tray*	to meet
retourner	*ruh-toor-nay*	to return
sembler	*sahN-blay*	to seem
signer	*see-nyay*	to sign
téléphoner	*tay-lay-foh-nay*	to telephone
travailler	*trah-vah-yay*	to work
voyager	*vwah-yah-zhay*	to travel

Table 7.5 Common ir Verbs

agir	*ah-zheer*	to act
avertir	*ah-vehr-teer*	to warn
blanchir	*blahN-sheer*	to bleach, whiten
choisir	*shwah-zeer*	to choose
finir	*fee-neer*	to finish
guérir	*gay-reer*	to cure
jouir	*zhoo-eer*	to enjoy
maigrir	*meh-greer*	to become thin
obéir	*oh-bay-eer*	to obey
punir	*pew-neer*	to punish
réfléchir	*ray-flay-sheer*	to reflect, think
réussir	*ray-ew-seer*	to succeed

Table 7.6 Common re Verbs

attendre	*ah-tahNdr*	to wait (for)
descendre	*deh-sahNdr*	to go (come) down
entendre	*ahN-tahNdr*	to hear
perdre	*pehrdr*	to lose
répondre	*ray-pohNdr ah*	to answer
vendre	*vahNdr*	to sell

The Least You Need to Know

➤ Subject pronouns can be used to replace any subject noun.

➤ Any verb that follows a subject noun or pronoun must be properly conjugated.

➤ There are different rules for conjugating verbs belonging to the *er, ir,* and *re* families.

➤ The easiest way to indicate that you're asking a question is to raise the intonation in your voice.

Part 2

Travel

Chapter 8

Meetings and Greetings

In This Chapter

➤ Greetings and salutations

➤ All about *être* (to be)

➤ The different professions

➤ Getting the information you need

You planned your trip in Chapter 7, and the time has come to put what you've learned to good use. Now that you can create simple French sentences (using subject nouns, pronouns, and regular verbs) and ask yes-no questions, you're ready to engage in a short conversation.

While you're sitting on the plane on your way to a glorious vacation in a French-speaking country, you might want to strike up a conversation with the person sitting next to you. If that person speaks French, you're in luck. This is an excellent opportunity for you to introduce yourself and, perhaps, to get a few helpful hints and recommendations about places to visit, restaurants to go to, and things to do in the country you're visiting.

Making Friends

Even though you've read every travel book in your local bookstore, you may still be a little nervous about your trip. What you really need to do is speak to someone from the country—someone who lives there and can fill you in on everything you can do and see and everywhere to go. Where can you find this person? Probably sitting right next to you on the plane! There's plenty of time before you arrive at your destination, so why not strike up a conversation?

Since you don't know the person at all, a formal approach is *de rigueur* (mandatory). A typical opening conversation might start with many of these phrases:

Bonjour	*bohN-zhoor*	Hello.
Bonsoir	*bohN swahr*	Good evening.
monsieur	*muh-syuh*	Sir
madame	*mah-dahm*	Miss, Mrs.
mademoiselle	*mahd-mwah-zehl*	Miss
Je m'appelle	*zhuh mah-pehl*	My name is (I call myself)
Comment vous appelez-vous?	*kohN-mahN voo zah-play voo*	What is your name?
Comment allez-vous?	*kohN-mahN tah-lay voo*	How are you?
Très bien.	*treh byaN*	Very well.
Pas mal.	*pah mahl*	Not bad.
Comme ci comme ça.	*kohm see kohm sah*	So so.

During an informal opening conversation (between young people or friends), you might use these phrases:

Salut!	*sah-lew*	Hi!
Je m'appelle.	*zhuh mah-pehl*	My name is (I call myself)
Comment t'appelles- tu?	*kohN-mahN tah-pehl tew*	What's your name?
Ça va?	*sah vah*	How's it going?
Ça marche?	*sah mahrsh*	How's it going?
Ça va.	*sah vah*	O.K.
Ça marche.	*sah mahrsh*	O.K.

To Be or Not To Be

If you'd really like to get to know the person you are talking to, ask him or her a few questions about himself or herself: Where he or she is from, for example. You'll also want to respond correctly when others ask where you are from. To do this, you will need the verb *être* (to be). Just as it is in English, the verb *to be* (*être*) is irregular, and all of its forms must be memorized. Because you will be using this verb so frequently, make it a top priority to memorize its forms. Compare the conjugations in Table 8.1. As you will see, there are more irregular forms in French than there are in English.

Table 8.1   The Verb être (to be)

je suis	*zhuh swee*	I am
tu es	*tew eh*	you are
il, elle, on est	*eel (ehl) (ohN) eh*	he, she, one is
nous sommes	*noo sohm*	we are
vous êtes	*voo zeht*	you are
ils, elles sont	*eel (ehl) sohN*	they are

Do you detect an unfamiliar accent when speaking to an acquaintance? Get ready to satisfy your curiosity by using the verb être to ask about a person's origins. You're ready to proceed:

Formal use:

Vous êtes d'où?	*voo zeht doo*	Where are you from?

Informal use:

Tu es d'où?	*tew eh doo*	Where are you from?
Je suis de _____ (city).	*zhuh swee duh*	I am from _____ (city).

To express the state you come from, keep the following in mind:

Use *de* (from) for all feminine states; that is, any state ending in *e* and for any state whose name has an adjective:

As a Rule

Out of respect, older women in France are generally referred to and addressed as *Madame* (Mrs.), whether they are married or not. At what age is one considered "older"? It's hard to say—perhaps it's just a look that one develops. When in doubt, use *Madame*. *Mademoiselle* (Miss, Ms.) is used for younger women.

Pitfall

It's considered quite a *faux pas* to address someone informally if a strong friendship or relationship has not been established. One would not *tutoyer* (use *tu*) a new business acquaintance or a stranger. Never use the familiar form *tu* when speaking to someone you don't know well. It's considered very rude and insulting.

Je suis de Maine.

Je suis de New York.

Use *du* (from) for all masculine states; that is, states ending in any letter other than *e*.

Je suis du Vermont.

Use *des* (from) to say that you come from the U.S.

Je suis des États-Unis.

What's Your Line?

You can also use *être* to ask about a person's job or to talk about your own job. The feminine forms are given in parentheses in Table 8.2. Some occupations have only masculine or feminine forms despite the gender of the person employed. Other professions use the same word for masculine and feminine employees, but require the gender-appropriate noun marker (le [un] or la [une]).

Pitfall
The indefinite article *un* (une) is not used when expressing someone's profession (Je suis professeur. Elle est artiste), unless the profession is qualified by an adjective (Je suis un bon professeur. Elle est une artiste célèbre).

Formal use:

| Quel est votre métier? | *kehl eh vohtr may-tyay* | What is your profession? |

Informal use:

| Quel est ton métier? | *kehl eh tohN may-tyay* | What is your profession? |
| Je suis... | *zhuh swee...* | I am... |

Table 8.2 Professions

Profession	Pronunciation	Meaning
agent de police m.	*ah-zhahN duh poh-lees*	police officer
avocate	*ah-voh-kah(t)*	lawyer
bijoutier (bijoutière)	*bee-zhoo-tyay (bee-zhoo-tyehr)*	jeweler
caissier (caissière)	*keh-syay (keh-syehr)*	cashier
coiffeur (coiffeuse)	*kwah-fuhr (kwah-fuhz)*	hairdresser
commerçante	*koh-mehr-sahN(t)*	merchant
dentiste m.	*dahN-teest*	dentist

Profession	Pronunciation	Meaning
docteur m.	*dohk-tuhr*	doctor
électricien(ne)	*ay-lehk-tree-syaN (ay-lehk-tree-syehn)*	electrician
étudiante	*ay-tew-dyahN (ay-tew-dyahNt)*	student
facteur (factrice)	*fahk-tuhr (fahk-trees)*	postal worker
gérante	*zhay-rahN(t)*	manager
infirmier (infirmière)	*aN-feer-myay (ahN-feer-myehr)*	nurse
mécanicien(ne)	*may-kah-nee-syaN (may-kah-nee-syehn)*	mechanic
médecin m.	*mayd-saN*	doctor
musicien(ne)	*mew-zee-syaN (mew-zee-syehn)*	musician
pompier m.	*pohN-pyay*	firefighter
secrétaire m. or f.	*seh-kray-tehr*	secretary
serveuse f.	*sehr-vuhz*	waitress

Idioms with être

Imagine that you are on the phone with your French-speaking relative, Uncle Gaston. You think you hear him say to you, "Je suis en train de préparer le dîner." Hearing the cognates *train*, *preparer*, and *diner*, you immediately assume that Uncle Gaston is a chef on one of France's trains, perhaps on the T.G.V. (Train à Grande Vitesse—a very modern and fast train). But how could this be? The last you heard, he was a nephrologist at a leading teaching hospital in Paris. Did he have a change of heart? If you think you hear something that sounds wildly implausible, chances are you're right. Just when you think you have a handle on the language, *idioms*, those linguistic bugaboos, are ready to trip you up. In this case, your Uncle was using an idiomatic expression that means he's busy preparing dinner (bouillabaisse perhaps?). Table 8.3 will show you some new idioms with *être*.

As a Rule
To refer to a woman who's in a profession that always uses the masculine word form, simply add the word *femme* (fahm/woman) before the job title: Elle est femme pilote/She's a woman pilot.

Table 8.3 Idioms with être

être à	*ehtr ah*	to belong to
être d'accord (avec)	*ehtr dah-kohr*	to agree (with)
être de retour	*ehtr duh ruh-toor*	to be back
être en train de + infinitive	*ehtr ahN traN duh*	to be in the act of, busy
être sur le point de + infinitive	*ehtr sewr luh pwaN duh*	to be on the verge of

Make sure to conjugate the verb when you use it in context:

Ce journal est à moi.	This newspaper is mine.
Je suis d'accord.	I agree.
Est-il de retour?	Is he back?
Nous sommes en train de manger.	We are busy eating.
Es-tu sur le point de finir?	Are you on the verge of finishing?

Become Very Nosy

Picture this: That sublime hunk in seat 6B—you think he's cute. What phrases do you need to probe more deeply and develop the relationship of your dreams? You have a million questions and you want thorough answers. You're going to have to ask *information questions* to find out all the relevant facts you seek. Whatever the situation or problem, you'll be able to see it through with the words and expressions in Table 8.4.

Table 8.4 Information Questions

à quelle heure	*ah kehl uhr*	at what time
à qui	*ah kee*	to whom
à quoi	*ah kwah*	to what
avec qui	*ah-vehk kee*	with whom
avec quoi	*ah-vehk kwah*	with what
de qui	*duh kee*	of, about, from whom
de quoi	*duh kwah*	of, about, from what
combien (de + noun)	*kohN-byaN (duh)*	how much, many
comment	*kohN-mahN*	how

où	*oo*	where
d'où	*doo*	from where
pourquoi	*poor-kwah*	why
quand	*kahN*	when
qui	*kee*	who, whom
que	*kuh*	what
qu'est-ce que	*kehs-kuh*	what

Obtaining Information the Easy Way

You're ready to make your move. What's your opening line? Something corny like, "Excuse me, where are you from?" Or, "Where are you going?" Or perhaps you have a more interesting question that will break the ice. No matter how you choose to pursue your line of questioning, you'll find that the easiest way to ask for information is to put the question word (as listed in Table 8.4) immediately after the verbal phrase or thought. Here are some questions you might want to ask a traveling companion:

Vous voyagez (Tu voyages) **avec qui**?

Vous voyagez (Tu voyages) **pourquoi**?

Vous voyagez (Tu voyages) **comment**?

Vous parlez (Tu parles) **de qui? de quoi**?

Vous regardez (Tu regardes) **quoi**?

Vous êtes (Tu es) **d'où**?

Vous habitez (Tu habites) **où** en France?

Le vol (the flight) arrive **quand? à quelle heure**?

Un soda coûte **combien**?

Obtaining Information by Using est-ce que

Information questions can also be asked by using *est-ce que*. This is done by putting the question word at the very beginning of the sentence and then adding *est-ce que* before the verbal phrase or thought:

Avec qui est-ce que vous voyagez (tu voyages)?

Pourquoi est-ce que vous voyagez (tu voyages)?

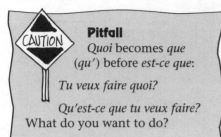

Pitfall
Quoi becomes *que* (*qu'*) before *est-ce que*:

Tu veux faire quoi?

Qu'est-ce que tu veux faire?
What do you want to do?

Comment est-ce que vous voyagez (tu voyages)?

De qui? De quoi est-ce que vous parlez (tu parles)?

Qu'est-ce que vous regardez (tu regardes)?

D'où est-ce que vous êtes (tu es)?

Où est-ce que vous habitez (tu habites) en France?

Quand? À quelle heure est-ce que le vol (the flight) arrive?

Combien est-ce que un soda coûte?

Obtaining Information by Using Inversion

Finally, you can use inversion to ask information questions. Put the question word(s) (as listed in Table 8.4) before the inverted subject pronoun and conjugated verb form:

Avec qui voyagez-vous (voyages-tu)?

Pourquoi voyagez-vous (voyages-tu)?

Comment voyagez-vous (voyages-tu)?

De qui? De quoi parlez-vous (parles-tu)?

Que regardez-vous (regardes-tu)?

D'où êtes-vous (es-tu)?

Où habitez-vous (habites-tu) en France?

Quand? À quelle heure le vol (the flight) arrive-t-il?

Combien coûte-t-il un soda?

You will probably ask for information in a variety of different ways. No doubt you'll choose the way that feels more comfortable and seems to flow. Most of the time, however, you will probably tack the question word or phrase onto the end of your statement (Vous êtes d'où?). Why not? It's easy and it works. Using *est-ce que* may be your choice on occasion, especially if you have a noun subject (A quelle heure est-ce que l'avion arrive?). At other times, you might find it preferable to invert (Que cherches-tu?). Whichever way you choose, you will be perfectly understood and will get the information you need.

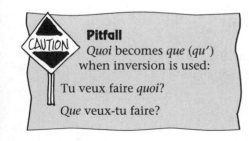

Pitfall
Quoi becomes *que* (*qu'*) when inversion is used:

Tu veux faire quoi?

Que veux-tu faire?

Ask Away

Read each of the following paragraphs. Ask as many questions as you can, based on the information given to you in each selection. In paragraph A, you are asking about Robert. In paragraph B, you must ask Georgette questions about herself:

➤ **A.** Robert est des États-Unis. Il voyage avec sa famille en France en voiture. Ils passent deux mois en France. Is désirent visiter tous les villages typiques. Ils retournent à Pittsburgh en septembre.

➤ **B.** Je m'appelle Georgette. Je suis de Nice. Je cherche une correspondante américaine parce que je désire pratiquer l'anglais. Je parle anglais seulement quand je suis en classe. J'adore aussi la musique. Je suis sérieuse.

The Least You Need to Know

➤ Choose your words carefully! The greeting words you use depend upon your familiarity with that person.

➤ The verb *être* is one of the most useful verbs in French. It is essential to memorize it because it is irregular.

➤ You can ask yes/no questions by using intonation, the tag *n'est-ce pas, est-ce que* at the beginning of a sentence, and inversion.

➤ You can get information easily by learning a few key words and phrases, and by placing them at the end of the thought, before *est-ce que* at the beginning of the sentence, or before an inverted question form.

I'd Like to Get to Know You

In This Chapter

➤ Family members

➤ Expressing possession

➤ Making introductions

➤ All about *avoir* (to have)

➤ Descriptions

If you've successfully used the linguistic tools provided in the preceding chapter, then you should be well on your way to introducing yourself and making new friends. You certainly don't want to appear rude, so how about introducing your family members to your new acquaintances? Perhaps you, too, will meet a new friend and be introduced to members of his or her family. Whatever the circumstances, it helps to be prepared.

Let's say there is someone in particular you think you would like to meet. But before you make your introduction, you'd like to find out a few things about this person. This chapter will give you the tools you need to find out what your potential pal is really like.

What a Family!

How many times have you opened your mouth during the course of a conversation only to find that you've done a magnificent job of sticking your foot in it? If you're anything like me, it's probably happened more often than you care to remember. Have you ever (as I have done) mistaken someone's father for his grandfather? Or worse yet, someone's wife for his mother? I've learned not to make any assumptions when I meet someone. Table 9.1 will help you to avoid a potentially embarrassing situation.

Table 9.1 Family Members

Male	Pronunciation	Meaning	Female	Pronunciation	Meaning
le père	*luh pehr*	father	la mère	*lah mehr*	mother
le grand-père	*luh grahN-pehr*	grandfather	la grand-mère	*lah graN-mehr*	grandmother
le beau-père	*luh bo- pehr*	father-in-law	la belle-mère	*lah behl- mehr*	mother-in-law
l'enfant	*lahN-fahN*	child	l'enfant	*lahN-fahN*	child
le frère	*luh frehr*	brother	la soeur	*lah suhr*	sister
le demi-frère	*luh duh-mee frehr*	step-brother	la demi-soeur	*lah duh-mee suhr*	step-sister
le beau-fils	*luh bo- fees*	stepson, son-in-law	la belle-fille	*lah behl- fee-y*	step-daughter
le fils	*luh fees*	son	la fille	*lah fee-y*	daughter
l'oncle	*lohNkl*	uncle	la tante	*lah tahNt*	aunt
le cousin	*luh koo-zahN*	cousin	la cousine	*lah koo-zeen*	cousin
le neveu	*luh nuh-vuh*	nephew	la nièce	*lah nyehs*	niece
le mari	*luh mah-ree*	husband	la femme	*lah fahm*	wife
le gendre	*luh zhahNdr*	son-in-law	la belle-fille	*lah behl-fee-y*	daughter-in-law
le petit ami	*luh puh-tee tah-mee*	boyfriend	la petite amie	*lah puh-tee tah-mee*	girlfriend

So, you've got a large family. How much easier it is to group our kids, parents, and grandparents together when we speak about them. Here are some useful plurals and their spellings:

les enfants	*lay zahN-fahN*	the children
les parents	*lay pah-rahN*	the parents
les grands-parents	*lay grahN-pah-rahN*	the grandparents
les beaux-parents	*lay bo pah-rahN*	the in-laws

Are You Possessed?

Don't be upset, but you're probably possessed. That is, you're somebody's somebody: your mother's child, your friend's friend, your brother's sister, or your sister's brother. There are two ways to show possession in French: by using the preposition *de* and by using possessive adjectives.

Possession with de

To show possession in English, we put *'s* or *s'* after a noun. But there are no apostrophes in French. In order to translate *Roger's mother* into French, a speaker would have to say *The mother of Roger = la mère de Roger*. The preposition *de* means *of* and is used to express possession or relationship. *De* is repeated before each noun and becomes *d'* before a vowel:

> C'est le père de Jean et d'Anne.

> He's John and Anne's father.

If the possessor is referred to not by name but by a common noun such as *the boy* or *the parents* (*He is the boy's father:* The father of the boy; or *That's the parents' car:* The car of the parents), then *de* contracts with the definite articles *le* and *les* to express *of the,* as shown in Table 9.2.

Table 9.2 Contractions with de

de +	le	DU
de +	les	DES

Examples using contractions with *de* are:

> Ce sont les parents *du* garçon.

> Ce sont les parents *des* jeunes filles.

Express These Relationships

Now that you understand how to use *de* to express possession, how would you say: Michael's mother? André and Marie's father? The girls' grandparents? The boy's uncle? The family's grandfather? The child's brother?

As a Rule

No changes are necessary for **de + la** or **de + l'**.

Ce sont les parents *de la* fille.

Ce sont les parents *de l'*homme.

Possessive Adjectives

The possessive adjectives *my*, *your*, *his*, *her*, and so on, show that something belongs to someone. In French, possessive adjectives agree with the nouns they describe (the person or thing that is possessed) and not with the subject (the person possessing them). See how this compares with English:

English	French
He loves *his* mother.	Il aime *sa mère*.
She loves *her* mother.	Elle aime *sa mère*.
He loves *his* father.	Il aime *son père*.
She loves *her* father.	Elle aime *son père*.

As a Rule
The French use *mon*, *ton*, and *son* before feminine nouns beginning with a vowel to prevent a clash between two pronounced vowel sounds. This allows the language to flow:

mon ami   my male friend
mon amie   my female friend

Son and *sa* both mean *his* or *her* because the possessive adjective agrees with the noun it modifies, not with the subject. Therefore, *her father = son père* because *son* agrees with the word *père*, which is masculine; and *his mother = sa mère* because *sa* agrees with the word *mère*, which is feminine. This difference makes French very tricky to English speakers. Just remember that it is important to know the gender (masculine or feminine) of the noun possessed. When in doubt, look it up! Table 9.3 summarizes the use of possessive adjectives.

Table 9.3 Possessive Adjectives

Used before masculine singular nouns or feminine singular nouns beginning with a vowel	Used before feminine singular nouns beginning with a consonant only	Used before all plural nouns
mon (*mohN*) my	ma (*mah*) my	mes (*may*) my
ton (*tohN*) your (fam.)	ta (*tah*) your (fam.)	tes (*tay*) your (fam.)
son (*sohN*) his, her	sa (*sah*) his, her	ses (*say*) his, her
notre (*nohtr*) our	notre (*nohtr*) our	nos (*no*) our
votre (*vohtr*) your (pol.)	votre (*vohtr*) your (pol.)	vos (*vo*) your (pol.)
leur (*luhr*) their	leur (*luhr*) their	leurs (*luhr*) their

State Your Preference

Do you have a favorite song, color, restaurant, vacation spot? We all have our own individual preferences. What are yours? Express them by using the correct possessive adjective (mon, ma, mes).

Pitfall
There is no elision with possessive adjectives because there are no final vowels to drop. Never use *m'*, *t'*, or *s'* to express *his* or *her*.

Examples:

acteur favori	Mon acteur favori est Danny DeVito.
acteurs favoris	Mes acteurs favoris sont Mel Gibson et Patrick Swayze.

actrices favorites	restaurants favoris	couleur favorite
chanson (song) favorite	sport favori	film favori

Let Me Introduce You

Let me introduce myself. My name is Gail. And I'd love for you to meet my husband, Doug, who's helped me tremendously with this book. Do you know my sons Eric and Michael? Eric is a computer wiz. This manuscript couldn't have been typed without him. And Michael, well, he's my source of moral support. Now, let's make some introductions in French:

Permettez-moi de me présenter. Je m'appelle _____.

Pehr-meh-tay mwah duh muh pray-zahN-tay. Zhuh mah-pehl _____.

You might ask about a companion:

Vous connaissez (Tu connais) mon cousin , Roger?

voo koh-neh-say (tew koh-neh) mohN koo-zahN roh-zhay?

If the answer is *no* (*non*), then you would say:

Je vous présente (Je te présente) mon cousin, Roger.

zhuh voo pray-zahNt (zhuh tuh pray-zahNt) mohN koo-zahN roh-zhay.

or

C'est mon cousin, Roger.

seh mohN koo-zahN roh-zhay.

To express pleasure at having met someone, you might say:

Formally

> Je suis *content(e) [heureux (heureuse), enchanté(e)]* de vous connaître.
> *zhuh swee kohN-tahN [zuh-ruh(z), zahN-shahN-tay] duh voo koh-nehtr*
> I am glad (happy, delighted) to know you.

Informally

> Enchanté(e), C'est un plaisir.
> *ahN-shahN-tay, seh tuhN pleh-zeer*
> Delighted. It's a pleasure.

The correct reply to an introduction is:

> Moi de même.
> *mwah dmehm*
> The pleasure is mine.

Can You?

Are you interested in initiating a conversation and getting your family or traveling companion involved? If so, see if you can do the following in French:

1. Introduce yourself to someone.

2. Ask someone if they know a member of your family.

3. Introduce a member of your family to somone.

4. Express pleasure at having met someone.

5. Respond to someone who says how glad they are to have met you.

Taking the Conversation a Little Further

Perhaps you would like to discuss how many children you have or your age; or you might want to describe family members or friends who aren't present. A verb that you will find most helpful is *avoir* (to have). Like the verb *être* (to be), *avoir* is an irregular verb, and all of its forms (as seen in Table 9.4) must be memorized.

Table 9.4 The Verb avoir (to have)

j'ai	*zhay*	I have
tu as	*tew ah*	you have
il, elle, on a	*eel,(ehl),(ohN) ah*	he, she, one has
nous avons	*noo zah-vohN*	we have

| vous avez | *voo zah-vay* | you have |
| ils, elles ont | *eel, (ehlz) ohN* | they have |

Idioms with *avoir*

In Chapter 4, you were given many idioms with *avoir* that express physical conditions. To refresh your memory, review Chapter 4.

Now you are ready for some new *avoir* idioms. Perhaps you would like to thank a family for giving you the *opportunity* to stay in their home. You might be tempted to give a French twist to our word *opportunity*. After all, *opportunité* does have a French ring to it. When you look up your creation (*opportunité*) in a bilingual dictionary, you will find that the word does exist, but it doesn't mean what you had hoped (in fact, it means *expediency, advisability, fitness*). To avoid other mistakes, study the *avoir* idioms in Table 9.5.

Table 9.5 Idioms with *avoir*

avoir l'occasion de	*ah-vwahr loh-kah-zyohN duh*	to have the opportunity to
avoir de la chance	*ah-vwahr duh lah shahNs*	to be lucky
avoir l'habitude de	*ah-vwahr lah-bee-tewd duh*	to be accustomed to
avoir l'intention de	*ah-vwahr laN-tahN-syohn duh*	to intend to
avoir le temps de	*ah-vwahr luh tahN duh*	to have the time to
avoir lieu	*ah-vwahr lyuh*	to take place

Make sure to conjugate the verb when you use it in context:

J'ai l'occasion de voyager	I have the opportunity to travel.
Tu as de la chance.	You're lucky.
J'ai l'habitude de dîner à at six heures.	I'm accustomed to dining at six o'clock.
Avez-vous l'intention de partir bientôt?	Do you intend to leave soon?
Ils n'ont pas le temps d' attendre.	They don't have the time to wait.
Le rendez-vous a lieu à midi.	The meeting is taking place at noon.

Using *avoir*

Avoir is a verb that you'll be constantly using. Now that you've taken the time to learn all of its forms and useful idiomatic expressions, see if you can properly complete the following thoughts:

avoir de la chance   avoir l'occasion de

avoir l'habitude de   avoir le temps de

avoir l'intention de   avoir lieu

1. Tu ne travailles pas. Alors tu _____ aider tes parents.

2. Il regarde la télévision tous les jours. Il _____ regarder la télévision.

3. Vous avez gagné (won) la loterie. Vous _____

4. Elles sont riches. Elles _____ visiter la France chaque année (every year).

5. J'étudie le français. Un jour j'_____ d'aller (to go) à Paris.

6. La cérémonie _____ aujourd'hui (today).

What's He/She Like?

I've been blabbing about myself for several chapters now. Are you curious to know what I'm like? Do you have a mental picture of what a French author looks like? Did you guess brunette (thank you, L'Oréal), brown eyes, 5'4", thin, and young at heart? (I'd tell you my real age, but my students might be curious enough to read this book and discover the answer to a very well-kept secret.) That's me.

If you want to describe a person, place, thing, or idea in detail, you must use adjectives. French adjectives always agree in gender (masculine or feminine) and number (singular or plural) with the nouns or pronouns they modify. In other words, all the words in a French sentence must match:

Her father is happy.   Son père est *content*.

Her mother is happy.   Sa mère est *contente*.

Fortunately, many adjectives follow the same, or almost the same, rules for gender and plural formation as the nouns you've studied in Chapter 6.

Gender of Adjectives

With most adjectives, you form the feminine by simply adding an *e* to the masculine form, as shown in Table 9.6. You will notice that a pronunciation change occurs when an *e* is added after a consonant. That consonant, which was silent in the masculine, is now pronounced in the feminine form. When the *e* is added after a vowel, there is no change in pronunciation.

Table 9.6 Forming Feminine Adjectives

Masculine		Feminine		Meaning
âgé	*ah-zhay*	âgée	*ah-zhay*	old, aged
américain	*ah-may-ree-kahN*	américaine	*ah-may-ree-kehn*	American
amusant	*ah-mew-zahN*	amusante	*ah-mew-zahNt*	amusing, fun
bleu	*bluh*	bleue	*bluh*	blue
blond	*blohN*	blonde	*blohNd*	blond
charmant	*shahr-mahN*	charmante	*shahr-mahNt*	charming
content	*kohN-tahN*	contente	*kohN-tahNt*	glad
court	*koor*	courte	*koort*	short
dévoué	*day-voo-ay*	dévouée	*day-voo-ay*	devoted
élégant	*ay-lay-gahN*	élégante	*ay-lay-gahNt*	elegant
fatigué	*fah-tee-gay*	fatiguée	*fah-tee-gay*	tired
fort	*fohr*	forte	*fohrt*	strong
français	*frahN-seh*	française	*frahN-sehz*	French
grand	*grahN*	grande	*grahNd*	big
haut	*o*	haute	*ot*	tall, big
intelligent	*aN-teh-lee-zhahN*	intelligente	*aN-teh-lee-zhahNt*	intelligent
intéressant	*aN-tay-reh-sahN*	intéressante	*aN-tay-reh-sahNt*	interesting
joli	*zhoh-lee*	jolie	*zhoh-lee*	pretty
lourd	*loor*	lourde	*loord*	heavy
occupé	*oh-kew-pay*	occupée	*oh-kew-pay*	busy
ouvert	*oo-vehr*	ouverte	*oo-vehrt*	open
parfait	*pahr-feh*	parfaite	*pahr-feht*	perfect
petit	*puh-tee*	petite	*puh-teet*	small
poli	*poh-lee*	polie	*poh-lee*	polite
prochain	*proh-shahN*	prochaine	*proh-shehn*	next
situé	*see-tew-ay*	située	*see-tew-ay*	situated

If an adjective already ends in an *e*, it is not necessary to make any changes at all. Both the masculine and feminine forms are spelled and pronounced exactly the same (see the adjectives in Chapter 3, pages 27–29).

célèbre (*say-lehbr*) famous

célibataire (*say-lee-bah-tehr*) single

chauve (*shov*) bald

comique (*koh-meek*) comical

drôle (*drohl*) funny

facile (*fah-seel*) easy

faible (*fehbl*) weak

formidable (*fohr-mee-dahbl*) great

honnête (*oh-neht*) honest

maigre (*mehgr*) thin

malade (*mah-lahd*) sick

mince (*maNs*) thin

moderne (*moh-dehrn*) modern

pauvre (*pohvr*) poor

propre (*prohpr*) clean

sale (*sahl*) dirty

splendide (*splahN-deed*)

sympathique (*saN-pah-teek*) nice

triste (*treest*) sad

vide (*veed*) empty

If a masculine adjective ends in *x*, the feminine is formed by changing *x* to *se,* which gives the feminine ending a *z* sound, as seen in Table 9.7.

Table 9.7 Adjectives Ending in eux and euse

Masculine		Feminine	
affectueux	*ah-fehk-tew-uh*	affectueuse	*ah-fehk-tew-uhz*
ambitieux	*ahN-bee-syuh*	ambitieuse	*ahN-bee-syuhz*
courageux	*koo-rah-zhuh*	courageuse	*koo-rah-zhuhz*
curieux	*kew-ryuh*	curieuse	*kew-ryuhz*
dangereux	*dahNzh-ruh*	dangereuse	*dahNzh-ruhz*
délicieux	*day-lee-syuh*	délicieuse	*day-lee-syuhz*
furieux	*few-ryuh*	furieuse	*few-ryuhz*
généreux	*zhay-nay-ruh*	généreuse	*zhay-nay-ruhz*
heureux (happy)	*uh-ruh*	heureuse	*uh-ruhz*
malheureux (unhappy)	*mahl-uh-ruh*	malheureuse	*mahl-uh-ruhz*
paresseux (lazy)	*pah-reh-suh*	paresseuse	*pah-reh-suhz*
sérieux	*say-ryuh*	sérieuse	*say-ryuhz*

If a masculine adjective ends in *f,* the feminine is formed by changing *f* to *ve.* See Table 9.8 for pronunciation changes.

Table 9.8   Adjectives Ending in f and ve

Masculine		Feminine	
actif	*ahk-teef*	active	*ahk-teev*
attentif	*ah-tahN-teef*	attentive	*ah-tahN-teev*
imaginatif	*ee-mah-zhee-nah-teef*	imaginative	*ee-mah-zhee-nah-teev*
impulsif	*aN-pewl-seef*	impulsive	*aN-pewl-seev*
intuitif	*aN-tew-ee-teef*	intuitive	*aN-tew-ee-teev*
naïf	*nah-eef*	naïve	*nah-eev*
neuf (new)	*nuhf*	neuve	*nuhv*
sportif	*spohr-teef*	sportive	*spohr-teev*
vif lively	*veef*	vive	*veev*

If a masculine adjective ends in *er*, the feminine is formed by changing *er* to *ère*, as shown in Table 9.9.

Table 9.9   Adjectives Ending in er and ère

Masculine		Feminine		Meaning
cher	*shehr*	chère	*shehr*	dear, expensive
dernier	*dehr-nyay*	dernière	*dehr-nyehr*	last
entier	*ahN-tyay*	entière	*ahN-tyehr*	entire
étranger	*ay-trahN-zhay*	étrangère	*ay-trahN-zhehr*	foreign
fier	*fyehr*	fière	*fyehr*	proud
léger	*lay-zhay*	légère	*lay-zhehr*	light
premier	*pruh-myay*	première	*puh-myehr*	first

Some masculine adjectives double the final consonant and then add *e* to form the feminine, as shown in Table 9.10.

Table 9.10   Adjectives that Double Their Consonants

Masculine		Feminine		Meaning
ancien	*ahN-syaN*	ancienne	*ahN-syehn*	ancient, old
bas	*bah*	basse	*bahs*	low

continues

Table 9.10 Continued

Masculine		Feminine		Meaning
bon	*bohN*	bonne	*bohn*	good
européen	*ew-roh-pay-aN*	européenne	*ew-roh-pay-ehn*	European
gentil	*zhahN-tee-y*	gentille	*zhahN-tee-y*	nice, kind
gros	*gro*	grosse	*gros*	fat, big
mignon	*mee-nyohN*	mignonne	*mee-noyhn*	cute

Finally, the adjectives in Table 9.11 list irregular feminine forms that must be memorized.

Table 9.11 Irregular Adjectives

Masculine		Feminine		Meaning
beau*	*bo*	belle	*behl*	beautiful
blanc	*blahN*	blanche	*blahNsh*	white
complet	*kohN-pleh*	complète	*kohN-pleht*	complete
doux	*doo*	douce	*doos*	sweet, gentle
faux	*fo*	fausse	*fos*	false
favori	*fah-voh-ree*	favorite	*fah-voh-reet*	favorite
frais	*freh*	fraîche	*frehsh*	fresh
long	*lohN*	longue	*lohNg*	long
nouveau*	*noo-vo*	nouvelle	*noo-vehl*	new
vieux*	*vyuh*	vieille	*vyay*	old

*The French use special forms: bel, nouvel, and vieil **before** masculine nouns beginning with a vowel or vowel sound to prevent a clash between two pronounced vowel sounds. This allows the language to flow.*

un bel appartement   un nouvel appartement   un vieil appartement

If the adjective comes **after** the noun, then the regular masculine form is used:

L'appartement est beau.   L'appartement est nouveau.   L'appartement est vieux.

More Than One? What Are They Like?

Perhaps you'd like to describe a physical or personality trait that is common to more than one of your family members. This is now a relatively simple task to perform because adjectives are often made plural in the same way as the nouns you've already studied.

The plural of most adjectives is formed by adding an unpronounced *s* to the singular form:

As a Rule
The masculine singular adjective *tout* (all) becomes *tous* in the plural.

Singular	Plural
timide	timide(s)
charmant(e)	charmant(e)s
joli(e)	joli(e)s
fatigué(e)	fatigué(e)s

If an adjective ends in *s* or *x*, it is unnecessary to add the *s*:

Singular	Plural
exquis	exquis
heureux	heureux

Most masculine singular adjectives ending in *al* change *al* to *aux* in the plural:

Singular	Plural
spécial	spéciaux

For the irregular, masculine, singular adjectives *beau, nouveau,* and *vieux,* the problem of having two conflicting vowel sounds (one at the end of the adjective and the other at the beginning of the noun that follows) is eliminated by adding an *s* or an *x* when the plural is formed. This eliminates the need for a plural form for the special masculine singular adjectives *bel, nouvel,* and *vieil* that are used only before nouns beginning with a vowel or a vowel sound. Note the plural formation for these masculine adjectives.

Singular	Plural	Example
beau	beaux	de beaux films
bel	beaux	de beaux appartements
nouveau	nouveaux	de nouveaux films
nouvel	nouveaux	de nouveaux appartements
vieux	vieux	de vieux films
vieil	vieux	de vieux appartements

What's Your Position?

As a Rule
If more than one adjective is being used in a description, put each adjective in its proper position:

une bonne histoire intéresante

une large et jolie avenue

un homme charmant et intelligent

In French, most adjectives are placed after the nouns they modify. Compare this with English, where we do the opposite:

un homme *intéressant*   an *interesting* man

Adjectives showing:

BEAUTY: beau, joli

AGE: jeune, nouveau, vieux

GOODNESS (or lack of it): bon, gentil, mauvais, vilain

SIZE: grand, petit, court, long, gros, large

generally precede the nouns they modify. Remember **BAGS,** and you'll have no trouble with these adjectives:

   un beau garçon   a handsome boy

   une large avenue   a wide avenue

Complete the Descriptions

How would you describe the Eiffel Tower, the car of your dreams, the mayor of your city? Here's an opportunity to give your opinions about certain things by using appropriate adjectives. Complete your descriptions carefully using the rules you've learned.

   1. La Tour Eiffel est une _____ tour _____.

   2. Les film français sont de _____ films _____.

3. Le président des États-Unis est un _____ homme _____.

4. Les boutiques parisiennes sont de _____ boutiques _____.

5. Le musée du Louvre est un _____ musée _____.

Personal Ads

Read the following personal ads taken from a few
French magazines and newspapers. Describe the
person writing the ad and the type of person being
sought.

As a Rule
Des becomes *de*
before an adjective.

FRANCAIS, 25 ans, plein de charme, romantique et cultivé aimerait rencontrer Jeune Française pour sorties sympathiques

27 ANS, excellent situation de dentiste, célibataire, BC.BG, il est dynamique et sympa, il est sentimental, il voudrait faire connaissance d'une J.F. tendre en vue de relations sérieuses et durables.

JEUNE AMERICAIN, 26 ans, séduisant sincère, intelligent, bonne situation financière, 1m79, cherche française pariant anglais. App. Victor

Ingénieur, Alexis, 30 ans, du charme et de l'élégance. C'est un homme sincère, courtois, généreux, qui souh. renc. une J.F. simple et naturelle pour s'investir dans une union durable. Célib.

FRANCINE, maman divorcée, simple, sage et dévouée, 35 ans, technicienne, offre son charme et sa tranquillité, à monsieur stable, courtois, aimant les enfants, la nature et la vie paisible.

Homme d'affaire, la trentaine, distingué, raffiné, aisé, généreux. Bel homme. Aimant le beau (Porsche, Cartier), désire combler belle jeune femme 20/25 ans, pour vie dorée, luxueuse et enviée.

The Least You Need to Know

➤ There is no *'s* in French. To show possession use the following formula: thing possessed + *de* + possessor.

➤ To show possession using an adjective, the adjective must agree with the person or thing possessed, not with the possessor.

➤ *Avoir* is an important irregular verb that expresses not only physical conditions, but also luck, intention, and opportunity.

➤ Adjectives agree in number and gender with the nouns they describe.

➤ Many adjectives follow the same rules for gender and plural formation as nouns.

➤ Irregularities must be memorized.

Chapter 10

Finally, You're at the Airport

> **In This Chapter**
>
> ➤ What you need to know about airplanes and airports
>
> ➤ All about *aller* (to go)
>
> ➤ Giving and receiving directions
>
> ➤ What to say if you don't understand something

Congratulations! You've planned a trip, you've gotten on the plane, and you've had a very pleasant conversation with the person sitting next to you. You've gotten the names of some good restaurants, places you want to be sure to visit, and perhaps the phone number of someone to call who will show you around town.

Your plane hasn't even landed yet, but you are mentally preparing for all the things you'll have to do before you even start off for your hotel: you must get your bags, go through customs, change some money, and find a means of transportation to get to your hotel. By the end of this chapter, you'll have accomplished these things and more.

The Plain Plane

A plane ride is often long and tedious. Sometimes you might experience some minor inconveniences or delays. During your trip, you might want to see about changing your seat, or perhaps you have some questions for the flight crew. Maybe they've stuck you in the smoking section, and you're a militant nonsmoker; or your traveling companion is seated a few rows in front of you, and you'd like to join him or her; or perhaps you'd simply like to ask the crew about takeoff and landing. The words and phrases in Table 10.1 will help you get information and solve simple problems you may encounter on board.

Cultural Tidbits

When your flight finally does arrive at the airport, you'll see the sign *Bienvenue (Welcome)*. If a friend or relative is there to greet you, expect to hear them wish you welcome by saying *Bienvenue*. A more formal greeting is:

Soyez le bienvenue (addressed to one male)

Soyez la bienvenue (addressed to one female)

Soyez les bienvenus (addressed to more than one male or a mixed group of males and females)

Soyez les bienvenues (addressed to more than one female)

Table 10.1 Inside the Plane

airline	la ligne aérienne	*lah lee-nyuh ahy-ryehn*
airline terminal	l'aérogare (f.), le terminal	*lahy-roh-gahr, luh tehr-mee-nahl*
airplane	l'avion (m.)	*lah-vyohN*
airport	l'aéroport	*lahy-roh-pohr*
aisle	le couloir	*luh kool-wahr*
on the aisle	côté couloir	*koh-tay kool-wahr*
board, embark	embarquer	*ahN-bahr-kay*
crew	l'équipage (m.)	*lay-kee-pahzh*
deboard, disembark, exit	débarquer	*day-bahr-kay*
emergency exit	la sortie (l'issue) de secours	*lah sohr-tee (lee-sew) duh suh-koor*
gate	la porte	*lah pohrt*

landing	l'atterrissage	*lah-teh-ree-sahzh*
life vest	le gilet de sauvetage	*luh zhee-leh duh sohv-tahzh*
(non) smokers	(non) fumeurs	*(nohN) few-muhr*
row	le rang	*luh rahN*
seat	la place, le siège	*lah plahs, luh syehzh*
takeoff	le décollage	*luh day-koh-lahzh*
trip	le voyage	*luh vwah-yahzh*
by the window	côté fenêtre	*koh-tay fuh-nehtr*

Airline Advice

If you've flown before, you know that airlines always have instructions about boarding, safety, and emergency procedures. Once on board, you will find an emergency card in your seat pocket, and your flight attendant will demonstrate any number of devices, from seat belts to oxygen masks. Read the following information to see if you can decipher the information the airline is trying to convey:

> **En cabine...**
>
> Pour votre confort et votre sécurité, n'emportez avec vous qu'un seul bagage de cabine.
>
> N'y placez pas d'objets considerés comme dangereux (armes, couteaux, ciseaux, etc.). Ils seront retirés lors des contrôles de sécurité.

What advice are they giving about your bags?

> **En soute...** (In the hold...)
>
> Choisissez des bagages solides, fermant à clé. Fixez à l'intérieur et à l'extérieur une étiquette d'identification. Évitez les articles suivants: médicaments, devises (securities), chèques, papiers d'affaires ou importants, bijoux et autres objets de valeur. Conservez-les avec vous en cabine.

On the Inside

There is a lot to do after you are inside the airport, but don't worry—there will be plenty of signs to point you in the right direction. Sometimes it's hard to judge where to go first. My first stop is usually the bathroom. After that, I slowly progress from one area to the next, taking care of all my business at a slow and steady pace. Table 10.2 will give you all the words you'll need to know after you're in the airport as well as outside on the way to your first destination!

Table 10.2   Inside the Airport

arrival	l'arrivée	*lah-ree-vay*
baggage claim area	la bande, les bagages (m.)	*lah bahnde, lay bah-gahzh*
bathrooms	les toilettes (f.)	*lay twah-leht*
bus stop	l'arrêt de bus	*lah-reh duh bews*
car rental	la location de voitures	*lah loh-kah-syohN duh vwah-tewr*
carry-on luggage	les bagages à main	*lay-bah-gahzh ah maN*
cart	le chariot	*luh shah-ryoh*
departure	le départ	*luh day-pahr*
destination	la destination	*lah dehs-tee-nah-syohN*
elevators	les ascenseurs (m.)	*lay-zah-sahN-suhr*
entrance	l'entrée	*lahN-tray*
exit	la sortie	*lah-sohr-tee*
flight	le vol	*luh vohl*
information	les renseignements (m.)	*lay rahN-seh-nyuh-mahN*
lost and found	les objets trouvés	*lay zohb-zheh troo-vay*
miss the flight	manquer (rater) le vol	*mahN-kay (rah-tay) luh vohl*
money exchange	le bureau de change	*luh bew-ro duh shahNzh*
passport control	le contrôle des passeports	*luh kohN-trohl day pahs-pohr*
porter	le porteur	*luh pohr-tuhr*
security check	le contrôle de sécurité	*luh kohN-trohl duh say-kew-ree-tay*
stop-over	l'escale	*lehs-kahl*
suitcase	la valise	*lah vah-leez*
taxis	les taxis	*lay tahk-see*
ticket	le billet, le ticket	*luh bee-yeh, luh tee-keh*

Signs Everywhere

With airport security at a maximum today due to terrorist threats and bomb scares, you can be sure that you will see many signs indicating the rules and procedures that must be followed. It is very important that you understand what you may and may not do. Even if you break a rule unintentionally, it can be scary to be approached by a *gendarme* speaking a language in which you have limited fluency. Following are the signs you can expect to see in Charles de Gaulle airport. Read them carefully and then match each sign with the information it gives you:

AVIS AUX PASSAGERS

Il est formellement interdit par la loi de transporter une arme dissimulée à bord d'un avion.

Les règlements en vigueur imposent l'inspection des passagers et des bagages à main lors de contrôle de sécurité.

Cette inspection peut être refusé. Les passagers refusant cette inspection ne seront pas autorisés à passer le contrôle de sécurité.

A

Chariot reservé aux passagers; utilisation interdite au delà du trottoir de l'aérogare.

B

ATTENTION:

Pour des raisons de sécurité, tout objet abandonné peut être détruit par les services de police.

Les passagers sont donc instamment priés de conserver leurs bagages avec eux.

C

ATTENTION:
Ne mettez pas votre sécurité en péril:n'acceptez aucun bagage d'une autre personne.

D

Veuillez présenter tous vos bagages à l'enregistrement, y compris vos bagages à main.

E

TRANSPORT DES ARMES À FEU
Les armes à feu transportées dans les bagages enregistrés doivent être déchargés et faire l'objet d'une déclaration auprès de nos services.

Les passagers transportant des armes sans les déclarer ou chargées sont passibles d'une amende de 1000 dollars ou équivalent.

F

Which sign is telling you that:

1. If you leave something behind, it might be destroyed ___

2. All of your baggage will be checked, even carry-ons ___

3. You can be searched for hidden weapons ___

4. You may carry a weapon if you declare it ___

5. You can only use the baggage cart within the airport ___

6. You shouldn't carry a suitcase for someone else ___

Going, Going, Gone

It's easy to get lost in sprawling international airports. To get yourself back on track, you'll need to know how to ask the right questions. One of the verbs you'll use a lot is *aller* (to go), an irregular verb that must be memorized (see Table 10.3 for conjugation).

Table 10.3   The Verb aller (to go)

je vais	*zhuh veh*	I go
tu vas	*tew vah*	you go
il, elle, on va	*eel, (ehl) (ohN) vah*	he, she, one goes
nous allons	*noo zah-lohN*	we go
vous allez	*voo zah-lay*	you go
ils, elles vont	*eel (ehl) vohN*	they go

As a Rule
Use the preposition *à* when you want to express going to or staying in a city.

Je vais à Lille. I'm going to Lille.

Ils restent à Strasbourg.
They're staying in Strasbourg.

Can You Tell Me How to Get to...?

If the airport is unfamiliar to you, you may need to ask for directions. This is relatively easy to do. There are two different ways of asking:

Où est le comptoir?
oo eh luh kohN-twahr?
Where is the counter?

Le comptoir, s'il vous plaît.
luh kohN-twahr seel voo pleh.
The counter, please.

Où sont les bagages?
oo sohN lay bah-gahzh?
Where is the baggage claim?

Les bagages, s'il vous plaît.
lay bah-gahzh seel voo pleh.
The baggage claim, please.

So That's Where It Is

Sometimes, the place you are trying to find is right in front of you. For instance, suppose that you're trying to locate the ticket counter. With all the noise and confusion, you lose your bearings, and you don't realize that you are standing near the very place you are trying to find. When you ask the gentlemen next to you for directions, he may reply:

Voici le comptoir.
vwah-see luh kohN-twahr.
Here is the counter.

Voilà le comptoir.
vwah-lah luh kohN-twahr.
There is the counter.

Giving and Receiving More Complicated Directions

If the place you want to get to is not within pointing distance, you'll need other directions. The verbs in Table 10.4 will be very helpful in getting you where you want to go or perhaps in helping someone else who is lost.

Table 10.4   Verbs Giving Directions

aller	*ah-lay*	to go
continuer	*kohN-tee-new-ay*	to continue
descendre	*day-sahNdr*	to go down
marcher	*mahr-shay*	to walk
monter	*mohN-tay*	to go up
passer	*pah-say*	to pass
prendre	*prahNdr*	to take
tourner	*toor-nay*	to turn
traverser	*trah-vehr-say*	to cross

When someone directs you to a location, that person is giving you a command. The subject of a command is understood to be *you* since *you* are being told where to go or what to do. Because there are two ways to say *you* in French (the familiar *tu* and the polite, and always plural, *vous*), there are two different command forms. Choose the form that best suits the situation. To form commands, simply drop the *tu* or *vous* subject pronoun:

> Va tout droit.   Allez à gauche.
> *vah too drwah.*   *ah-lay ah gohsh.*
> Go straight ahead.   Go to the left.

Using Commands

Imagine for a moment that, in Orly Airport, a Hungarian tourist approaches and asks you for directions. He doesn't speak English and you don't know a word of Hungarian. Fortunately, you both bought Idiot's Guides and know a little French. Help the poor lost Hungarian man by practicing your

As a Rule
For *er* verbs only, drop the final *s* from the *tu* form in all commands.

Pitfall
Two verbs that have very irregular command forms are *être* and *avoir*. Although they are used infrequently, you should memorize them:

	être	avoir
Tu form	Sois	Aie!
	swah	*ay*
	Be!	Have!
Vous form	Soyez!	Ayez
	swah-yay	*ay-yay*
	Be!	Have!

commands. Complete Table 10.5 by filling in the missing command forms and their meanings.

Table 10.5 Command Forms

Verb	Tu	Vous	Meaning
aller	Va!	Allez!	Go!
continuer			
descendre			
marcher			
monter			
passer			
prendre (Chapter 11)	Prends!	Prenez!	Take!
tourner			
traverser			

As a Rule
To be very polite, use *veuillez* + infinitive to say please:

Veuillez entrer. (vuh-yay ahN-tray.) Please enter.

Prepositions

Prepositions are used to show the relation of a noun to another word in a sentence. Refresh your memory with the idiomatic expressions for direction and location in Chapter 4 that are, in fact, prepositional phrases. Then add these simple prepositions in Table 10.6 that might also be useful for giving or receiving directions.

Table 10.6 Prepositions

à	*ah*	to, at
après	*ah-preh*	after
avant	*ah-vahN*	before
chez	*shay*	at the house (business) of
contre	*kohNtr*	against
dans	*dahN*	in
de	*duh*	from
derrière	*deh-ryehr*	behind
devant	*duh-vahN*	in front of

en	*ahN*	in
entre	*ahNtr*	between
loin (de)	*lwaN (duh)*	far (from)
par	*pahr*	by, through
pour	*poor*	for, in order to
près (de)	*preh (duh)*	near
sans	*sahN*	without
sous	*soo*	under
sur	*sewr*	on
vers	*vehr*	toward

Contractions

In certain cases, contractions form with the prepositions *à* and *de*, whether they are used alone or as part of a longer expression:

	Le	Les
à	au	aux
de	du	des

Allez à la douane.   La porte est à côté de la douane.

Allez à l'entrée.   La porte est à côté de l'entrée.

BUT

Allez **au** bureau de change.   La porte est à côté **du** bureau de change.

Allez **aux** bagages.   La porte est à côté **des** bagages.

> **As a Rule**
> There are no contractions with *la* and *l'*.

Are You Dazed and Confused?

What if someone gives you directions, and you don't understand? Perhaps the person to whom you are speaking is mumbling, speaking too fast, has a strong accent, or uses words you don't know. Don't be embarrassed. Ask for help in a kind, polite manner. You'll find the phrases in Table 10.7 to be an invaluable aid if you need to have something repeated or if you need more information.

Table 10.7 Expressing Lack of Understanding and Confusion

Excusez (Excuse)-moi	*ehk-skew-zay (ehk-skewz) mwah*	Excuse me
Pardon	*pahr-dohN*	Pardon me
Je ne comprends pas	*zhuh nuh kohN-prahN pah*	I don't understand
Je ne vous (t') ai pas entendu.	*zhuh nuh voo zay (tay) pah zahN-tahN-dew*	I didn't hear you
Répétez (Répète), s'il vous (te) plaît	*ray-pay-tay (ray-peht)seel voo (tuh) pleh*	Please repeat it
Parlez (Parle) plus lentement.	*pahr-lay (pahrl) plew lahNt-mahN*	Speak more slowly
Qu'est-ce que vous avez (tu as) dit?	*kehs-kuh voo zah-vay (tew ah) dee?*	What did you say?

Cultural Tidbits

It always pays to know the word for *thank you!* After getting directions from a French-speaking person, you may respond with a simple *merci* (*mehr-see*), which means *thank you*. If you are feeling profoundly grateful, you may wish to say *merci beaucoup*, meaning *thank you very much*. In either case, the person will likely respond *Je vous en prie* (*zhuh voo zahN pree*), which means *not at all*. (This phrase may also mean *Please* or *Please do*). Another possible reply is *De rien* (*duh ryaN*), which simply means *You're welcome*.

Get There!

You've been invited to spend your vacation in Canada at a friend's house. You've got all your bags and you're ready to leave the airport now. You take out the directions he gave you to his house and realize they are in French! Trace the correct route and then put an X on the map where his house should be.

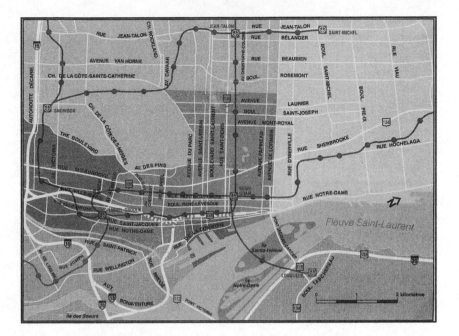

Prends le bus numéro 7. Quand tu arrives en ville, descends à l'avenue Mont-Royal. Prends l'avenue Mont-Royal et tourne à droite à la rue St.-Denis. Va tout droit. Passe par le boulevard St.-Joseph. Tu vas voir une école sur ta gauche. Puis tu vas voir une église à ta droite. Juste après l'église, tourne à gauche. Prends l'avenue Laurier. Passe près du cinéma. Juste après le cinéma, à la prochaine rue, tourne à droite. C'est l'avenue du Parc. Ma maison est là, sur la gauche, au coin de l'avenue du Parc et de l'avenue Laurier.

The Least You Need to Know

➤ The irregular verb *aller* is used to give directions and to speak about health and well-being.

➤ There are a few verbs that are tremendously useful in giving and taking directions: aller (to go), continuer, descendre, marcher, monter, passer, prendre (to take), tourner, and traverser (to cross).

➤ Leave out the subject (*tu* or *vous*) when you give a command.

Chapter 11

Getting to the Hotel

In This Chapter

➤ Planes, trains, and automobiles—the best way of getting around the city

➤ All about *prendre* (to take)

➤ Renting a car

➤ Cardinal numbers

➤ Telling time

You'll probably find that it's far less painful and far more time-consuming than you thought to get through customs, find your bags, and change some money into francs. If you're lucky, you will have *transfers* (transportation provided as part of your travel package) to your hotel and someone waiting to whisk you away. If not, then you must figure out on your own how you are going to get to the hotel. This chapter discusses your options.

Cultural Tidbits

If it's Paris you're visiting, the R.A.T.P. (Régie Autonome des Transports Parisiens) directs the user-friendly bus and subway system. Green Parisian buses post their route and destination on the outside, front of the bus and their major stops on the bus's sides. The route of each line is indicated on a sign at every stop it makes. Free bus maps (autobus Paris—Plan du Réseau) are readily available at tourist offices and some métro booths. Because tickets may not be purchased aboard the bus, they must be bought ahead of time at a métro station or bureau de tabac (tobacconist).

Planes, Trains, and Automobiles

From the airport, there are several different means of transportation that can get you to your hotel: bus, subway, train, taxi, or car. To make the decision that is right for you, keep the following considerations in mind: Do you really want to carry your bags on a bus or the subway? (Remember what you packed!) Although taxis are fast and efficient, they are costly. Do you feel up to renting a car in a foreign country where you are unfamiliar with the traffic laws and street signs? Think carefully before you make a choice.

l'auto (f.)	*lo-to*	car
la voiture	*lah vwah-tewr*	car
le taxi	*le tahk-see*	taxi
le bus (l'autobus)	*le bews (loh-toh-bews)*	bus
le train	*luh traN*	train
le métro	*luh may-tro*	subway

Taking the Best Means of Transportation

However you decide to get where you are going, you will need to use the irregular verb *prendre* (*prahNdr*) (to take) to express which mode of transportation you have chosen. *Prendre* is a tricky verb: all singular forms end in a nasal sound, but the third person plural, *ils/elles*, is pronounced quite differently. The double *n*s eliminate the need for an initial nasal sound and give the first *e* a more open sound. Pay close attention to Table 11.1.

Table 11.1 The Verb prendre (to take)

je prends	*zhuh prahN*	I take
tu prends	*tew prahN*	you take
il, elle, on prend	*eel (ehl) (ohN) prahN*	he, she, one takes
nous prenons	*noo pruh-nohN*	we take
vous prenez	*voo pruh-nay*	you take
ils, elles prennent	*eel (ehl) prehn*	they take

If you've done your homework well, you should be able to tell someone which means of transportation you use to get to the following places: work and/or school, the supermarket, the nearest department store, downtown, a neighboring city.

Something New

Travelers interested in visiting from England and Belgium may now make use of the Chunnel. Although you can't drive through these new tunnels, *Le Shuttle* carries freight and cars with passengers (up to 180 vehicles) between Folkestone, England and Calais, France. Just drive a car onto a train at one end and drive off at the other—in just 35 minutes. Service is available 24 hours a day, and at peak times, trains depart every 15 minutes. No reservations are accepted, so drivers will be accommodated on a first-come, first-served basis. Drivers pay a charge per car, regardless of the number of occupants.

The other Chunnel service, *Eurostar*, carries only passengers (each train carries 800 people) and provides through service from London to Paris and London to Brussels.

Which Do You Prefer?

When you ask questions about the mode of transportation you've chosen, you'll use the interrogative adjective *quel* (which, what). Just like all adjectives, *which* agrees with the noun it modifies. Table 11.2 shows you how easy it is to make a match between the correct form of *quel* (keeping gender and number in mind) and the noun that follows it.

Table 11.2 The Possessive Adjective quel

	Masculine	Feminine
Singular	quel	quelle
Plural	quels	quelles

Be prepared for questions like these:

Quel bus est-ce que vous prenez (tu prends)?
kehl bews ehs-kuh vous pruh-nay (tew prahN)
Which bus are you taking?

Quelle marque de voiture est-ce vous louez (tu loues)?
kehl mahrk duh vwah-tewr ehs-kuh voo loo-ay (tew loo)
What make of car are you renting?

Using quel

Did you ever have a conversation with a friend who rambles on and on about a fabulous film she's just seen, but never mentions the title? You're about ready to explode from frustration when she finally decides to come up for air. You grab your chance and quickly interject: Which film? Here are some typical answers that don't give enough information. Pursue your line of questioning by using *quel*:

J'aime le film. *Quel film?*

Je prends le train.

J'aime la couleur.

J'achète(buy) les jolies blouses.

Je lis (read) de bons journaux.

Je loue une voiture.

Je cherche de bonnes cassettes.

Je regarde le match.

Je prépare des plats délicieux.

Fill 'er Up

If you are adventurous, you might want to rent a car at *une location de voitures*. Check out rates of a few car rentals before you make a decision because rates vary from agency to agency. Keep in mind that gasoline is very expensive in most foreign countries, usually more than double the price Americans generally pay. Familiarize yourself with all driving and traffic laws. The following phrases are very useful when renting a car:

Je voudrais louer une (give make of car).
zhuh voo-dreh loo-ay ewn _____.
I would like to rent a _____.

Je préfère la transmission automatique.
zhuh pray-fehr lah tranhz-mee-syohN o-toh-mah-teek.
I prefer automatic transmission.

Quel est le tarif à la journée (à la semaine) (au kilomètre)?
kehl eh luh tah-reef ah lah zhoor-nay (ah la suh-mehn) (o kee-lo-mehtr)?
How much does it cost per day (per week) (per kilometer)?

Quel est le montant de l'assurance?
kehl eh luh mohn-tahN duh lah-sew-rahNs?
How much is the insurance?

Le carburant est compris?
luh kahr-bew-rahN eh kohN-pree?
Is the gas included?

Acceptez-vous des cartes de crédit? Lesquelles?
ahk-sehp-tay voo day kahrt duh kray-dee? lay-kehl?
Do you accept credit cards? Which ones?

If you've decided to rent a car, take a tip from me: Carefully inspect the car—inside and out—because you never know what might go wrong after you're on the road. Make sure there is *un cric (uhN kreek)* a jack and *un pneu de secours (uhN pnuh duh suh-koor)* a spare tire in the trunk.

Outside the Car

la batterie	*lah bah-tree*	battery
la poignée	*lah pwah-nyay*	door handle
le carburateur	*luh kahr-bew-rah-tuhr*	carburetor
le coffre	*luh kohfr*	trunk
le phare	*luh fahr*	headlight
le moteur	*luh moh-tuhr*	motor
le pare-choc	*luh pahr-shohk*	bumper
l'essuie-glace (m.)	*leh-swee glahs*	windshield wiper
le capot	*luh kah-po*	hood
le radiateur	*luh rahd-yah-tuhr*	radio
le feu arrière	*luh fuh ah-ryehr*	tail light
la transmission	*lah trahNz-mee-syohN*	transmission
le ventilateur	*luh vahN-tee-lah-tuhr*	fan
le réservoir à essence	*luh ray-sehr-vwahr ah eh-sahNs*	gas tank

l'aile	*lehl*	fender
la plaque d'immatriculation	*lah plahk dee-mah-tree-kew-lah-syohN*	license plate
le pneu	*luh pnuh*	tire
la roue	*lah roo*	wheel

Inside the Car

l'accélérateur (m.)	*lahk-say-lay-rah-tuhr*	accelerator
le clignotant	*luh klee-nyoh-tahN*	directional signal
le changement de vitesses	*luh shahNzh-mahN duh vee-tehs*	gear shift
le klaxon	*luh klahk-sohN*	horn
l'allumage	*lah-lew-mahzh*	ignition
la radio	*lah rahd-yo*	radio
le volant	*luh voh-lahN*	steering wheel
les freins (m.)	*lay fraN*	brakes
la pédale d'embrayage	*lah pay-dahl dahN-brah-yahzh*	clutch pedal
la boîte à gants	*lah bwaht ah gahN*	glove compartment
le frein à main	*luh fraN ah maN*	hand brake
le coussin (sac) gonflable	*luh koo-saN (sahk) gohn-flahbl*	air bag
le freinage anti-blocage	*luh freh-nahzh ahn-tee bloh-kahzh*	antilock brake system

In Europe, distance is measured by kilometers. Refer to Table 11.4 for the approximate equivalents.

Table 11.4 Distance Measures (Approximate)

Miles	Kilometers
.62	1
3	5
6	10
12	20
31	50
62	100

> ### Cultural Tidbits
>
> The French use the word *feu* (which really means "fire") to refer to a traffic light. Just as in the United States, you are required to stop *au feu rouge* (at the red light) and to go *au feu vert* (at the green light). Should you get stopped for running *un feu rouge* by a *gendarme,* you could always try using your foreign nationality as an excuse: *Mais, je suis américain(e).* Perhaps a simple apology might work: *Pardon (Excusez-moi). Je le regrette.*

Point Me in the Right Direction

By all means, learn those road signs—some of them are not as obvious as they should be. It took a one-week vacation and a near accident in Saint-Martin for me to figure out that the sign with a horizontal line through it meant NO ENTRY. Here are some road signs you need to be familiar with before you venture out on your own in a car.

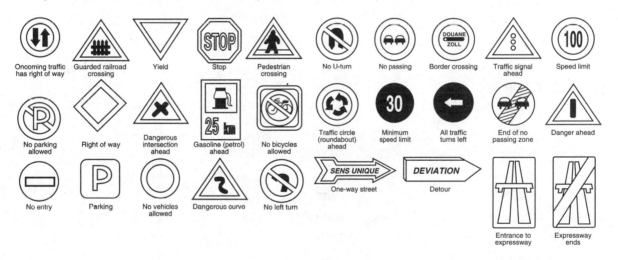

My husband and I were driving along when all of a sudden we came to a fork in the road. I screamed, "Quick, go this way!" Unfortunately, he went "that" way. Maybe next time I'll remember to tell him whether to go east or west, north or south. If you plan on driving, make sure to know your compass directions. They're all masculine.

au nord	à l'est	au sud	à l'ouest
o nohr	*ah lehst*	*o sewd*	*ah lwehst*
to the north	to the east	to the south	to the west

Pitfall

When you begin, you may find that learning the numbers from 70 to 100 will take a little mathematical finesse. But unless you are stymied by simple addition, you'll get the hang of it in no time.

How Much Is It?

In order to tell someone what flight or bus you are taking or to figure out how much a rental car is going to set you back, you'll need to learn the French numbers listed in Table 11.5. Believe it or not, these very same numbers will come in handy when you want to tell time, count to ten, or reveal your age.

Table 11.5 Cardinal Numbers

zéro	*zay-ro*	0
un	*uhN*	1
deux	*duh*	2
trois	*trwah*	3
quatre	*kahtr*	4
cinq	*saNk*	5
six	*sees*	6
sept	*seht*	7
huit	*weet*	8
neuf	*nuhf*	9
dix	*dees*	10
onze	*ohNz*	11
douze	*dooz*	12
treize	*trehz*	13
quatorze	*kah-tohrz*	14
quinze	*kaNz*	15
seize	*sehz*	16
dix-sept	*dee-seht*	17
dix-huit	*dee-zweet*	18
dix-neuf	*dee-znuhf*	19
vingt	*vaN*	20
vingt et un	*vaN tay uhN*	21
vingt-deux	*vaN-duh*	22
trente	*trahNt*	30

quarante	*kah-rahNt*	40
cinquante	*saN-kahNt*	50
soixante	*swah-sahNt*	60
soixante-dix	*swah-sahNt-dees*	70
soixante et onze	*swah-sahNt ay ohNz*	71
soixante-douze	*swah-sahNt-dooz*	72
soixante-treize	*swah-sahNt-trehz*	73
soixante-quatorze	*swah-sahNt-kah-tohrz*	74
soixante-quinze	*swah-sahNt-kaNz*	75
soixante-seize	*swah-sahNt-sehz*	76
soixante-dix-sept	*swah-sahNt-dee-seht*	77
soixante-dix-huit	*swah-sahNt-dee-zweet*	78
soixante-dix-neuf	*swah-sahNt-dee-znuf*	79
quatre-vingts	*kahtr-vaN*	80
quatre-vingt-un	*kahtr-vaN-uhN*	81
quatre-vingt-deux	*kahtr-vaN-duh*	82
quatre-vingt-dix	*kahtr-vaN-dees*	90
quatre-vingt-onze	*kahtr-vaN-onze*	91
quatre-vingt-douze	*kahtr-vaN-dooz*	92
cent	*sahN*	100
cent un	*sahN uhN*	101
deux cents	*duh sahN*	200
deux cent un	*duh sahN uhN*	201
mille	*meel*	1000
deux mille	*duh meel*	2000
un million	*uhN meel-yohN*	1,000,000
deux millions	*duh meel-yohN*	2,000,000
un milliard	*uhN meel-yahr*	1,000,000,000
deux milliards	*duh meel-yahr*	2,000,000,000

When numbers are used before plural nouns beginning with a vowel, the pronunciation of the numbers changes to allow for elision:

Before a Consonant	Before a Vowel Sound
deux jours (*duh zhoor*)	deux oncles (*duh zohNkl*)
trois cartes (*trwah kahrt*)	trois opinions (*trwah zoh-pee-nyohN*)
quatre valises (*kaht vah-leez*)	quatre hôtels (*kaht ro-tehl*)
cinq dollars (*saN doh-lahr*)	cinq années (*saN kah-nay*)
six femmes (*see fahm*)	six hommes (*see zohm*)
sept francs (*seht frahN*)	sept heures (*seh tuhr*)
huit mois (*wee mwah*)	huit enfants (*wee tahN-fahN*)
neuf billets (*nuhf bee-yeh*)	neuf artistes (*nuh fahr-teest*)
dix personnes (*dee pehr-sohn*)	dix ans (*dee zahN*)

Cultural Tidbits

The French write the number one with a little hook on top. In order to distinguish a 1 from the number 7, they put a line through the 7 when they write it: 7.

In numerals and decimals, where we use commas the French use periods and vice versa:

English	French
1,000	1.000
.25	0,25
$9.95	$9,95

French numbers are a little tricky until you get used to them. Look carefully at Table 11.5 and pay special attention to the following:

➤ The conjunction *et* (and) is used only for the numbers 21, 31, 41, 51, 61, and 71. Use a hyphen in all other compound numbers through 99.

➤ *Un* becomes *une* before a feminine noun:

vingt et un hommes et vingt et une femmes

➤ To form 71-79, use 60 + 11, 12, 13, and so on.

➤ To form 91-99, use 80 (4 20s) + 11, 12, 13, and so on.

➤ 80 (quatre-vingts) and the plural of *cent* for any number over 199 drop the *s* before another number, but not before a noun:

quatre-vingts dollars	80 dollars
quatre-vingt-trois dollars	83 dollars
deux cents dollars	200 dollars
deux cent cinquante dollars	250 dollars

➤ Do not use *un* (one) before *cent* and *mille*.

➤ *Mille* doesn't change in the plural.

As a Rule
The **f** sound in neuf becomes a v sound when liaison is made with **heures** (hours, o'clock) and **ans** (years):

Il est neuf heures.	Il a neuf ans.
eel eh nuh vuhr.	*Eel ah nuh vahN*
It is nine o'clock.	He is nine years old.

What's Your Number?

Parisian phone numbers consist of eight numbers grouped in pairs of two. The regional code for Paris is (1). You must dial this number before the phone number when calling from outside the city. How would you ask the operator for these numbers?

45 67 89 77   48 21 15 51   46 16 98 13   43 11 72 94   41 34 80 61   42 85 59 02

What Time Is It?

Now that you are familiar with French numbers, it will be relatively easy to learn how to tell time, as explained in Table 11.6. A question that you will probably ask or hear asked very often is:

Quelle heure est-il?

kehl uhr eh-teel?

What time is it?

Table 11.6   Telling Time

Il est une heure.	*eel eh tewn nuhr*	It is 1:00.
Il est deux heures cinq.	*eel eh duh zuhr saNk*	It is 2:05.
Il est trois heures dix.	*eel eh trwah zuhr dees*	It is 3:10.
Il est quatre heures et quart.	*eel eh kahtr uhr ay kahr*	It is 4:15.
Il est cinq heures vingt.	*eel eh saN kuhr vaN*	It is 5:20.
Il est six heures vingt-cinq	*eel eh see zuhr vaN-saNk*	It is 6:25.

continues

Table 11.6 Continued

Il est sept heures et demie.	*eel eh seh tuhr ay duh-mee*	It is 7:30.
Il est huit heures moins vingt-cinq.	*eel eh wee tuhr mwaN vaN-saNk*	It is 7:35 (25 minutes to eight).
Il est neuf heures moins vingt.	*eel eh nuh vuhr mwaN vaN*	It is 8:40 (20 minutes to nine).
Il est dix heures moins le quart.	*eel eh dee zuhr mwaN luh (uhN) kahr*	It is 9:45 (a quarter to ten).
Il est onze heures moins dix.	*eel eh ohN zuhr mwaN dees*	It is 10:50 (10 minutes to eleven).
Il est midi moins cinq.	*eel eh mee-dee mwaN saNk*	It is 11:55 (5 minutes to noon).
Il est minuit.	*eel eh mee-nwee*	It is midnight.

➤ To express the time after the hour, the number of minutes is simply added; use *et* only with *quart et demi(e)*.

➤ To express time before the hour, use *moins le* (before, less, minus).

➤ To express half past noon or midnight, use the following:

Il est midi et demi.

Il est minuit et demi.

➤ With all other hours, *demie* is used to express half past.

It's not just enough to know how to say what time it is—you might want to know *at what time* an activity is planned or whether it is taking place in the morning, afternoon, or evening. Imagine that you asked someone at what time a play was being presented, and he responded, *"Il y a deux heures."* You might mistake this as meaning "at two o'clock" or "there are two hours" which, to you, means you have two hours before the play begins. In fact, you've missed the play because it started two hours ago. The expressions in Table 11.7 will help you deal with time.

Table 11.7 Time Expressions

une seconde	*ewn suh-gohNd*	a second
une minute	*ewn mee-newt*	a minute
une heure	*ewn nuhr*	an hour
du matin	*dew mah-taN*	in the morning (A.M.)

de l'après-midi	*duh lah-preh mee-dee*	in the afternoon (P.M.)
du soir	*dew swahr*	in the evening (P.M.)
à quelle heure	*ah kehl uhr*	at what time?
à minuit précis	*ah mee-nwee pray-see*	at exactly midnight
à une heure précise	*ah ewn uhr pray-seez*	at exactly 1:00
à deux heures précises	*ah duh zuhr pray-seez*	at exactly 2:00
vers deux heures	*vehr duh zuhr*	at about 2:00
un quart d'heure	*uhN kahr duhr*	a quarter of an hour
une demi-heure	*ewn duh-mee uhr*	a half hour
dans une heure	*dahN zew nuhr*	in an hour
jusqu'à deux heures	*zhew-skah duh zuhr*	until 2:00
avant trois heures	*ah-vahN trwah zuhr*	before 3:00
après trois heures	*ah-preh trwah zuhr*	after 3:00
depuis quelle heure	*duh-pwee kehl uhr*	since what time?
depuis six heures	*duh-pwee see zuhr*	since 6:00
il y a une heure	*eel yah ewn nuhr*	an hour ago
par heure	*pahr uhr*	per hour
tôt (de bonne heure)	*to (duh boh nuhr)*	early
tard	*tahr*	late
en retard	*ahN ruh-tahr*	late (in arriving)

The Least You Need to Know

➤ The irregular verb *prendre* is used when taking transportation.

➤ *Quel* is an adjective expressing *which*.

➤ If you plan on renting a car, you'll need to know French numbers and the metric system.

➤ Tell time easily by giving the hour and the number of minutes past the hour.

GOING UP?

Chapter 12

Hooray, You've Made It to the Hotel!

In This Chapter

➤ Getting the most from your hotel

➤ Ordinal numbers

➤ Shoe verbs

You've successfully chosen a suitable means of transportation to get you where you want to go. Now, as you ride along, you try to get a feel for your new environment. You can hardly wait to get to your hotel so you can unpack and start your glorious vacation. Just as your patience is wearing thin, you catch a glimpse of your hotel in the distance. Your first impression reassures you that you've chosen wisely.

Are you a traveler who is happy with the bare minimum in accommodations? Do you feel that because you won't be spending much time in your room, you'd be wasting money on something that you wouldn't truly enjoy? Perhaps you'd rather spend more money on consumables: food, drink, side trips, and souvenirs. Or, on the other hand, are you someone who prefers the creature comforts of home at the very least and, at most, outright luxury. Do you want it all and expect to be treated royally? In this chapter, you will learn how to get the room and the services you expect from your hotel.

What a Hotel! Does It Have...?

Before leaving home, you will probably want to check with your travel agent or the hotel management to be sure that the hotel you've chosen has the amenities you desire. Depending upon your requirements, you will need to know the words for everything from *bathroom* to *swimming pool*. In the 1970s, my husband and I backpacked around Europe with a copy of Arthur Frommer's *Europe on $5 a Day* under our arms. We hadn't made any reservations, so most nights we had to take whatever room we could get. In Paris, we wound up in a small room in the red-light district. The room didn't have its own bathroom, and we were not thrilled with having to share the W.C. down the hall—sometimes the wait was unbearable. Even with reservations, you may end up with some surprises—but it never hurts to ask questions when you are making your arrangements. See Table 12.1 for a basic list of hotel amenities.

Table 12.1   Hotel Facilities

bar	le bar	*luh bahr*
business center	le centre d'affaires	*luh sahNtr dah-fehr*
cashier	la caisse	*lah kehs*
concierge (caretaker)	le (la) concierge	*luh (lah) kohN-syehrzh*
doorman	le portier	*luh pohr-tyay*
elevator	l'ascenseur (m.)	*lah-sahN-suhr*
fitness center	le club santé	*luh klewb sahN-tay*
gift shop	la boutique	*lah boo-teek*
laundry and dry cleaning service	la blanchisserie	*lah blahN-shees-ree*
maid service	la gouvernante	*lah goo-vehr-nahNt*
restaurant	le restaurant	*luh rehs-toh-rahN*
swimming pool	la piscine	*lah pee-seen*
valet parking	l'attendance (f.) du garage	*lah-tahN-dahNs dew gah-rahzh*

Cultural Tidbits

In French buildings, the ground floor is called *le rez-de-chaussée*, and the basement is called *le sous-sol* (literally, the "under ground"). The "first floor" is really on the second story of any building. A typical French elevator pad will look like this:

4

3

2

1

rez-de-ch.

s-s

When I was planning a trip to Martinique, my travel agent told me about a terrific hotel whose best rooms had balconies facing the ocean. She described the views as breathtaking. Unfortunately, we were not able to confirm a room with a balcony at the time of the reservation, but I figured I'd give it a shot after we arrived. As fate would have it, a travel agent and her large family arrived just as we did. She, too, was eager to trade up to a room with a view. Unfortunately, she was not able to make herself understood to the French-speaking staff. My husband and I, however, were rewarded for our fluency—we got a spectacular room overlooking the ocean! Study Table 12.2 to get a jump on the others, just as we did.

Table 12.2 Getting What You Want Nicely Furnished

a single (double) room	une chambre à un (deux) lits	*ewn shahNbr ah uhN (duh) lee*
air conditioning	la climatisation	*lah klee-mah-tee-zah-syohN*
alarm clock	le réveil	*luh ray-vehy*
balcony	le balcon	*luh bahl-kohN*
bathroom (private)	la salle de bains (privée)	*lah sahl duh baN (pree-vay)*
key	la clé (clef)	*lah klay (klay)*
on the courtyard	coté cour	*koh-tay koor*
on the garden	côté jardin	*koh-tay zhahr-daN*

continues

135

Table 12.2   Continued

on the sea	côté mer	*koh-tay mehr*
safe (deposit box)	le coffre	*luh kohfr*
shower	la douche	*lah doosh*
telephone (dial-direct)	le téléphone (direct)	*luh tay-lay-fohn (dee-rehkt)*
television (color)	la télévision (en couleurs)	*lah tay-lay-vee-zyohN (ahN koo-luhr)*
toilet facilities	le W.C.	*luh doobl-vay say*

Cultural Tidbits

In many foreign countries, the sink and bathtub (and/or shower) are located in what is called the bathroom, while the toilet and bidet are in the W.C. (water closet). Showers are often the hand-held type and are not affixed to the wall, which sometimes makes them rather difficult to negotiate.

Expressing Need

Don't you just hate it when your hotel skimps on towels? They often give four small bath towels and expect them to be enough for a couple with two kids. I alone could use three just for myself: hair, top half, and bottom half. Imagine how the rest of my family feels when they're left with my soggy remains! If you need something for your room to make your stay more enjoyable, the following phrases may help you:

Je voudrais	*zhuh voo-dreh*	I would like
Il me faut un (une)(des)	*eel muh foh tuhN (tewn) (day)*	I need a (some)
J'ai besoin d'un (une)	*zhay buh-zwaN duhN (ewn)*	I need a (for plural use de + noun)

Okay. You're all checked in, you've even unpacked, and now you're ready for a nice hot bath. But wait! The housekeeper has forgotten to provide you with any towels at all! Rather than making your sheets do double duty, call the front desk and ask for towels. The management, after all, is there to make sure that your stay is enjoyable. Table 12.3 lists a few things you might need.

Table 12.3   Necessities

une serviette	*ewn sehr-vyeht*	a towel
un drap de bain	*uhN drah dbaN*	a beach towel
une savonnette	*ewn sah-voh-neht*	a bar of soap
des cintres (m.)	*day saNtr*	hangers
un oreiller	*uhN noh-reh-yay*	a pillow
une couverture	*ewn koo-vehr-tewr*	a blanket
des glaçons (m.)	*day glah-sohN*	ice cubes
un cendrier	*uhN sahN-dree-yay*	an ashtray
de l'eau minérale	*duh lo mee-nay-rahl*	mineral water
un rouleau de papier hygiénique	*uhN roo-lo duh pah-pyay ee-zhyay-neek*	a roll of toilet paper
des mouchoirs en papier	*day moo-shwahr ahN pah-pyay*	tissues
un transformateur	*uhN trahnz-fohr-mah-tuhr*	a transformer (an electric adaptor)

Just in Case

When you check into a hotel room there is usually a sign or two tacked onto the inside of the entry door. These notices often give important information to guests. Read a copy of the sign that I copied off the back of my hotel room door the last time I was in Paris. What did it tell everyone to do?

CONDUITE À TENIR EN CAS D'INCENDIE

En cas d'incendie dans votre chambre si vous ne pouvez pas maîtriser le feu :
--Gagnez la sortie en fermant bien la porte de votre chambre et en suivant le balisage (floor lights).
--Prévenez la réception

En cas d'audition du signal d'alarme :
--Gagnez la sortie en refermant bien la porte de votre chambre et en suivant le balisage.
--Si la fumée rend le couloir ou l'escalier impracticable :
    Restez dans votre chambre;
    Manifestez votre présence à la fenêtre, en attendant l'arrivée des sapeurs-pompiers.

Going to the Top

We've all had an elevator experience where we've felt like a large sardine in a small can. When you're pushed to the back or squished to the side, you have to hope that a kind and gentle soul will wiggle a hand free and ask: *Quel étage, s'il vous plaît (kehl ay-tahzh seel voo pleh)*? You will need the ordinal numbers in Table 12.4 to give a correct answer: *Le deuxième étage, s'il vous plaît (luh duh-zyehm ay-tahzh see voo pleh)*.

Table 12.4 Ordinal Numbers

premier (première)	*pruh-myay (pruh-myehr)*	1st
deuxième (second[e])	*duh-zyehm (suh-gohN[d])*	2nd
troisième	*trwah-zyehm*	3rd
quatrième	*kah-tree-yehm*	4th
cinquième	*saN-kyehm*	5th
sixième	*see-zyehm*	6th
septième	*seh-tyehm*	7th
huitième	*wee-tyehm*	8th
neuvième	*nuh-vyehm*	9th
dixième	*dee-zyehm*	10th
onzième	*ohN-zyehm*	11th
douzième	*doo-zyehm*	12th
vingtième	*vaN-tyehm*	20th
vingt et un (e)ième	*vaN-tay-uhN (ewn)-nyehm*	21st
soixante-douzième	*swah-sahNt doo-zyehm*	72nd
centième	*sahN-tyehm*	100th

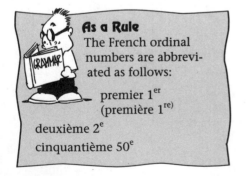

As a Rule
The French ordinal numbers are abbreviated as follows:

premier 1er
(première 1re)
deuxième 2^{e}
cinquantième 50^{e}

➤ *Premier* and *second* are the only ordinal numbers that must agree in gender (masculine or feminine) with the noun they describe. All other ordinal numbers must agree in number with the noun:

son premier fils	his (her) first son
sa première fille	his (her) first daughter
Les dixièmes anniversaires de mariage sont spéciaux.	Tenth wedding anniversaries are special.

➤ Except for *premier* and *second*, *ième* is added to all cardinal numbers to form the ordinal number. Drop the silent *e* before *ième*.

➤ Note that *u* was added in *cinquième,* and *v* replaced *f* in *neuvième*.

➤ *Second(e)* is generally used in a series that does not go beyond two.

➤ There is no elision with *huitième* and *onzième*. The definite article *le* or *la* does not drop its vowel:

le huitième jour	the eighth day
la onzième personne	the eleventh person

➤ In French, cardinal numbers precede ordinal numbers:

les deux premières fois	the first two times

As a Rule

If you are going to memorize anything, it should be these phrases. Give them a good workout—you won't regret it!

s'il vous plaît
seel voo pleh
please

merci
mehr-see
thank you

de rien
duh ryaN
you're welcome

(il n'y a) pas de quoi
(eel nyah pah) duh kwah
you're welcome

I'm Afraid There'll Have to Be a Change

Imagine that you want to sample a famous French delicacy, eat in a special restaurant, pay with your credit card, or buy a special gift. Naturally, you'll want some recommendation and will probably get opinions from everyone from the concierge to the chambermaid. In the course of your conversations, you'll have to use many verbs to get the information you seek. There are a few categories of regular *er* verbs whose endings require spelling changes in certain forms. In some instances, this is necessary to maintain the proper sound of the verb. In other instances, it's just one of the idiosyncrasies of the language. You should familiarize yourself with some of these verbs in each group because they are high-frequency words that you will use and see quite often.

These verbs are referred to as *shoe verbs* because the rules of conjugation work as if you put the subject pronouns that follow one set of rules within the shoe, and the others, outside the shoe. To make that more clear, look at the pronouns that go in and out of the shoe:

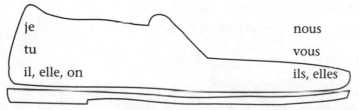

je   nous

tu   vous

il, elle, on   ils, elles

139

In other words, for all verbs in these categories, *je, tu, il, elle, on, ils,* and *elles* will follow one set of rules, while *nous* and generally, but not always, *vous* will follow a different set of rules. Now let's look at the different categories.

cer Verbs

For *cer* verbs, the *nous* form needs ç to maintain the soft sound of the *c* (s). This cedilla is added before the vowels *a, o,* and *u*.

placer (to place, set)	
je place	nous plaçons
tu places	vous placez
il, elle, on place	ils, elles placent

Other verbs conjugated just like *placer* include:

annoncer	*ah-nohN-say*	to announce
avancer	*ah-vahN-say*	to advance (be fast—clocks and watches)
commencer (à)	*koh-mahN-say (ah)*	to begin
menacer	*muh-nah-say*	to threaten
remplacer	*rahN-plah-say*	to replace
renoncer à	*ruh-nohN-say ah*	to give up, renounce

Using cer Verbs

You should find *cer* verbs quite easy since there is really only one small change involved. Practice vocabulary and conversation by completing the sentence with the correct form of the appropriate verb from the list in the preceding section:

1. Le spectacle (commencer) _____ à neuf heures.

2. Nous (renoncer à) _____ à faire des projets.

3. Tu (remplacer) _____ ta valise?

4. Ma montre (avancer) _____.

5. Ils (annoncer) _____ le départ du train.

ger Verbs

For *ger* verbs, the *nous* form needs an extra *e* to maintain the soft sound of the *g* (zh). This extra *e* is always added after *g* before the vowels *a*, *o*, and *u*.

manger (to eat)	
je mange	nous mangeons
tu manges	vous mangez
il, elle, on mange	ils, elles mangent

Other verbs that are conjugated just like *manger* are:

arranger	*ah-rahn-zhay*	to arrange
changer	*shahN-zhay*	to change
corriger	*koh-ree-zhay*	to correct
déranger	*day-rahN-zhay*	to disturb
diriger	*dee-ree-zhay*	to direct
nager	*nah-zhay*	to swim
obliger	*oh-blee-zhay*	to oblige
partager	*pahr-tah-zhay*	to share, divide
ranger	*rahN-zhay*	to tidy

Using ger Verbs

Like *cer* verbs, *ger* verbs have only one change to memorize. Giving the correct form of the verb in each sentence should prove to be a snap:

1. La fille de chambre/(ranger) _____ la chambre.

2. Tu/(déranger) _____ les autres clients.

3. Nous/(partager) _____ notre sandwich parce qu'il est très grand.

4. Vous/(nager) _____ bien.

5. Ils/(arranger) _____ tout.

141

yer Verbs

In *yer* verbs, the *y* is retained in the *nous* and *vous* forms. Within the shoe, an *i* is used instead of the *y*:

employer (to use)	
j'emploie	nous employons
tu emploies	vous employez
il, elle, on emploie	ils, elles emploient

Other verbs that are conjugated just like *employer* are:

ennuyer	*ahN-nwee-yay*	to bother, bore
envoyer	*ahN-vwah-yay*	to send
nettoyer	*neh-twah-yay*	to clean

> **As a Rule**
>
> Verbs ending in *ayer* may or may not change *y* to *i* in the forms in the shoe:
>
> essayer (de)
> *eh-say-yay (duh)*
> to try (to)
>
> payer
> *peh-yay*
> to pay, to pay for

payer (to use)	
je paie (paye)	nous payons
tu paies (payes)	vous payez
il, elle, on paie (paye)	ils, elles paient (payent)

essayer (to try)	
j'essaie (essaye)	nous essayons
tu essaies (essayes)	vous essayez
il, elle, on essaie (essaye)	ils, elles essaient (essayent)

Using yer Verbs

Do you feel confident with *yer* verbs? Keep the shoe image in your mind and remember that *y* changes to *i*. Now have a go at conjugating the verbs below.

1. Tu (payer) _____ trop.

2. Il (employer) _____ un plan de la ville.

3. Vous (ennuyer) _____ les autres.

4. La fille de chambre (nettoyer) _____ bien.

5. J' (essayer) _____ de parler français.

e+consonant+er Verbs

Verbs with a silent *e* in the syllable before the *er* infinitive ending (*acheter*: to buy; *peser*: to weigh) change the silent *e* to *è* for all forms in the shoe. Within the shoe, all the endings of the verbs are silent.

acheter (to buy)	
j'achète (*ah-sheht*)	nous achetons (*ahsh-tohN*)
tu achètes (*ah-shcht*)	vous achetez (*ahsh-tay*)
il, elle, on achète (*ah-sheht*)	ils, elles achètent (*ah-sheht*)

Notice the difference in pronunciation of the verb inside and outside the shoe. Within the shoe, the first *e* has an accent grave, and *è* is pronounced. Outside the shoe, the first *e* is unpronounced.

Other verbs that are conjugated just like *acheter* are:

achever	*ahsh-vay*	to finish, complete
amener	*ahm-nay*	to bring, lead to
emmener	*ahNm-nay*	to take, lead away
enlever	*ahN-lvay*	to take off, remove
peser	*puh-zay*	to weigh
promener	*prohm-nay*	to walk

As a Rule
Because all of the endings within the shoe are silent, adding an accent grave (è) to the silent *e* before the ending gives sound to that silent *e*. This prevents having two syllables, one right after the other, with a silent *e*. (Two silent *e*s would make the word virtually impossible to pronounce. Imagine having to say *j'achète* if both *e*s were silent!)

Two verbs with silent *e* that double the consonant before the *er* infinitive ending, instead of adding the accent grave, are:

appeler (to call)	
j'appelle (*ah-pehl*)	nous appelons (*ah-plohN*)
tu appelles (*ah-pehl*)	vous appelez (*ah-play*)
il, elle, on appelle (*ah-pehl*)	ils, elles appellent (*ah-pehl*)

jeter (to throw)	
je jette (*zheht*)	nous jetons (*zhuh-tohN*)
tu jettes (*zheht*)	vous jetez (*zhuh-tay*)
il, elle, on jette (*zheht*)	ils, elles jettent (*zheht*)

Using e+consonant+er Verbs

It's very important to practice the correct spelling of *e + consonant + er* verbs—and not because spelling is so important. Let's face it, you're probably not going to be writing many letters in French. Why spend time on this? Because if you understand that accents give sounds to silent letters, then you'll be much more successful at perfecting your pronunciation. Take this opportunity to read and write at the same time:

1. (walk) Il _____ son chien.

2. (call) Vous _____ votre ami.

3. (take) J' _____ mon chapeau.

4. (throw) On _____ les papiers dans la poubelle.

5. (bring) Nous _____ nos enfants au cinéma.

é+consonant+er Verbs

Verbs with *é* in the syllable before the infinitive ending change *é* to *è* in the shoe, where the endings to the conjugated verb forms are all silent:

préférer (to prefer)	
je préfère (*pray-fehr*)	nous préférons (*pray-feh-rohN*)
tu préfères (*pray-fehr*)	vous préférez (*pray-feh-ray*)
il, elle, on préfère (*pray-fehr*)	ils, elles préfèrent (*pray-fehr*)

Other verbs that are conjugated just like *préférer* are:

célébrer	*say-lay-bray*	to celebrate
espérer	*ehs-pay-ray*	to hope
posséder	*poh-say-day*	to own, possess
protéger	*proh-tay-zhay*	to protect
répéter	*ray-pay-tay*	to repeat

Using é+consonant+er Verbs

Once again, using accents correctly will ensure that you're speaking properly. You can practice vocabulary, spelling, and pronunciation all in one fell swoop by completing the following sentences:

1. (celebrate) Je _____ mon anniversaire demain.

2. (Repeat) _____ la phrase, s'il vous plaît.

3. (protect) Nous _____ nos amis.

4. (hope) Ils _____ voyager.

5. (owns) Elle _____ une jolie voiture.

The Least You Need to Know

➤ To be happy in your hotel, learn the vocabulary for facilities and furnishings in order to ask for what you want and need.

➤ Ordinal numbers (except for *premier:* first) are formed by adding *ième* to the cardinal number.

➤ "Shoe verbs" follow a pattern of conjugation that resembles the outline of a shoe. Remember the shoe, and you'll remember how to conjugate the verb.

Part 3

Fun and Games

Chapter 13

What's the Weather?

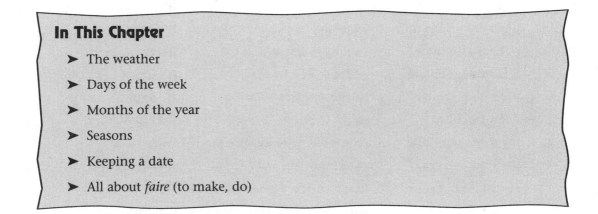

In This Chapter

➤ The weather

➤ Days of the week

➤ Months of the year

➤ Seasons

➤ Keeping a date

➤ All about *faire* (to make, do)

Your hotel is fabulous. Your room suits you to a *T* and has all the creature comforts, and then some. But it is time to get up and out. Before you head to the lobby, you glance out the window and notice that the sky is overcast, and you want to be prepared in case it rains. By the way, what are you going to do if that happens?

If you were at home, you'd probably tune into the weather channel to get the latest forecast. You could give this approach a shot, but remember, in a French-speaking country, all the announcers will be speaking French—and when it comes to weather, your knowledge of cognates won't take you too far. In this chapter, you'll tackle the weather report, and you'll also learn what you need to know to find out the hours at museums, movie theatres, and other places that may beckon on a rainy day.

It's 20 Degrees, but They're Wearing Shorts!

Let's say that you've turned on the television and manage to understand the weatherman when he reports that it is 20 degrees. But it's summer—how can this be? Is it possible that *La météo* (the forecast) is wrong? Perhaps it's time to consult the friendly *concierge* (caretaker/manager) at the front desk. The phrases in Table 13.1 will help you talk about the weather.

Table 13.1   Weather Expressions

Quel temps fait-il?	*kehl tahN feh-teel*	What's the weather?
Il fait beau.	*eel feh bo*	It's beautiful.
Il fait chaud.	*eel feh sho*	It's hot.
Il fait du soleil.	*eel feh dew soh-lehy*	It's sunny.
Il fait mauvais.	*eel feh moh-veh*	It's nasty (bad).
Il fait froid.	*eel feh frwah*	It's cold.
Il fait frais.	*eel feh freh*	It's cool.
Il fait du vent.	*eel feh dew vahN*	It's windy.
Il fait des éclairs (m.)	*eel feh day zay-klehr*	It's lightning.
Il fait du tonnerre.	*eel feh dew toh-nehr*	It's thundering.
Il fait du brouillard.	*eel feh dew broo-yahr*	It's foggy.
Il y a du brouillard.	*eel yah dew broo-yahr*	It's foggy.
Il fait humide.	*eel feh tew-meed*	It's humid.
Il y a de l'humidité.	*eel yah duh lew-mee-dee-tay*	It's humid.
Il y a des nuages.	*eel yah day new-ahzh*	It's cloudy.
Le ciel est nuageux.	*luh syehl eh new-ah-zhuh*	It's cloudy.
Le ciel est couvert.	*luh syehl eh koo-vehr*	It's overcast.
Il pleut.	*eel pluh*	It's raining.
Il pleut à verse.	*eel pluh ah vehrs*	It's pouring.
Il neige.	*eel nehzh*	It's snowing.
Il y a des rafales (f.).	*eel yah day rah-fahl*	There are gusts of wind.
Il y a de la grêle.	*eel yah duh lah grehl*	There's hail.
Il y a des giboulées (f.)	*eel yah day zhee-boo-lay*	There are sudden showers.

Before you get to the réception (or concierge's desk), you suddenly remember that the French use Celsius (centigrade) rather than Fahrenheit. This means that when it is 20 degrees Celsius—it's a pleasant 68 degrees Fahrenheit.

To convert Fahrenheit to Centigrade, subtract 32 from the Fahrenheit temperature and multiply the remaining number by 5/9. This will give you the temperature in degrees Centigrade.

To convert Centigrade to Fahrenheit, multiply the Centigrade temperature by 9/5, then add 32. This will give you the temperature in degrees Fahrenheit.

What's the Temperature?

You never were that great in math, but you're determined to have a pretty good idea of what the temperature is. You arm yourself with a mini–solar calculator and ask the concierge:

Il fait quelle temperature?

eel feh kehl tahN-pay-rah-tewr?

What's the temperature?

If someone asks you what the temperature is (and you happen to know!), respond with the phrase *il fait* followed by the number of degrees. If it is below zero, throw a *moins* (minus) before the number.

Il fait moins dix.	Il fait zéro.	Il fait soixante.
eel feh mwaN dees	*eel feh zay-ro*	*eel feh swah-sahNt*
It's 10 below.	It's zero.	It's sixty degrees.

But It Says in the Paper...

French newspapers, like American newspapers, contain weather information, complete with maps and symbols. Take a look at the following map to see if you can decipher the symbols. If you have trouble, consult the guide for help.

MÉTÉO

Brouillards et fraîcheur puis soleil

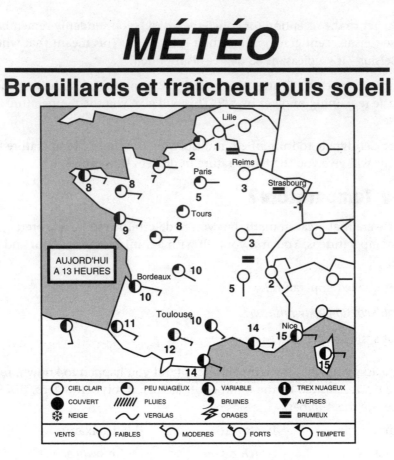

brouillards	*broo-yahr*	fog		
fraîcheur	*freh-shuhr*	chilly		
soleil	*soh-lehy*	sun		
ciel clair	*syehl klehr*	clear sky		
couvert	*koo-vehr*	cloudy		
neige	*nehzh*	snow		
peu nuageux	*puh new-ah-zhuh*	slightly cloudy		
pluies	*plwee*	rain		
verglas	*vehr-glah*	sleet		
variable	*vah-ree-yahbl*	changeable		
bruines	*brween*	drizzle		

orages	*oh-rahzh*	storms
très nuageux	*treh new-ah-zhuh*	very cloudy
averses	*ah-vehrs*	showers (heavy rain)
brumeux	*brew-muh*	hazy, foggy
vent	*svaN*	winds
faibles	*fehbl*	weak
modérés	*moh-day-ray*	moderate
fort	*fohr*	strong
tempête	*tahN-peht*	storm

The Forecast

You're undecided about what to do today. So, you open the newspaper to the weather page to get a better idea of what plans would be appropriate. According to the headline, what weather is predicted for this day?

You're intrigued by the French weather map you see and decide to bone up on your forecast reading abilities. Give the temperature and the weather for the following cities in France at 1 p.m.:

Lille	Strasbourg	Tours
Reims	Paris	Nice

What Day Is It?

If you're anything like me, the day your vacation starts is the day your watch comes off. You get so involved in having a good time that you lose all track of time. Every day seems like Saturday or Sunday, and you frequently have to ask: "What day is it, anyway?" If you're on a sightseeing vacation, you really have to keep track of the days of the week so that you don't wind up at the attraction you were dying to see on the day that it's closed. That can happen very easily in Paris, where schedules differ from museum to museum. When you study the days of the week in Table 13.2, you'll notice that they all end in *di*, except for Sunday, which begins with *di*.

Pitfall

Unlike our calendars, French calendars start with Monday. Don't let this confuse you when you give a quick glance. You want to make sure that you get to that appointment on the right day.

Table 13.2 Days of the Week

lundi	*luhN-dee*	Monday
mardi	*mahr-dee*	Tuesday
mercredi	*mehr-kruh-dee*	Wednesday
jeudi	*zhuh-dee*	Thursday
vendredi	*vahN-druh-dee*	Friday
samedi	*sahm-dee*	Saturday
dimanche	*dee-mahNsh*	Sunday

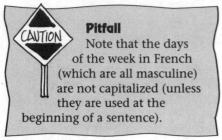

Pitfall
Note that the days of the week in French (which are all masculine) are not capitalized (unless they are used at the beginning of a sentence).

To express *on* when talking about a certain day, the French use the indefinite article *le*:

Le lundi je vais en ville.
luh luhN-dee zhuh veh zahN veel.
On Monday(s) I go downtown.

On what days do you go to the movies; go to the supermarket; do laundry; go out with friends; eat out; work hard?

This Is the Best Time of the Month

It's August and you want to go to Nice. Disappointment sets in when your travel agent says, "Sorry. There's nothing available." So, you book your own trip to Paris during this same time period. When you get there, the city is empty. Where *is* everyone? In France, many stores and businesses are closed during the month of August, when everyone seems to head south to La Côte d'Azur (the Riviera) for a vacation. Table 13.3 gives you the months of the year. Thus, when you glance through all those glossy vacation brochures, you can figure out the best time to take your trip.

Pitfall
Like the days of the week, all months in French are masculine and are not capitalized (unless they are used at the beginning of a sentence).

Table 13.3 Months of the Year

janvier	*zhahN-vyay*	January
février	*fay-vree-yay*	February
mars	*mahrs*	March
avril	*ah-vreel*	April

mai	*meh*	May
juin	*zhwaN*	June
juillet	*zhwee-eh*	July
août	*oo(t)*	August
septembre	*sehp-tahNbr*	September
octobre	*ohk-tohbr*	October
novembre	*noh-vahNbr*	November
décembre	*day-sahNbr*	December

To make clear that something is expected to happen *in* a certain month, use the preposition *en*. For example:

Je vais en France en avril.

zhuh veh zahN frahNs ahN nah-vreel

I am going to France in April.

As a Rule
August is pronounced two ways: *oo* and *oot*. Both are equally correct.

Practice this usage with everyday information. In which month does your birthday fall? When do you usually take a vacation? During which month do you watch the most TV or play your favorite sport?

The Four Seasons

Some seasons are better for traveling in certain countries than in others. Make sure to plan a trip when the weather will be great so you don't have to worry about hurricanes, storms, or other adverse conditions. Maybe you're not a traveler, but enjoy doing crossword puzzles where clues often call for "season (fr.)." Perhaps you'd like to know what sports and activities are performed in each season. Whatever your reason, Table 13.4 gives you the names of the seasons:

Table 13.4 The Seasons

l'hiver	*lee-vehr*	winter
le printemps	*luh praN-tahN*	spring
l'été	*lay-tay*	summer
l'automne	*lo-tohn*	autumn, fall

To express *in* with the seasons, the French use the preposition *en* for all the seasons, except the spring, when *au* is used:

> Je vais en France en hiver (en été, en automne, **au** printemps).
>
> *zhuh veh zahN frahNs ahN nee-vehr (ahN nay-tay, ahN o-tohn, o praN-tahN)*
>
> I'm going to France in the winter (summer, fall, spring).

In which season do you go to the beach; watch a football game; go on outdoor picnics; watch the leaves turn colors?

You Have a Date for What Date?

Do you also lose track of the date while you're away from home or work? The date is something people tend to forget on a fairly regular basis, especially when they're on vacation. (I finally broke down and bought a minicomputer so that I can always have a calendar on hand.) A few words you will need to know when making plans are:

un jour	*uhN zhoor*	a day
une semaine	*ewn suh-mehn*	a week
un mois	*uhN mwah*	a month
un an	*uhN nahN*	a year
une année	*ewn ah-nay*	a year

As a Rule

The word for *year*, *an*, is used with cardinal numbers one, two, three, and so on, unless an adjective is used to describe the word *year*. In that case, the word *année* is used. Sometimes, either word is acceptable.

un an	one year
une année	a year
deux bonnes années	two good years
quelques années	some years
l'an dernier	last year
l'année dernière	last year

You've decided to take the plunge and get a new French coif. Perhaps you're on a business trip and have to arrange for an important meeting. Or maybe you've decided to make unexpected travel plans. Whatever the reason, you'll have to know how to express the date for your appointment.

➤ Dates in French are expressed as follows:

(le) day of week + (le) (cardinal) number + month + year

lundi onze juillet 1996

lundi le onze juillet 1996

le lundi onze juillet 1996

➤ The first day of each month is expressed by *premier*. Cardinal numbers are used for all other days:

le premier janvier   January 1st

le deux janvier   January 2nd

➤ Just as in English, years are usually expressed in hundreds. When the word for *thousand* is written in dates only, *mil* is often used instead of *mille*:

1996 dix-neuf cent quatre-vingt seize

    mil neuf cent quatre-vingt seize

➤ In order to get information about the date, you need to ask the following questions:

Quelle est la date d'aujourd'hui?   Quel jour est-ce aujourd'hui?

kehl eh lah daht doh-zhoor-dwee?   *kehl zhoor ehs oh-zhoor-dwee?*

What is today's date?   What day is today?

OR

Quel jour sommes-nous aujourd'hui?

kehl zhoor sohm noo oh-zhoor-dwee?

What day is today?

The answer to your questions would be one of the following:

C'est aujourd'hui   Aujourd'hui nous sommes
+ (day) date   + (day) date

sehh toh-zhoor-dwee   *oh-zhoor-dwee noo sohm*

Today is   Today is

Heaven help those of us who forget important dates. It's not done intentionally, but it often creates problems. Practice what you've learned by giving the day and dates for these important events of the year:

> **Pitfall**
>
> When the French write the date in numbers, the sequence is day + month + year. In the U.S., we tend to lead with the month, followed by the day, and then the year. Notice how different this looks:
>
> | French | English |
> | --- | --- |
> | le 22 avril 1977 | April 22, 1977 |
> | 22.4.77 | 4/22/77 |
> | le trois mai 1995 | May 3, 1995 |
> | 3.5.95 | 5/3/95 |

your birthday, the birthday of a friend, Thanksgiving, New Year's, Mother's Day, Valentine's Day, Father's Day, Memorial Day

When you have to make plans and schedule your time wisely, you'll need certain time-related words and expressions. Keep the expressions in Table 13.5 in mind when time is of the essence.

Table 13.5   Time Expressions

dans _____	*dahN*	in
il y a _____	*eel yah*	ago
par _____	*pahr*	per
pendant _____	*pahN-dahN*	during
prochain(e)	*proh-shahN (proh-shehn)*	next
dernier (dernière)	*dehr-nyah (dehr-nyehr)*	last
passé(e)	*pah-say*	last
la veille	*la vehy*	eve
avant-hier	*ah-vahN yehr*	day before yesterday
hier	*yehr*	yesterday
aujourd'hui	*oh-zhoor-dwee*	today
demain	*duh-maN*	tomorrow
après-demain	*ah-preh duh-maN*	day after tomorrow
le lendemain	*luh lahN-duh-maN*	next day
dès _____	*deh*	from
d'aujourd'hui en huit	*doh-zhoor-dwee ahN weet*	a week from today
de demain en quinze	*duh duh-maN ahN kaNz*	two weeks from tomorrow

What's the Date?

Yesterday? Tomorrow? Two weeks from today? What if you don't have a calendar on you and you need the exact date? Practice your understanding of the phrases above. If today were *le sept août*, give the date for the following:

avant-hier	de demain en huit	d'aujourd'hui en quinze
demain	la veille	il y a sept jours

What Do You Make of This?

A French friend has phoned and says to you, "Il fait si beau aujourd'hui. On fait du golf?" We've already seen that, in speaking about the weather, we can use the irregular verb *faire*, in an impersonal way: *il fait* + the weather condition. The verb *faire*, shown in Table 13.6, means *to make* or *to do*, and is often used to speak about household chores. *Faire* can also be used to speak about playing a sport, even though it translates poorly into English. So, will you be playing golf with your friend today?

Table 13.6   The Verb faire (to make, to do)

je fais	*zhuh feh*	I make, do
tu fais	*tew feh*	you make, do
il, elle, on fait	*eel (ehl, ohN) feh*	he (she, one) makes, does
nous faisons	*noo fuh-zohN*	we make, do
vous faites	*voo feht*	you make, do
ils, elles font	*eel (ehl) fohN*	they make, do

Expressions with faire

Let's say you don't want to talk about sports or the weather. How else can you use the verb *faire* to your best advantage? There are many useful idioms with the verb *faire*. If your host asked you, *"Voudriez-vous faire une partie de tennis?"* would you think he was inviting you to a tennis party? Common sense and a knowledge of cognates would trick you into thinking so. In reality, he'd only be inviting you to play in a match. Similarly, if he told you, *"Je l'ai fait exprès"* would you think he did something in a rush? Again, your knowledge of English would make you think so. Actually, whatever he did, he did it on purpose. You can see why it is very important to study the idiomatic expressions with *faire* in Table 13.7.

Table 13.7   More Idioms with faire

faire attention à	*fehr ah-tahN-syohN ah*	to pay attention to
faire des achats (emplettes)	*fehr day zah-shah (ahN-pleht)*	to go shopping
faire des courses	*fehr day koors*	to do errands (shop)
faire exprès	*fehr ehks-preh*	to do on purpose
faire la connaissance de	*fehn lah koh-neh-sahNs duh*	to meet, become acquainted with
faire la queue	*fehr lah kuh*	to stand on line
faire une partie de	*fehr ewn pahr-tee duh*	to play a game of
faire une promenade	*fehr ewn prohm-nahd*	to take a walk
faire un voyage	*fehr uhN vwah-yahzh*	to take a trip
faire venir	*fehr vuh-neer*	to send for

Make sure to conjugate the verb when you use it in context:

Je fais les courses le lundi.   I go on errands on Mondays.

Ils font un voyage en France.   They are taking a trip to France.

Faites venir le médecin.   Send for the doctor.

Using faire

Because the verb *faire* has so many different uses, it's quite important to practice it thoroughly. After you feel confident with the conjugation of *faire* and have learned its various idioms, complete the following sentences:

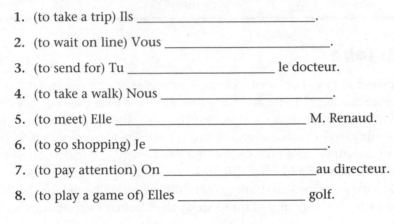

1. (to take a trip) Ils _____.

2. (to wait on line) Vous _____.

3. (to send for) Tu _____ le docteur.

4. (to take a walk) Nous _____.

5. (to meet) Elle _____ M. Renaud.

6. (to go shopping) Je _____.

7. (to pay attention) On _____au directeur.

8. (to play a game of) Elles _____ golf.

The Least You Need to Know

➤ Use "il fait" to express weather conditions and the temperature.

➤ To express the date, use the day of the week + the number of the day + the month + the year.

➤ The irregular verb *faire* is used to discuss sports and household chores and in some very useful idiomatic expressions.

Chapter 14

Let's Sightsee

In This Chapter

➤ Sightseeing delights

➤ Animals are everywhere

➤ How to make suggestions and plans

➤ How to give your opinion

➤ Other countries

➤ How to use the pronoun *y*

The weather in today's paper is calling for a mild and sunshiny day. It's perfect weather to have a café au lait at a sidewalk café, visit Notre Dame, and finally take a stroll down the Champs-Elysées. You've checked your guidebook to see what's open and at what times. Now it's time to take out your metro or bus map and plan your day so that you can leisurely enjoy the sights you long to see.

In this chapter you will be given a choice of things to do and interesting places to visit. You will become proficient in making suggestions and giving your opinions about things. And if you should decide to travel far and wide, you will be able to get there—in French.

Where Do You Want to Go?

There's so much to do and so much to see in all of the French-speaking countries. Are you in the mood for sightseeing or relaxing? Do you want to pack your day with activity or do you prefer to proceed at a leisurely pace? The brochures you've picked up at your hotel or at the tourist office offer many suggestions. Table 14.1 gives you the words and phrases you need to talk about your choices.

Table 14.1   Where to Go and What to Do

Le Lieu (luh lyuh)/the Place	L'Activité (lahk-tee-vee-tay)/the Activity
l'aquarium (*lah-kwah-ryuhm*)/ the aquarium '	voir les poissons/see the fish
l'église (*lay gleez*)/the church	voir l'architecture /see the architecture
la boîte de nuit (*lah bwaht duh nwee*), le cabaret (*luh kah-bah-reh*)/the nightclub	voir un spectacle/see a show
la cathédrale (*lah kah-tay-drahl*)/ the cathedral	voir les vitraux /see the stained glass windows
la foire (*lah fwahr*)/the fair	regarder les expositions/look at the exhibits
la fontaine (*lah fohn-tehn*)/the fountain	regarder les jets d'eau/look at the spray of water
la place (*lah plahs*)/the public square	voir la statue/see the statue
le carnaval (*luh kahr-nah-vahl*)/ the carnival	regarder le défilé, les chars /look at the parade, floats
le château (*luh shah-to*)/the castle	voir les salles/see the room
le cirque (*luh seerk*)/the circus	voir les spectacles/see the shows
le jardin (*luh zhahr-daN*)/the garden	voir les fleurs/see the flowers
le jardin zoologique, le zoo (*luh zhahr-daN zoh-oh-loh-geek, luh zo*)/the zoo	voir les animaux/see the animals
le marché aux puces (*luh mahr-shay o pews*)/the flea market	regarder la marchandise /look at the merchandise
le musée (*luh mew-say*)/the museum	voir les tableaux, les scupltures/see the paintings, sculptures
le parc d'attractions (*luh pahrk dah-trahk-syohN*)/amusement park	monter sur les manèges/go on the rides
le quai (*luh kay*)/the quay	faire une croisière/take a cruise

Cultural Tidbits

Euro-Disney's theme park is just 20 miles east of Paris (45 minutes by train), at Marne-La-Vallée. The 29 attractions in 5 different "lands" (Main St. USA, Fantasyland, Discoveryland, Frontierland, and Adventureland), six hotels, artificial lakes and entertainment grounds cover an area one-fifth the size of Paris. The Disney company claims that the food in Euro-Disney is the best in all of its theme parks. It would be surprising if it weren't! Before the grand opening, there was quite a debate about serving wine in the park. The French were adamant about maintaining their tradition while the Americans wanted to uphold their sense of family values. It took some persuading, but the French finally prevailed. Today, beer and wine can be enjoyed, but not abused, at Euro-Disney.

What Do You Want to See?

So will it be the exquisite painting and sculptures of a particular museum, the stained glass windows of a cathedral, the luxurious rooms of a château, or perhaps a famous monument? To express what you would like to see or are going to see, you will need the irregular verb *voir* (to see) that is presented in Table 14.2. *Voir* is similar to a shoe verb in that the *nous* and *vous* forms change. These forms do not, however, look like the infinitive. In this case, the forms inside the shoe do! Consider *voir* a reverse shoe verb.

Table 14.2   The Verb voir (to see)

je vois	*zhuh vwah*	I see
tu vois	*tew vwah*	you see
il, elle, on voit	*eel, (ehl, ohN) vwah*	he, she, one sees
nous voyons	*noo vwah-yohN*	we see
vous voyez	*voo vwah-yay*	you see
ils, elles voient	*eel (ehl) vwah*	they see

I See...

You've visited the Tuileries Gardens and walked along the banks of the Seine. You're having a wonderful time taking in all the sights. You're so captivated by everything around you that you feel you must express what you see: a parade, a fountain, animals, stained glass windows, a garden, flowers.

Making Suggestions in More Ways Than One

You've always had your heart set on seeing the Folies Bergères. The glamorous ads, posters, and pictures you've seen have enticed you and piqued your curiousity. You don't know, however, how the others in your group feel about accompanying you. Live it up! Make the suggestion. There are two options in French that you'll find quite simple.

As a Rule
With *on* use the third person singular form (il) of the verb.

You may use the pronoun *on* + the conjugated form of the verb that explains what it is you want to do:

Ohn va aux Folies Bergères?	On fait une croisière?
ohN vah o foh-lee behr-zhehr	*ohN feh tewn krwah-zyehr*
How about going to the Folies Bergères?	How about going on a cruise?

As a Rule
When using this command form, it is unnecessary to use the subject pronoun *nous*.

Another way to propose an activity is to use the command form that has **nous** as its understood subject:

Allons aux Folies Bergères!	Faisons une croisière!
ah-lohN zo foh-lee behr-zhehr	*fuh-zohN zewn krwah-zyehr*
Let's go to the Folies Bergères!	Let's go on a cruise!

Making Suggestions

It's a gorgeous day and you're eager to go out and have a great time. Suggest five things that we can do together and express each suggestion in two different ways.

Other Phrases You Might Find Useful

If you're feeling rather confident with the language at this point, you might want to take a more sophisticated approach. There are a number of phrases you can use, all of which are followed by the infinitive of the verb (The familiar forms [tu] are in parenthesis.):

Ça vous (te) dit de…	*sah voo (tuh) dee duh*	Do you want to…
Ça vous (t')intéresse de…	*sah voozaN(taN)-tay-rehs duh*	Are you interested in…
Ça vous (te) plairait de…	*sah voo (tuh) pleh-reh duh…*	Would it please you to…
Vous voulez (Tu veux…)	*voo voo-lay (tew vuh)*	Do you want to…

Ça vous (te) dit de (d')

Ça vous (t') intéresse de (d')   aller au cinéma?

Ça vous (te) plairait de (d')   faire une croisière?

Vous voulez (Tu veux)

Any of the phrases listed above can be made negative by using *ne…pas:*

Ça *ne* te dit *pas* de (d')

(Don't you want to…?)

Ça *ne* t'intéresse *pas* de (d')   aller au cinéma?

(Aren't you interested in…)   (going to the movies?)

Ça *ne* te plairait *pas* de (d')   faire une croisière?

(Wouldn't it please you to…)   (go on a cruise?)

Tu *ne* veux *pas*

(Don't you want to…?)

Only petulant teenagers give abrupt yes or no answers to questions. Most of the rest of us say "yes, but…" or "no, because…." If you'd like to elaborate on your answer, here's what you'll have to do: change the pronoun *vous* or *te* (t') from the question to *me* (m') in your answer.

As a Rule
Remember to use *d'* instead of *de* before a vowel.

Oui (Si), ça me dit de (d')

Oui (Si), ça m'intéresse de (d') aller au cinéma.

Oui (Si), ça me plairait de (d') faire **une** croisière.

Oui (Si), je veux

Non, ça ne me dit pas de (d')

Non, ça ne m'intéresse pas de (d') aller au cinéma.

Non ça ne me plairait pas de (d') faire **de** croisière.

Non, je ne veux pas

As a Rule
When answering a negative question *yes, si* is used instead of *oui.* When answering in the negative *un, une,* and *des* become *de.*

What Do You Think?

How do you feel about a suggestion that was made to you? Does the activity appeal to you? If so, then you would say:

J'aime la musique classique.   J'adore l'opéra.   Je suis fana de ballet.

When you do something or go somewhere new, different, exotic, out of the ordinary, you're bound to have an opinion on whether you liked it or not. Was it fun? You had a good time? You were amused? Give your positive opinion by saying:

C'est (*seh*)…   super (*sew-pehr*)!   extra (*ehks-trah*)!

chouette (*shoo-eht*)! great   formidable! great   génial (*zhay-nyahl*)! fantastic
                                 (*fohr-mee-dahbl*)

superbe (*sew-pehrb*)!   sensationnel   magnifique (*mah-nyee-feek*)!
                                 (*sahN-sah-syoh-nehl*)!

merveilleux (*mehr-veh-yuh*)!

Perhaps you don't like the suggestion presented. Maybe the activity bores you. To express your dislikes you might say:

Je n'aime pas	*zhuh nehm pah*	I don't like
Je déteste	*zhuh day-tehst*	I hate
Je ne suis pas fana de	*zhuh nuh swee pah fah-nah duh*	I'm not a fan of

Je n'aime pas la musique classique.

Je déteste l'opéra.

Je ne suis pas fana de ballet.

Just to be a good sport, you tried it anyway. It was just as you thought: not your cup of tea. To give your negative opinion about an activity you could say:

C'est…

la barbe (*lah bahrb*)	boring
désagréable (*day-zah-gray-ahbl*)	
affreux (*ah-fruh*)	frightful, horrible
horrible (*oh-reebl*)!	
dégoûtant (*day-goo-tahN*)	disgusting
ennuyeux (*ahN-nwee-yuh*)	boring

| embêtant (*ahN-beh-tahN*) | boring |
| ridicule (*ree-dee-kewl*) | ridiculous |

Beyond the Blue Horizon

Years ago, when my husband and I backpacked throughout Europe, we used our French in every single country we visited (except England, naturally). Since France borders Belgium, Luxembourg, Germany, Switzerland, Italy, and Spain, it is easily understood why French would be spoken and understood in all of those countries, and why the people in France are familiar with those languages as well. Furthermore, due to France's importance in the European Economic Community (formerly, the Common Market), French is spoken in all other European countries too. Your travels may take you to many different places where French is spoken. It would prove quite helpful to learn the French names of the countries in Tables 14.4 and 14.5, especially those countries in Europe.

Table 14.4   Feminine Countries

l'Algérie	*lahl-zhay-ree*	Algeria
l'Allemagne	*lahl-mah-nyuh*	Germany
l'Angleterre	*lahN-gluh-tehr*	England
l'Autriche	*lo-treesh*	Austria
la Belgique	*lah behl-zheek*	Belgium
la Chine	*lah sheen*	China
l'Égypte	*lay-zheept*	Egypt
l'Espagne	*lehs-pah-nyuh*	Spain
la France	*lah frahNs*	France
la Grèce	*lah grehs*	Greece
Haïti	*ah-ee-tee*	Haiti
l'Italie	*lee-tah-lee*	Italy
la Pologne	*lah poh-loh-nyuh*	Poland
la Roumanie	*lah roo-mah-nee*	Rumania
la Russie	*lah rew-see*	Russia
la Suisse	*lah swees*	Switzerland
la Tunisie	*lah tew-nee-zee*	Tunisia

As a Rule

In order to talk correctly about travel **to**, **in**, or **from** a country, city, state, or province, it is necessary to learn the gender (masculine or feminine) of the place to which you are referring.

As a Rule

If you look closely at the names of the feminine countries, you will notice that, except for Haïti (which is also the only country in the group that does not use a definite article: *la*, *l'*), they all end in *e*. This makes them very easy to identify.

Table 14.5 Masculine Countries

le Canada	*luh kah-nah-dah*	Canada
le Cambodge	*luh kahN-bohdzh*	Cambodia
les États-Unis	*lay zay-tah-zew-nee*	United States
Israël	*eez-rah-ehl*	Israel
le Japon	*luh zhah-pohN*	Japan
le Liban	*luh lee-bahN*	Lebanon
le Maroc	*luh mah-rohk*	Morocco
le Mexique	*luh mehk-seek*	Mexico
le Zaïre	*luh zah-eer*	Zaire

Do your travels take you far and wide? Are you fortunate enough to be able to plan a trip to another continent? The names of the seven continents in Table 14.6 are also feminine.

Table 14.6 The Continents

l'Afrique	*lah-freek*	Africa
l'Amérique du Nord	*lah-may-reek dew nohr*	North America
l'Amérique du Sud	*lah-may-reek dew sewd*	South America
l'Antarctique	*lahn-tahrk-teek*	Antarctica
l'Asie	*lah-zee*	Asia
l'Australie	*loh-strah-lee*	Australia
l'Europe	*lew-rohp*	Europe

Going to Stay?

On your next trip to Europe, will you be going to Italy? Will you be staying with your relatives in Spain or in Portugal? To express that you are going *to* or staying *in* another country use the preposition *en* to express *to*, and also to express *in* before the names of feminine countries, continents, provinces, islands, and states and before masculine countries starting with a vowel:

As a Rule
Three masculine countries are exceptions to the rule and end in *e*. Israël does not use the definite article *l'*.

I am going to Italy.
Je vais en Italie.
zhuh veh zahN nee-tah-lee

I'm staying in Spain.
Je reste en Espagne.
zhuh rehst ahN nehs-pah-nyuh

I am going to travel to (in) Israel.
Je vais voyager en Israël.
zhuh veh vwah-yah-zhay ahN neez-rah-ehl

The preposition *au* (*aux* for plurals) is used to express *to, in* before the names of some masculine countries, islands, provinces, and states that start with a consonant:

I am going to Japan.
Je vais au Japon.
zhuh veh zo zhah-pohN

I am staying in the United States.
Je reste aux États-Unis.
zhuh rehst o zay-tah-zew-nee

Use *dans le* to express *to, in* before geographical names that are modified by an adjective:

Je vais dans le Dakota du Nord.
J'habite dans l'État de New Jersey.

Coming

Every traveler has an accent, albeit sometimes almost imperceptible, that alerts native speakers to the fact that he (or she) is from another region or country. My French nasal sounds give me away as a New Yorker. My consultant Roger's "th" that comes out "z," is typically French. And the fact that my friend Carlos drops his final "s" is a dead give-away that he's a native Hispanic. If your accent reveals your identity and you want to say that you are from (or that you are coming from) a country, use the preposition *de* to express *from* before the names of feminine countries, continents, provinces, islands, and states and before masculine countries starting with a vowel:

As a Rule
Remember that the preposition *de* (from) combines with *le* to become *du*, and *de* combines with *les* to become *des*.

I am from France.
Je suis de France.
zhuh swee duh frahNs

I am from Israel.
Je suis d'Israël.
zhuh swee deez-rah-ehl

The preposition *de* + the definite article *(le, l', les)* is used to express *from* before masculine countries and geographical names that are modified by an adjective:

I am from Canada.
Je suis du Canada.
zhuh swee dew kah-nah-dah

I am from the United States.
Je suis des États-Unis.
zhuh swee day-zay-tah-zew-nee

I am from beautiful France.
Je suis de la belle France.
zhuh swee duh lah behl frahns

I am from North America.
Je suis de l'Amérique du Nord.
zhuh swee duh lah-may-reek dew nohr

Where Are You Going?

Start your sentence with *Je vais* (I'm going) and tell what country you are going to if you plan to see: a bullfight, the Great Wall, Mexican jumping beans, the Moscow circus, the leaning Tower of Pisa, Big Ben, the pyramids, the Eiffel Tower, home.

Y Gads!

You probably looked at this section and thought: "Oops, the author spelled the title wrong." Or perhaps you're gloating because you found a typographical mistake in the book—even authors and editors are human. Everyone who looks at *Y Gads!* wants to take out a red pen and correct it. It's obvious to me that they didn't study their French well enough to see that I'm just trying to be cute. You see, *y* (ee) is a French pronoun that generally refers to or replaces previously mentioned places or locations and may also refer to things or ideas. The pronoun *y* usually replaces the preposition *à (au, a l', à la, aux)* or other prepositions of location, shown in Table 14.7 + a noun .

Pitfall
Never use *y* to refer to people. *Y* only refers to places, things, or ideas.

Table 14.7 Prepositions of Location

chez	*shay*	at the house (business) of
contre	*kohNtr*	against
dans	*dahN*	in
derrière	*deh-ryehr*	behind
devant	*duh-vahN*	in front of
en	*ahN*	in
entre	*ahNtr*	between
sous	*soo*	under
sur	*sewr*	on
vers	*vehr*	toward

You received a letter today from your French friend. I, of course, would never open your mail, but I sure am curious about that letter. Is it on your desk? Are you going to answer it immediately? Are you going to go to France to visit your friend? Are you going to stay at your friend's house? Will your family say, "Go there and have a good time"? All of these questions can be answered in French by using the pronoun *y*.

Y means *there* when the place has already been mentioned, and can also mean it, them, in it/them, to it/them, or on it/them.

As a Rule

Y is only used to replace *de* + noun when *de* is part of a prepositional phrase showing location:

La douane est *à côté des* bagages.

La douane *y* est.

Il va à Paris.	Mon billet est dans ma poche.	Je réponds à la lettre.
He goes there.	My ticket is in it (there).	I answer it.
Il *y* va.	Mon billet *y* est.	J'*y* réponds.
eel ee vah	*mohN bee-yeh ee eh*	*zhee ray-pohN*

Sometimes *y* is used in French and is not translated into English:

La valise est sur la table?	Is the valise on the table?
Oui, elle *y* est.	Yes, it is.

Y is placed before the verb to which its meaning is tied. When there are two verbs, *y* is placed before the infinitive:

J'*y* vais.	I am going there.
Je n'*y* vais pas.	I'm not going there.
Je désire *y* aller.	I want to go there.
N'*y* va pas.	Don't go there.

In an affirmative command *y* changes position and is placed immediately after the verb and is joined to it by a hyphen:

Vas-*y*! (*vah zee*)	Go (there)! (Familiar)
Allez-*y*! (*ah-lay zee*)	Go (there)! (Polite)

Using y

Word has gotten out that you'll be going to Europe this summer. Your nosy next door neighbor has heard the rumor and can't wait to pump you for information. Use *y* to efficiently answer her questions and make a rapid getaway:

1. Vous allez en France?

2. Vous restez à Paris?

3. Vous passez vos vacances chez votre famille?

4. Vous allez descendre en ville?

5. Vous allez dîner dans des restaurants élégants?

6. Vous allez penser à votre travail?

Make a Suggestion

Let's say you are planning a trip with a group of friends. Your friends are spirited and lively—and none are shy about expressing an opinion about where the group should go. It's your turn to react to the various suggestions:

As a Rule
The familiar command forms of *er* verbs (regular and irregular) retain there final *s* before *y*. This is to prevent the clash of two vowel sounds together. Remember to put a liaison (linking) between the final consonant and *y*.

Example: aller en Italie
Allons-y!
N'y allons pas!

voyager en Grèce

aller à l'aquarium

rester dans un hôtel chic

passer la journée au carnaval

assister à une exposition d'art moderne

The Least You Need to Know

➤ To suggest an activity use *on* + the conjugated verb or the *nous* form conjugated without *nous*.

➤ Simple phrases can express your likes (C'est super!) and dislikes (C'est la barbe!).

➤ Countries that end in *e* are usually feminine. The rest are masculine.

➤ The pronoun *y* can be substituted for a preposition + a location. *Y* means *there*.

Chapter 15

I Wanna Shop Till I Drop

In This Chapter

➤ Stores and what they sell

➤ Clothing, colors, sizes, materials, and designs

➤ All about *mettre* (to put [on])

➤ Getting what you like

➤ This, that, these, and those (a.k.a. demonstrative adjectives)

You've visited just about everything on your "Must See" list, compiled with the help of your friends. For the time being you've had your fill of sightseeing. Now you would like to pick up some souvenirs of your trip, or those gifts you promised family and friends at home.

Are you particular about what you buy? Is it important to you to pick out the "perfect" gift or memento? Do you spend time agonizing over the right color, size, material, design? Or is shopping a chore and you choose almost anything you feel will be appropriate? This chapter will help you make the decisions that are best for you. Read and study all the information before you "shop till you drop."

Now That's My Kinda Store!

Today has been designated as a shopping day. Do you prefer to browse in a small boutique or are you attracted by a large, elegant mall (*un centre commercial*—uhN sahNtr koh-mehr-syahl) such as le Forum des Halles in Paris or the underground Place Bonaventure in Montreal. Table 15.1 will point you in the direction of stores that might interest you and the merchandise you can purchase in them.

Table 15.1 Stores (Les magasins—lay mah-gah-zaN)

la parfumerie, perfume store *lah par-fuhN-ree*	du parfum, perfume
la librairie, book store *lah lee-breh-ree*	des livres, books
le magasin de fleuriste, florist *luh mah-gah-saN duh fluh-reest*	des fleurs, flowers
la boutique, boutique *lah boo-teek*	des vêtements, clothing
le grand magasin, department store *luh grahN mah-gah-zaN*	presque tout, almost everything
le bureau de tabac, tobacconist *luh bew-ro duh tah-bah*	du tabac, tobacco, des cigarettes (f.), cigarettes, des pipes (f.), pipes, des cigares (f.), cigars, des allumettes (f.), matches, des briquets (m.), lighters
le kiosk à journaux, newsstand *luh kee-ohsk ah zhoor-noh*	des journaux (m.), newspapers, des revues (f.), des magazines (m.), magazines
le magasin de disques, record store *luh mah-gah-zaN duh deesk*	des disques (m.), records, des cassettes (f.), cassettes, des C.D. (m.), compact disks
la bijouterie, jewelry store *lah bee-zhoo-tree*	des bijoux (m.), jewels, des bagues (f.), rings, des bracelets (m.), bracelets, des montres (f.), watches, des boucles (f.) d'oreille, earrings, des colliers (m.), necklaces
la maroquinerie, leather goods store *lah mah-roh-kaN-ree*	des portefeuilles (m.), wallets, des sacs (m.), pocket books, des valises (f.), suitcases, des serviettes (f.), briefcases
le magasin de souvenirs, souvenir shop *luh mah-gah-zaN duh soo-vuh-neer*	des tee-shirt (m.), T-shirts, des posters (m.), posters, des monuments en miniature (m.), miniature monuments, des tableaux (m.), paintings

Cultural Tidbits

Do you want to bring home something that is inexpensive (what could be cheaper than a $20 T-shirt!), elegant, typically French, and appropriate to both genders? For as little as $10 you can purchase an original watercolor painted by an artist in Montmartre, along the banks of the Seine, or in front of a wide variety of tourist attractions.

Know Your Jewels

Some people feel, and rightfully so, that they can get a very good bargain when they purchase jewelry in a foreign country because they can avoid certain taxes and duties. Here's the living proof of that. In honor of our wedding anniversary my husband purchased a beautiful watch for me during a trip to Saint Martin (French side, of course). The exact watch, a well-known brand name, was double the price in a popular stateside store, reputed far and wide to give the best deals on jewelry. He really got an incredible deal.

As a Rule

If you want to say that you are going to a store or that you'll be at a store, remember to use *à* (to, at) + the definite article (*au, à la, à l'*): au grand magasin, à la parfumerie.

If you know your prices and are a good shopper, or if you're simply in the mood to buy some jewelry, you can use Table 15.2 to get exactly what you want.

Table 15.2 Jewels (les bijoux—lay bee-zhoo)

amethyst	une améthyste	*ewn ah-may-teest*
aquamarine	une aige-marine	*ewn ehg mah-reen*
diamond	un diamant	*uhN dee-ah-mahN*
emerald	une émeraude	*ewn aym-rod*
ivory	un ivoire	*uhN nee-vwahr*
jade	un jade	*uhN zhahd*
onyx	un onyx	*uhN noh-neeks*
pearls	des perles (f.)	*day pehrl*
ruby	un rubis	*uhN rew-bee*
sapphire	un saphir	*uhN sah-feer*
topaz	une topaze	*ewn toh-pahz*
turquoise	une turquoise	*ewn tewr-kwahz*

If you are buying jewelry you might want to ask:

Est-ce en or?	*ehs ahN nohr*	Is it gold?
Est-ce en argent?	*ehs ahN nahr-zhahN*	Is it silver?

Clothing

It's simply impossible to take a trip to France, the fashion capital of the world, and not come home with at least one article of clothing. You want to have one French label so that you can brag that you are *dans le vent* (*dahN luh vahN*), in fashion. Table 15.3 will help you in your quest for something *au courant*.

Table 15.3   Clothing (les vêtements—lay veht-mahN)

For One and All		
bathing suit	le maillot	*luh mah-yo*
bikini	le bikini	*luh bee-kee-nee*
string bikini	la ficelle	*lah fee-sehl*
belt	la ceinture	*lah saN-tewr*
bikini briefs	le slip	*luh sleep*
boots	les bottes (f.)	*lay boht*
gloves	les gants (m.)	*lay gahN*
handkerchief	le mouchoir	*luh moo-shwahr*
hat	le chapeau	*luh shah-po*
jacket	la veste	*lah vehst*
outer jacket	le blouson	*luh bloo-zohN*
jeans	le jean	*luh zheen*
jogging suit	le survêt, le jogging	*luh sewr-veh, luh zhoh-geeng*
overcoat	le manteau	*luh mahN-to*
pants	le pantalon	*luh pahN-tah-lohN*
pullover	le pull	*luh pewl*
pajamas	le pyjama	*luh pee-zhah-mah*
raincoat	l'imperméable (m.)	*laN-pehr-may-ahbl*
robe	la robe de chambre	*lah rohb duh shahNbr*
sandals (f.)	les sandales	*lay sahN-dahl*

For One and All

scarf	l'écharpe (f.), le foulard	*lay-shahrp, luh foo-lahr*
shirt (man-tailored)	la chemise	*lah shuh-meez*
shoes	les chaussures (f.), les souliers (m.)	*lay sho-sewr, lay sool-lyay*
shorts	le short	*luh shohrt*
sneakers	les tennis	*lay tuh-nees*
socks	les chaussettes (f.)	*lay sho-seht*
T-shirt	le tee-shirt	*luh tee-shehrt*
umbrella	le parapluie	*luh pah-rah-plwee*
underwear	les sous-vêtements (m.)	*lay soo-veht-mahN*
vest	le gilet	*luh zhee-leh*

You want to make sure that you get your right size. Tell the salesperson:

Je porte du…	petit	moyen	grand
zhuh pohrt dew	*puh-tee*	*mwah-yaN*	*grahN*
I wear…	small	medium	large
Ma taille est…	petite	moyenne	grande
Ma tahy eh…	*puh-teet*	*mwah-yehn*	*grahNd*
My size is…	small	medium	large

For shoes you would say:

Je chausse du… + size
zhuh shohs dew
I wear shoe size…

Cultural Tidbits

All products in France (except medicine, food, and books) have a T.V.A. *(taxe à la valeur ajoutée)*, a value-added tax added on to the price of the item. This tax varies depending on the purchase. Visitors from outside the European Economic Community (E.E.C.) may receive a reimbursement of the tax if they spend above a certain amount (often 13 percent on a minimum purchase of 2,000F). Visitors from within the E.E.C. must spend more to receive the discount. So always save your sales receipts and present them at the T.V.A. desk at the airport.

Colors

My friend Vivian, an *artiste*, has taught her four-year-old daughter to describe things as chartreuse, teal, aubergine, and tangerine. I, on the other hand, see the world in primary colors. Whether you go for the *exotique* or the *ordinaire*, Table 15.4 will help you with the basic colors that will get you by.

Table 15.4   Colors (les couleurs—lay koo-luhr)

beige	beige	*behzh*	gray	gris(e)	*gree(z)*
black	noir(e)	*nwahr*	green	vert(e)	*vehr(t)*
blue	bleu(e)	*bluh*	orange	orange	*oh-rahNzh*
brown	brun(e)	*bruhN (brewn)*	pink	rose	*roz*
purple	mauve	*mov*	white	blanc(he)	*blahN(sh)*
red	rouge	*roozh*	yellow	jaune	*zhon*

Materials

While travelling, you might be tempted to make a clothing purchase. Do you find linen sexy? Do you love the feel of silk? Do you crave the coolness of cotton? Is leather a turn-on? Are you into wrinkle-free? We choose or reject different fabrics for a wide variety of reasons. Table 15.5 will help you pick the material you prefer for your special purchases:

Table 15.5   Materials (Les tissus—lay tee-sew)

cashmere	en cachemire	*ahN kahsh-meer*
corduroy	en velours côtelée	*ahN vuh-loor koht-lay*
cotton	en coton	*ahN koh-tohN*
denim	en jean	*ahN zheen*
flannel	en flanelle	*ahN flah-nehl*
gabardine	en gabardine	*ahN gah-bahr-deen*
knit	en tricot	*ahN tree-ko*
leather	en cuir	*ahN kweer*
linen	en lin	*ahN laN*

silk	en soie	*ahN swah*
suede	en daim	*ahN daN*
wool	en laine	*ahN lehn*

Read the Labels

Have you ever accidentally washed a "dry clean only" shirt? Or, have you ever washed a 100% cotton pair of jeans that could never be worn again? Make sure to read all labels carefully for the following information:

non-rétrécissable	*nohN-ray-tray-see-sahbl*	non-shrinkable
lavable	*lah-vahbl*	washable
en tissu infroissable	*ahN tee-sew aN-frwah-sahbl*	wrinkle-resistant

You're Putting Me On

Now that your wardrobe is full, you will have to decide what to put on. The verb *mettre* in Table 15.7 will help you express this concept. Because it is an irregular verb, you should probably commit its forms to memory.

Table 15.7   The Verb mettre (to put [on])

je mets	*zhuh meh*	I put (on)
tu mets	*tew meh*	you put (on)
il, elle, on met	*eel (ehl, ohN) meh*	he, she, one puts (on)
nous mettons	*noo meh-tohN*	we put (on)
vous mettez	*voo meh-tay*	you put (on)
ils, elles mettent	*eel (ehl) meht*	they put (on)

What Do You Put On?

Does your life style demand an extensive wardrobe or are you strictly a jeans and T-shirt kind of person? Imagine that you've found yourself in the following situations. Describe in detail (including jewelry) what you put on to go to: work, the beach, a formal dinner party, your friend's house, skiing.

As a Rule
The regular *er* verb *porter* means to wear.

What's the Object?

I have an absolutely fabulous red dress. Imagine that I was telling you about it and said: "I put on my red dress to go to parties. I love my red dress. I wear my red dress very often." How tedious and boring! It sounds much better to say: "I put my red dress on to go to parties. I love it and I wear it often."

What did I do to improve my conversation? I stopped repeating **my red dress** (a direct object noun) and replaced it with it (a direct object pronoun). Just what exactly are direct objects? Let's take a closer look:

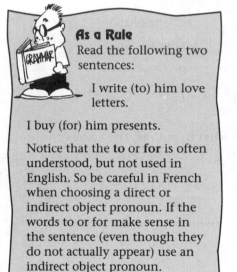

As a Rule
Read the following two sentences:

I write (to) him love letters.

I buy (for) him presents.

Notice that the **to** or **for** is often understood, but not used in English. So be careful in French when choosing a direct or indirect object pronoun. If the words to or for make sense in the sentence (even though they do not actually appear) use an indirect object pronoun.

Direct objects (which can be nouns or pronouns) answer the question **whom** or **what** the subject is acting upon and may refer to people, places, things, or ideas:

I see **the boy.**	I see **him.**
I like **the dress.**	I like **it.**
He pays **John and me.**	He pays **us.**

Indirect object nouns can be replaced by indirect object pronouns. Take the story of my friend Georgette who is crazy about her new boyfriend, Paul. This is what she told me: "I write to Paul. Then I read my love letters to Paul. I buy presents for Paul. I make cakes for Paul. I cook dinners for Paul." To get to the point more efficiently, all she had to say was: I write to Paul and then I read him (to him) my love letters. I buy him (for him) presents. I make him (for him) cakes and I cook him (for him) dinners."

How do indirect objects differ from direct objects? We'll need a closer look:

Indirect objects answer the question to whom the subject is doing something or for whom the subject is acting. Indirect objects only refer to people.

I speak **to the boys.**	I speak **to them.**
I buy a gift **for Mary.**	I buy a gift **for her.** (I buy her a gift.)
	He gives **(to) me** a tie every Christmas.

We use direct and indirect pronouns automatically in English all the time to prevent the constant, monotonous repetition of a word and to allow our conversation to flow naturally. Direct and indirect object nouns in French may be replaced by the pronouns in Table 15.8.

Table 15.8 Object Pronouns

Direct Object Pronouns			Indirect Object Pronouns		
me (m')	*muh*	me	me (m')	*muh*	me
te (t')	*tuh*	you (familiar)	te (t')	*tuh*	(to) you (familiar)
le (l')	*luh*	he, it	lui	*lwee*	(to) him
la (l')	*lah*	her, it	lui	*lwee*	(to) her
nous	*noo*	us	nous	*noo*	(to) us
vous	*voo*	you (polite)	vous	*voo*	(to) you
les	*lay*	them	leur	*luhr*	(to) them

The clue to the correct usage of an indirect object is the French preposition *à (au, à la, à l', aux)* followed by the name of or reference to a person. Some verbs like *répondre (à), téléphoner (à),* and *ressembler (à)* are always followed by *à* + person and will, therefore, always take an indirect object pronoun.

> **Pitfall**
> Be careful! Some verbs like *écouter* (to listen to), *chercher* (to look for), *payer* (to pay for), and *regarder* (to look at) take direct objects in French.

As you can see, you should have little problem using the direct or indirect object pronouns for me (to me), you, (to you), or us (to us) because these pronouns are all exactly the same. You must be careful, however, when expressing him, her, or to/for him, her, and them, or to/for them because there are now two sets of pronouns. Sometimes this does get a bit tricky. Remember to choose the pronoun that reflects the number and gender of the noun to which you are referring:

Elle met *le pantalon noir.*	Elle *le* met.
Il met *la chemise blanche.*	Il *la* met.
Je mets *mes gants bruns.*	Je *les* mets.
Il téléphone *à Marie.*	Il *lui* téléphone.
Il téléphone *à Marie et à Luc.*	Il *leur* téléphone.

Position of Object Pronouns

Although we can automatically place object pronouns in their proper place in English, correct placement in French does not follow English rules and requires some practice. Let's take a closer look.

181

Object pronouns are placed before the verb to which their meaning is tied (usually the conjugated verb). When there are two verbs, object pronouns are placed before the infinitive:

Je *la* mets.   Je *lui* parle.

Je ne *la* mets pas.   Je ne *lui* parle pas.

Je vais *la* mettre.   Je ne vais pas *lui* parler.

Ne *la* mets pas!   Ne *lui* parle pas!

In an affirmative command, object pronouns change position and are placed immediately after the verb and are joined to it by a hyphen. *Me* becomes *moi* when it follows the verb:

Mets-*la*!   Parle-*lui*!

Mettez-*la*!   Parlez-*lui*!

                                 Donnez-*moi* la robe!

Using Direct Object Pronouns

Imagine that you are on a shopping spree in the Samaritaine department store in Paris and your arms are loaded with all your "finds." Your friend joins you and questions your choices. Answer all his or her questions efficiently by using a direct object pronoun:

1. Aimez-vous le pantalon bleu?   4. Regardez-vous les chaussures brunes?

2. Prenez-vous les gants noirs?   5. Achetez-vous la chemise blanche?

3. Choisissez-vous la cravate rouge?   6. Adorez-vous le blouson beige?

Using Indirect Object Pronouns

Your friend doesn't know what to buy her friends and family members as gifts. Offer suggestions, following the examples:

Example: Paul/une radio   ses frères/une chemise
Offre-lui une radio.   Offre-leur une chemise.

1. Robert/une montre   4. ses soeurs/des robes

2. ses parents/un tableau   5. son amie/un bracelet

3. Luc et Michel/des cravates   6. sa grand-mère/un pull

Asking for What You Want

Sometimes you just want to browse and resent having a salesperson hover over you waiting to make a sale. At other times, you have specific wants and needs and require assistance. Here are some phrases to help you deal with most common situations.

Upon entering a store an employee might ask you:

Est-ce que je peux vous aider?	Puis-je vous aider?	Vous désirez?
ehs-kuh zhuh puh voo zeh-day	*pweezh voo zeh-day*	*voo day-zee-ray*
May I help you?		

If you are just browsing, you would answer:

Non, merci, je regarde (tout simplement).
nohN mehr-see zhuh ruh-gahrd (too saN-pluh-mahN)
No, thank you, I am (just) looking.

If you want to see or buy something, you would answer:

Oui, je voudrais voir…s'il vous plaît.	Je cherche…
wee zhuh voo-dreh vwahr…seel voo pleh	*zhuh shehrsh*
Yes, I would like to see…please.	I'm looking for…

And of course, if you're a shopper like I am, you'd want to know:

Y a-t-il des soldes?	Avez-vous cassé les prix?
ee ah teel day sohld?	*ah-vay-voo kah-say lay pree?*
Are there any sales?	Have you slashed your prices?

What Do You Prefer?

To be of proper assistance to you and to help you make the decision that's right for you the salesperson has to understand your preferences. Here are a few questions you may hear:

Quel pull est-ce que vous préférez?
kehl pewl esh-kuh voo pray-fay-ray
Which pullover do you prefer?

If you are deciding between two different items, the salesperson would ask which one(s) you preferred by using one of the interrogative adjectives in Table 15.9.

Table 15.9 Interrogative Adjectives

	Masculine	Feminine
Singular	lequel (*luh-kehl*)	laquelle (*lah-kehl*)
Plural	lesquels (*lay-kehl*)	lesquelles (*lay-kchl*)

These interrogative adjectives must agree with the nouns to which they refer:

Lequel de ces pulls est-ce que vous préférez?
luh-kehl duh say pewl ehs-kuh voo pray-fay-ray
Which one of these pullovers do you prefer?

Lesquelles de ces robes est-ce que vous prenez?
lay-kehl duh say rohb ehs-kuh voo pruh-nay
Which ones of these dresses are you taking?

To express your preference (to say *the … one* or *the … ones*), simply use the appropriate definite article plus an adjective that agrees. When speaking about the pullover you might say:

Je préfère le bleu clair.   Je préfère le grand.
zhuh pray-fehr luh bluh klehr   *zhuh pray-fehr luh grahN*
I prefer the light blue one.   I prefer the big one.

When speaking about the dresses you might say:

Je prends les petites.   Je prends la rouge et la bleue.
zhuh prahN lay puh-teet   *zhuh prahN lah roozh ay lah bluh*
I am taking the small ones.   I am taking the red one and the blue one.

Expressing Opinions

That shirt is you. You just love those pants. What a perfect jacket! If you are happy with an item you will want to express your pleasure by saying one of the following:

Ça me plaît.	*sah muh pleh*	I like it.
Ça me va.	*sah muh vah*	It suits (fits) me.
C'est agréable.	*seh tah-gray-ahbl*	It's nice.
C'est élégant(e).	*seh tay-lay-gahN*	It's elegant.
C'est pratique.	*seh prah-teek*	It's practical.

If you are unhappy with what you see, you might use:

Ça ne me plaît pas.	*sah nuh muh pleh pah*	I don't like it.
Ça ne me va pas.	*sah nuh muh vah pah*	It doesn't suit (fit) me.
Il (elle) est abominable.	*eel (ehl) eh tah-boh-mee-nahbl*	It's horrible.

Il (elle) est trop petit(e).	*eel (ehl) eh tro puh-tee(t)*	It's too small.
Il (elle) est trop serré(e).	*eel (ehl) eh tro suh-ray*	It's too tight.
Il (elle) est trop court(e).	*eel (ehl) eh tro koor(t)*	It's too short.
Il (elle) est trop long(ue).	*eel (ehl) eh tro lohN(g)*	It's too long.
Il (Elle) est trop criard(e).	*eel (ehl) eh tro kree-ahr*	It's too loud.
Il (Elle) est trop étroit(e).	*eel (ehl) eh tro pay-trwaht*	It's too narrow.

If you're not satisfied and want something else:

Je cherche quelque chose de plus (moins) + adjective
zhuh shehrsh kehl kuh shooz duh plew (mwaN)
I'm looking for something more (less)…

> **Pitfall**
> Remember to change verbs and adjectives to accommodate plural subjects:
>
> Ils sont trop étroits.
> Elles sont trop étroites.

I'll Take This, That, One of These, and Some of Those

While considering a purchase, it's not uncommon to ask a friend or salesperson for an opinion of this suit, that shirt, these shoes, or those ties. A demonstrative adjective points out someone or thing being referred to and allows you to be specific by expressing this, that, these, and those as shown in Table 15.10.

Table 15.10 Demonstrative Adjectives: This, That, These, Those

used before masculine singular nouns beginning with a consonant	used before masculine singular nouns beginning with a vowel	used before all feminine singular nouns	used before all plural nouns
ce (*suh*)	cet (*seht*)	cette (*seht*)	ces (*say*)
ce sac	cet imperméable	cette écharpe	ces sacs
		cette robe	ces écharpes

➤ Demonstrative adjectives precede the nouns they modify and agree with them in number and gender. The special masculine form *cet* is used to prevent a clash of two vowel sounds together.

➤ Demonstrative adjectives are repeated before each noun:

Ce pantalon et cette chemise sont formdables.

The Least You Need to Know

➤ To shop successfully in a French-speaking country you must use the metric system.

➤ To make your conversation more fluid, use object pronouns to replace object nouns.

➤ If you know how to ask for what you want, you'll probably get it.

➤ Demonstrative adjectives (ce, cet, cette, ces) agree in number and gender with the nouns they describe.

Munch munch

Chapter 16

Finally, A Home-Cooked Meal

In This Chapter

➤ Where to buy different foods

➤ How to read a wine label

➤ How to express quantity

➤ All about irregular *ir* verbs

➤ A special treat

In the last chapter you learned to shop for souvenirs, gifts, and some everyday odds and ends. You also picked out some fabulous French fashions and even managed, despite the metric system, to get the right size. Shopping is hard work and you've really worked up an appetite. It's a bit early for dinner. What should you do next?

Your best bet is to stop in one of the local food stores to pick up a snack to tide you over until your next meal. You can grab a sandwich (*un sandwich—uhN sahNd-weesh*) made on a long loaf of French bread (*une baguette—ewn bah-geht*), a pastry (*une pâtisserie—ewn pah-tees-ree*), or just a large chunk of cheese (*du fromage—dew froh-mahzh*). This chapter will provide you with many alternatives, and assure that you get the right quantities. In the end, there's a special treat.

Shopping Around

I loved going on a class trip to Paris in 1990 with my younger son, Michael. Like his mother, he's an incorrigible junk food addict and truly appreciates the sweet things in life. It seems that there are pastry shops on every corner in Paris and he and I enjoyed many an *éclair* together. Are you like us? Do you like to keep snacks in your hotel room, just in case you get the midnight munchies? Or have you rented a condo or an apartment and prefer to do your own cooking? In any French-speaking country you will be able to enjoy the culinary delights in the shops listed in Table 16.1.

Cultural Tidbits

Bread and rolls are generally sold in a *boulangerie*. You can choose from *croissants*, crescent rolls made from a puff-pastry dough; *pains au chocolat*, croissants filled with bittersweet chocolate; *brioches*, soft, sweet rolls made of butter, eggs, flour, and yeast; and *baguettes*, French loaves. Pastries, such as *éclairs*, *charlottes russes*, and *napoléons*, are sold in a *pâtisserie*.

Table 16.1   Food Shops and Provisions

l'épicerie	*lay-pees-ree*	grocery (vegetable) store
les légumes (m.)	*lay lay-gewm*	vegetables
les provisions (f.)	*lay proh-vee-zyohN*	provisions
la boucherie	*lah boosh-ree*	butcher shop
la viande	*lah vyahNd*	meat
la boulangerie	*lah boo-lahNzh-ree*	bakery
les desserts	*lay duh-sehr*	desserts
la charuterie	*lah shahr-keww-tree*	delicatessen
les viandes froides	*lay vyahNd frwahd*	coldcuts
la confiserie	*lah kohN-feez-ree*	candy store
les bonbons (m.)	*lay bohN-bohN*	candies
la crémerie	*lah kraym-ree*	dairy store
les produits (m.) laitiers	*lay proh-dwee leh-tyay*	dairy products
la fruiterie	*la frwee-tree*	fruit store

les fruits (m.)	*lay frwee*	fruits
la pâtisserie	*lah pah-tees-ree*	pastry shop
la pâtisserie	*lah pah-tees-ree*	pastry
la poissonnerie	*lah pwah-sohn-ree*	fish store
le poisson	*luh pwah-sohN*	fish
le hypermarché	*luh ee-pehr-mahr-shay*	large supermarket
le magasin de vins	*luh mah-gah-zaN duh vaN*	liquor store
les vins (m) et les spiritueux(m.)	*lay vaN ay lay spee-ree-tew-uh*	wines and liquors
le supermarché	*luh sew-pehr-mahr-shay*	supermarket

Where Are You Going?

You've scouted out the shops in the area where you are staying and now you're ready to venture out on your own and do some serious shopping. When it's time to stock up and you're ready to leave, use the verb *aller* and the preposition *à* + the appropriate definite article (*au, à la, à l'*) to indicate the store to which you are going:

> Je vais à l'épicerie.   I'm going to the grocery store.
>
> Je vais à la boulangerie.   I'm going to the bakery.

It is very common to use the preposition *chez* (to [at] the house [business] of) + *the person* to express where you are going:

➤ Je vais chez l' épicier (épicière).

➤ Je vais chez le (la) boulanger (boulangère).

Write where you would go to buy: vegetables, pastry, meat, fruits, fish, wine, candy, and milk.

Cultural Tidbits

Many French shoppers still do most of their shopping at smaller neighborhood shops, despite the convenience of the larger *supermarchés* or *hypermarchés*. Favoring quality over convenience, many French people would rather make numerous stops—at their favorite bread shop, cheese shop, butcher, and so forth—than settle for supermarket brands.

The delectable displays of food in the windows of various food stores across France just beckon you to enter and try something new and exotic. What foods (*aliments* m.) are among your favorites: fruits? vegetables? pastries? cheeses? Are you interested in trying different meat, poultry, game, or fish? Perhaps there's a wine that has caught your fancy? Tables 16.2–16.9 will help you enjoy the culinary experience of your choice.

Table 16.2 At the Grocery Store

Vegetables	Les Légumes	
asparagus	les asperges (f.)	*lay zahs-pehrzh*
broccoli	le brocoli	*luh broh-koh-lee*
carrot	la carotte	*lah kah-roht*
corn	le maïs	*luh mah-ees*
eggplant	l'aubergine	*lo-behr-zheen*
lettuce	la laitue	*lah leh-tew*
mushroom	le champignon	*luh shahN-pee-nyohN*
onion	l'oignon	*loh-nyohN*
pepper	le piment, le poivron	*luh pee-mahN, luh pwah-vrohN*
potato	la pomme de terre	*lah pohm duh tehr*
rice	le riz	*luh ree*
shallot	l'échalote (f.)	*lay-shah-loht*
spinach	les épinards (m.)	*lay zay-pee-nahr*
sweet potato	la patate douce	*lah pah-taht doos*
tomato	la tomate	*lah toh-maht*

Table 16.3 At the Fruit Store

Fruits	Les Fruits	
apple	la pomme	*lah pohm*
apricot	l'abricot (m.)	*lah-bree-ko*
banana	la banane	*lah bah-nahn*
blueberry	la myrtille	*lah meer-tee-y*
cherry	la cerise	*lah suh-reez*
date	la datte	*lah daht*
fig	la figue	*lah feeg*
grape	le raisin	*luh reh-zahN*
grapefruit	le pamplemousse	*luh pahNpl-moos*
lemon	le citron	*luh see-trohN*
melon	le melon	*luh muh-lohN*
orange	l'orange(f.)	*loh-rahNzh*
peach	la pêche	*lah pehsh*
pear	la poire	*lah pwahr*
pineapple	l'ananas (m.)	*lah-nah-nah*
prune	le pruneau	*luh prew-no*
raisin	le raisin sec	*luh reh-zaN sehk*
raspberry	la framboise	*lah frahN-bwahz*
strawberry	la fraise	*lah frehz*
Nuts	**Les Noix**	
almond	l'amande	*lah-mahNd*
chestnut	le marron	*luh mah-rohN*
hazelnut	la noisette	*lah nwah-zeht*
walnut	la noix	*lah nwah*

Table 16.4 At the Butcher or Delicatessen

Meats	Les Viandes	
bacon	le lard, le bacon	*luh lahr, luh bah-kohN*
beef	le boeuf	*luh buhf*
blood pudding	le boudin	*luh boo-daN*
bologna	la mortadelle	*lah mohr-tah-dehl*
brains	les cervelles (f.)	*lay sehr-vehl*
chopped meat	la viande hachée	*lah vyahNd ah-shay*
goat	la chèvre	*lah sheh-vruh*
ham	le jambon	*luh zhahN-bohN*
lamb	l'agneau (m.)	*lah-nyo*
liver	le foie	*luh fwah*
pâté	le pâté	*luh pah-tay*
pork	le porc	*luh pohr*
roast beef	le rosbif	*luh rohs-beef*
sausage	les saucisses (f.)	*lay so-sees*
spareribs	les basses côtes (f.)	*lay bahs kot*
sweetbreads	les ris de veau	*lay ree dvo*
tongue	la langue	*lah lahNg*
veal	le veau	*luh vo*
Fowl and Game	**La Volaille et le Gibier**	
chicken	le poulet	*luh poo-leh*
duck	le canard	*luh kah-nard*
goose	l'oie (f.)	*lwah*
pheasant	le faisan	*luh feh-zahN*
pigeon	le pigeon	*luh pee-zhohN*
quail	la caille	*lah kahy*
rabbit	le lapin	*luh lah-paN*
turkey	la dinde	*lah daNd*

Cultural Tidbits

Pâté is a paste (thicker than our traditional meat loaf), usually made with goose liver, but it may also be prepared with duck, pork, or chicken. Wine is added to the ground meat mixture and then it is baked in a loaf. The pâté is then allowed to cool and is served cold, often with bread or crackers. At times, pâté is baked in a decorated pastry crust (en croûte—ahN kroot), making it even more flavorful.

Table 16.5 At the Fish Store

Fish and Seafood	Le Poisson et les Fruits de Mer	
clam	la palourde	*lah pah-loord*
crab	le crabe	*luh krahb*
crawfish	les écrivisses	*lay zay-kruh-vees*
flounder	le carrelet	*luh kahr-leh*
frogs' legs	les cuisses de grenouille (f.)	*lay kwees duh gruh-nuhy*
halibut	le flétan	*luh flay-tahN*
herring	le hareng	*luh ah-rahN*
lobster	le homard	*luh oh-mahr*
mussel	la moule	*lah mool*
oyster	l'huître	*lwee-truh*
red snapper	la perche rouge	*lah pehrsh roozh*
salmon	le saumon	*luh so-mohN*
sardine	la sardine	*lah sahr-deen*
scallops	les coquilles	*lay koh-kee*
sea bass	le bar	*luh bahr*
shrimp	la crevette	*lah kruh-veht*
snail	l'escargot (m.)	*lehs-kahr-go*
sole	la sole	*lah sohl*
squid	le calmar	*luh kahl-mahr*
swordfish	l'espadon	*lehs-pah-dohN*
trout	la truite	*lah trweet*
tuna	le thon	*luh tohN*

Table 16.6   At the Dairy

Dairy Products Produits Laitiers

butter	le beurre	*luh buhr*
cheese	le fromage	*luh froh-mahzh*
cream	la crème	*lah krehm*
eggs	des oeufs (m.)	*day zuh*
yogurt	le yaourt	*luh yah-oort*

Table 16.7   At the Bakery and Pastry Shop

Breads and Desserts	Pains et Desserts	
apple turnover	le chausson aux pommes	*luh sho-sohN o pohm*
bread	le pain	*luh paN*
brioche	la brioche	*lah bree-ohsh*
cake	le gâteau	*luh gah-to*
chocolate croissant	le pain au chocolat	*luh paN o shoh-koh-lah*
cookie	le biscuit	*luh bees-kwee*
cream puffs	les choux à la crème (m.)	*lay shoo ah lah krehm*
crescent roll	le croissant	*luh krwah-sahN*
danish	la danoise	*lah dah-nwahz*
doughnut	le beignet	*luh beh-nyeh*
loaf of French bread	la baguette	*lah bah-geht*
pie	la tarte	*lah tahrt*
roll	le petit pain	*luh puh-tee paN*

Cultural Tidbits

If you are interested in maintaining a nutritious, healthy diet you might want to look for *une maison de régime* (*ewn meh-zohN duh ray-zheem*)—a health foods store, also referred to as *une diététique* (*ewn dee-ay-tay-teek*). Since product advertising is not as widespread in France as it is here in the U.S., the French rely on the professional advice of the store owner when it comes to purchasing products. Teas (especially herbal teas), vitamins, and breads are the most popular items sold in a French health foods store.

Table 16.8 At the Candy Store

Sweets	Les Sucreries	
candy	les bonbons (m.)	*lay bohN-bohN*
chocolate	le chocolat	*luh shoh-koh-lah*

Table 16.9 At the Supermarket

Drinks	Les Boissons	
beer	la bière	*lah byehr*
champagne	le champagne	*luh shahN-pah-nyuh*
cider	le cidre	*luh seedr*
coffee	le café	*luh kah-fay*
juice	le jus	*luh zhew*
hot chocolate (cocoa)	le chocolat	*luh shoh-koh-laht*
lemonade	le citron pressé	*lun see-trohN preh-say*
milk	le lait	*luh leh*
mineral water	l'eau minérale (f.)	*lo mee-nay-rahl*
carbonated	gazeuse	*gah-zuhz*
non-carbonated	plate	*plaht*
orangeade	l'orangeade (f.)	*loh-rahN-zhahd*
soda	le soda	*luh soh-dah*
tea	le thé	*luh tay*
wine	le vin	*luh vaN*

Cultural Tidbits

Would you love to snack on a peanut-butter-and-jelly sandwich? You're out of luck. Peanut butter (*le beurre de cacahouètes, luh buhr duh kah-kah-weht*) is not sold in France!

What's That Wine?

Have you ever looked at a wine label and wondered what all the information meant? We've come to the rescue with a convenient key that will help you make sense of wine labels. Both French and American governments have strict rules concerning wine and labeling, but in a nutshell, this is what you should know:

➤ The region where the wine was produced, such as Bourgogne (Burgundy), Bordeaux, Champagne

➤ Product of France

➤ The *appellation* of the wine (trademark), indicates the region in which the wine was produced and affirms that the grapes were grown, picked, fermented, and bottled according to strict government controls. Only better quality wines are marked with an *appellation*. Table wine is clearly marked as such, and has no *appellation* since it is of a lesser quality. A champagne label merely states: "Champagne."

➤ The quality of the wine (from the lowest to the highest):

vin de table

village wine (no vineyard is mentioned, probably meaning that the wine is made from a variety of grapes from different vineyards)

premier cru and grand cru: Premier and grand cru indicate that the grapes used to produce the wine were of a superior quality because they were grown on the most fertile land, under the best climatic conditions. Although premier cru is considered the ultimate, many *connaisseurs* prefer the taste of grand cru. The ordinary palate would not be able to distinguish between the two.

premier grand cru

➤ The town where the wine was bottled

➤ The name and origin of the shipper (for champagne, the champagne house is usually the shipper)

➤ The net contents

➤ The percentage of alcohol by volume

➤ The name and address of the importer

Information that may or may not be included on the label is:

➤ The vintage (the year the wine was bottled)

➤ The brand or château name

➤ Whether the wine was "estate" or "château" bottled

Cultural Tidbits

The only true champagne comes from the Champagne province in the northwest of France. All others are merely imitation sparkling wines. Here's why. French winegrowers patiently and carefully work all year to grow and harvest the most perfect grapes possible. These grapes are then separated according to their types, the villages they come from, and the date when they were picked. They are then pressed, and their juice is fermented in different vats. In the spring, the wine is bottled. According to French law and tradition, the wine then ferments a second time in the bottle (creating the bubbles) and ages in cellars for three, four, or five years in order to reach perfect maturity.

It's the Quantity That Counts

You've decided to go on a picnic with a friend in the French countryside and have stopped by a *charcuterie* to purchase some sandwich meat. You figure that a half pound ought to be sufficient. But when you get to the counter to order, you find that no one understands how much you want. Why are you having this problem and how will you get the right amount of meat? In France the metric system is used for measuring quantities of food: liquids are measured in liters and solids are measured in kilograms or fractions thereof. Since most of us are used to dealing with ounces, pounds, pints, quarts, and gallons, I've included a conversion chart to help you out until the metric system becomes second nature.

Table 16.10 Measuring Quantities of Food

Approximate Solid Measures

1 oz. = 28 grams	3/4 lb. = 375 grams
1/4 lb. = 125 grams	1.1 lb. = 500 grams
1/2 lb. = 250 grams	2.2 lb. = 1000 grams (1 kilogram)

Approximate Liquid Measures

1 oz. = 30 milliliters	16 oz. (1 pint) = 475 milliliters
32 oz. (1 quart) = 950 milliliters (approximately 1 liter)	1 gallon = 3.75 liters

Not having been brought up on the metric system myself, I can understand that you might still be a bit confused. So I've made it even easier for you. Sometimes it's just easier to ask for a box, bag, jar, etc., and to commit to memory the amounts we're accustomed to: a pound, a quart, etc. Consult Table 16.11 to easily get the amount you want or need.

Table 16.11 Getting the Right Amount

2 pounds of	un kilo de	*uhN kee-lo duh*
a bag of	un sac de	*uhN sahk duh*
a bar of	une tablette de	*ewn tah-bleht duh*
a bottle of	une bouteille de	*ewn boo-tehy duh*
a box of	une boîte de	*ewn bwaht duh*
a can of	une boîte de	*ewn bwaht duh*
a dozen	une douzaine de	*ewn doo-zehn duh*
a half pound of	deux cent cinquante grammes de	*duh sahN saN-kahNt grahm duh*
a jar of	un bocal de	*uhN boh-kahl duh*
a package of	un paquet de	*uhN pah-keh duh*
a pound of	un demi-kilo de, cinq cents grammes de	*uhN duh-mee kee-lo duh, saNk sahN grahm duh*
a quart of	un litre de	*uhN lee-truh duh*
a slice of	une tranche de	*ewn trahNsh duh*

You're on a diet but you must have "just a taste" of the chocolate mousse that your French host spent hours preparing for you. He starts filling your bowl and you try to motion: "enough." Too bad, he just keeps heaping it on. Now there's really a lot of mousse on your plate. Finally, there's just too much. Don't allow yourself to get into this bind. Here are some expressions that will help you limit the quantity you receive:

a little	un peu de	*uhN puh duh*
a lot of	beaucoup de	*bo-koo duh*
enough	assez de	*ah-say duh*
too much	trop de	*tro duh*

What's in the Fridge?

When you arrive at the check-in desk at your hotel in Saint Martin, you are delighted to find out that your room has been upgraded and there's a refrigerator at your disposal. You look out the window and there's a convenience store in walking distance. What snacks would you purchase for that occasional craving?

Cultural Tidbits

Be advised: it is not customary to receive a shopping bag in individual neighborhood stores. French shoppers usually bring along *un filet* (*uhN fee-leh*), a net bag where they stow their purchases. This bag is re-usable and is, therefore, environment-friendly. You may purchase one at a supermarket, drugstore, or variety store.

Getting What You Want

In a small, neighborhood store there will always be someone eager to help you. Be prepared for the questions that you might be asked and the proper way to give an answer that will get you what you want:

Vous désirez?	Est-ce que je peux vous aider?
voo day-zee-ray	*ehs-kuh zhuh puh voo zeh-day*
What would you like?	May I help you?

As a Rule

All of these expressions of quantity include the word *de* (of). Before a vowel *de* becomes *d'*. In all other instances, *de* never changes:

beaucoup de bonbons
a lot of candies

une douzaine d'oeufs
a dozen eggs

Your answer might begin:

Je voudrais…	Pourriez-vous me donner…?	s'il vous plaît
zhuh voo-dreh	*poo-ryay voo muh doh-nay*	*seel voo pleh*
I would like…	Could you give me…?	please

You might then be asked:

Et avec ça?	C'est tout?
ay ah-vehk sah	*seh too*
And with that?	Is that all?

An appropriate response would be to either give additional items that you want or to answer:

Oui, c'est tout, merci.
wee seh too mehr-see
Yes, that's all, thank you.

You're on your own. Tell a shopkeeper that you would like the following: a pound of ham, a liter of soda, a chocolate bar , a box of cookies, a bag of candy, a half pound of turkey.

ir Irregularities

Snacking is fine but now you're in the mood for a good dinner. Imagine walking along the port in Martinique and **smelling** the aromas emanating from the various restaurants. Of course you want to know what type of cuisine is being **served**. Let's take a closer look at these verbs and some other similar ones. The verb *servir* (to serve) and a few others that end in *ir* (*dormir*—to sleep, *partir*—to leave, *sentir*—to feel, smell, and *sortir*—to go out) do not follow the pattern of present tense conjugation for *ir* verbs that has already been studied. They drop the consonant before the *ir* of the infinitive in the singular forms and retain that consonant in the plural forms:

dormir (to sleep)		
je dors	*zhuh dohr*	I sleep
tu dors	*tew dohr*	you sleep
il, elle, on dort	*eel (ehl, ohN) dohr*	he (she, one) sleeps
nous dormons	*noo dohr-mohN*	we sleep
vous dormez	*voo dohr-may*	you sleep
ils, elles dorment	*eel (ehl) dohrm*	they sleep

partir (to leave)

je pars	*zhuh pahr*	I leave
tu pars	*tew pahr*	you leave
il, elle, on part	*eel (ehl, ohN) pahr*	he (she, one) leaves
nous partons	*noo pahr-tohN*	we leave
vous partez	*voo pahr-tay*	you leave
ils, elles partent	*eel (ehl) pahrt*	they leave

sentir (to smell, feel)

je sens	*zhuh sahN*	I smell, feel
tu sens	*tew sahN*	you smell, feel
il, elle, on sent	*eel (ehl, ohN) sahN*	he (she, one) smells, feels
nous sentons	*noo sahN-tohN*	we smell, feel
vous sentez	*voo sahN-tay*	you smell, feel
ils, elles sentent	*eel (ehl) sahNt*	they smell, feel

servir (to serve)

je sers	*zhuh sehr*	I serve
tu sers	*tew sehr*	you serve
il, elle, on sert	*eel (ehl, ohN) sehr*	he (she, one) serves
nous servons	*noo sehr-vohN*	we serve
vous servez	*voo sehr-vay*	you serve
ils, elles servent	*eel (ehl) sehrv*	they serve

sortir (to go out)

je sors	*zhuh sohr*	I go out
tu sors	*tew sohr*	you go out
il, elle, on sort	*eel (ehl, ohN) sohr*	he (she, one) goes out
nous sortons	*noo sohr-tohN*	we go out
vous sortez	*voo sohr-tay*	you go out
ils, elles sortent	*eel (ehl) sohrt*	they go out

It's a Puzzle to Me

Do you want to make sure that you have all those verb forms down pat? Practice can make perfect in a fun way. Complete the crossword with the correct forms of all the verbs.

Horizontalement

1. (leave) je
3. (sleep) you
7. (serve) ils
8. (server) nous
10. (sleep) elles
12. (go out) nous
14. (feel) ils
15. (leave) nous
17. (serve) il
18. (feel) vous
19. (serve) tu
20. (sleep) vous

Verticalement

1. (leave) elles
2. (go out) vous
3. (sleep) nous
4. (feel) il
5. (feel) nous
6. (serve) vous
9. (go out) ils
11. (sleep) il
13. (leave) elle
15. (leave) vous
16. (feel) je
17. (go out) tu
18. (go out) elle

The Treat's on Me

Why not impress your friends with this delicious treat from *Bon Appétit*: frozen chocolate mousse truffles? They are great and easy to prepare. You will need:

1/2 cup sugar

3 large egg yolks

3/4 cup heavy cream

8 oz. semisweet chocolate morsels

2 tablespoons Chambord or amaretto liqueur

3-4 oz. grated semisweet chocolate

Mix sugar and egg yolks in medium bowl until thick. Bring cream to a boil in a heavy saucepan. Add hot cream to the yolk mixture and beat gently until thoroughly mixed. Return mixture to saucepan and stir over medium heat until custard gets thick—about three minutes. **Do not boil.** Remove from heat. Add chocolate to custard mixture. Stir until melted and smooth. Add liqueur. Cover and freeze until firm (4–24 hours). For each truffle use 1 tablespoon of the mixture. Shape into round balls. Roll in grated chocolate. Arrange in a single layer in a container lined with waxed paper. Freeze. Serve frozen. Can be kept up to one month. Enjoy!

The Least You Need to Know

➤ Use the verb *aller* + *à* + the definite article to express where you are going to.

➤ Purchasing the correct amount of food in France requires a knowlege of the metric system.

➤ Ask for a box or a jar of something if you are not familiar with the metric system.

➤ Certain *ir* verbs follow a different pattern of conjugation and should be committed to memory.

Chapter 17

Let's Eat Out

In This Chapter

➤ How to order in a restaurant

➤ How to get exactly what you want

➤ Special diets

➤ Exclamations

Let's say you're in gay Paris. Alas, it is neither lunch nor dinner time, but using the lessons from the last chapter, you've managed to grab a snack to tide you over until your next real meal. Or maybe you've stocked your hotel room refrigerator, and are lying around your room snacking on *biscuits, fromage,* and *citronnade*—your new knowledge of the metric system helped you when ordering the right amount of cheese.

But now you are really hungry, and it is time to head out and find a place for dinner. The French are fanatical about food, and their haute cuisine is considered the finest and most sophisticated in the world. Indeed, when Americans started taking food more seriously, they turned to France for guidance and inspiration (remember, Boston's own Julia Child built her reputation around teaching French cooking). With all the French cooking terms that have crept into our culture, there are plenty of places at home to practice gastromic French—from menus to cookbooks and magazines. By the end of this chapter, you will be a pro at ordering from a French menu, even if you have certain dietary needs or restrictions. And if, perchance, you are dissatisfied with your meal, you will be able to send it back and get what you want.

Where Should We Go?

Wherever you decide to eat, France offers a wide variety of eating establishments to suit your hunger and your pocketbook. Are you going out for breakfast (*le petit déjeuner,* luh puh-tee day-zhuh-nay), lunch (*le déjeuner,* luh day-zhuh-nay), dinner (*le dîner,* luh dee-nay), or an early afternoon snack (*le goûter,* luh goo-tay)? If you're not in the mood for a formal restaurant, why not try:

➤ une auberge (*ewn o-behrzh*), an inn

➤ un bistro (*uhN bees-tro*), a small informal neighborhood pub or tavern

➤ une brasserie (*ew brahs-ree*), a large café serving quick meals

➤ une cabaret (*ewn kah-bah-reh*), a nightclub

➤ un café (*uhN kah-fay*), a small neighborhood restaurant where residents socialize

➤ un cafétéria (*uhN kah-fay-tay-ryah*), a self-service restaurant

➤ une casse-croûte (*ewn kahs-kroot*), a restaurant serving sandwiches

➤ une crêperie (*ewn krehp-ree*), a stand or restaurant serving *crêpes* (filled pancakes)

➤ un fast-food (*uhN fahst-food*), a fast food chain restaurant

➤ un self (*uhN sehlf*), a self-service restaurant

Which Restaurant?

You've opened up a tourist magazine where you've found ads for restaurants. Now you have to decide what you feel in the mood for this evening. Explore the ads and determine what you would expect to get in each of these restaurants:

Cultural Tidbits

What's the typical French breakfast, lunch, or dinner? For breakfast *un croissant* (uhN krwah-sahN), *une brioche* (ewn bree-ohsh), or *une tartine* (ewn tahr-teen, a piece of bread with butter or jam) is served with a bowl of hot chocolate (*un bol de chocolat,* uhN bohl duh shoh-koh-lah) or coffee. Eggs are eaten at dinnertime, as omelettes.

Lunch, in many parts of the country, still remains the main meal of the day and is served in many courses—appetizer, soup, entrée (main course), salad, cheese, dessert. Note that the French eat their salad after the main course. In some areas, business establishments still close for two hours at lunchtime to allow for a long, leisurely meal (for those not eating *sur le pouce,* on the run). This custom, however, is dying, especially with the infiltration of *le fast-food.* Two popular French lunches are *un croque-monsieur* (uhN krohk muh-syuh), a toasted ham and cheese sandwich, and *un croque-madame* (uhN krohk mah-dahm), the same sandwich with an egg on top. You can pick them up at a restaurant or on the run, along with *une crêpe* (ewn krehp), a pancake filled with cheese, seafood, meat, or a dessert, or *une mini-quiche* (ewn mee-nee keesh), an egg and cheese pie filled with vegetables, bacon, or ham.

Dinner is a lighter meal and is generally served after 7 p.m.

NOTRE SELECTIONS DE RESTAURANTS

Noms	*Spécialités*	*N°P*
LE SAINT-NICOLAS	CUISINE FINE TRADITONNELLE	4
LES QUATRES SAISONS (Abela Hôtel Monaco)	CUISINE FRANÇAISE SPECIALITES LIBANAISES	5
LE SAINT-BENOIT	CUISINE DE LA MER	6
TIP TOP BAR	SPECIALITES ITALIENNES	7
FLASHMAN'S	RESTAURATION ANGLAISE	13
STARS'N'BARS	CUISINE AMERICAINE MUSIQUE TOUS LES SOIRS	13
LE METROPOLE PALACE	CUISINE FRANÇAISE	15
LES AMBASSADEURS (Hôtel Métropole)	SPECIALITES LIBANAISES ET FRANÇAISE	15
LA PORTE D'OR	SPECIALITES VIETNAMIENNES ET CHINOISES	16
LE CHINA TOWN	SPECIALITES VIETNAMIENNES ET CHINOISES	16
CAFE MOZART	BUFFET CHAUD & FROID, GLACES, PATISSERIES	82
RESTAURANT DU PORT	POISSONS, SPECIALITES ITALIENNES	24
LA CANTINELLA	SPECIALITES ITALIENNES	Plan
SASS' CAFE	PIANO BAR	Plan
LE PARADISE	RESTAURANT GLACIER	56
L'ESCALE	SPECIALITES DE POISSONS	55
HARRY'S BAR	MENU HOMMES D'AFFAIRES	12

If you've chosen to dine in a restaurant, it might be necessary to reserve a table. When you call, make sure to include all the pertinent information:

Je voudrais réserver une table...
zhuh voo-dreh ray-sehr-vay ewn tahbl
I would like to reserve a table...

pour ce soir	pour demain soir	pour samedi soir
poor suh swahr	*poor duh-maN swahr*	*poor sahm-dee swahr*
for this evening	for tomorrow evening	for Saturday night

pour deux personnes
poor duh pehr-sohn
for two people

à huit heures et demie
ah wee tuhr ay duh-mee
at 8:30 p.m.

sur (à) la terrasse, s'il vous plaît.
sewr (ah) lah teh-rahs seel voo pleh
on the terrace, please (outdoors).

We're Eating Out

Practice what you've learned above by reserving a table for Friday evening, at 9:00 p.m., for six people. Also request a table outdoors.

But let's say that you did not reserve a table and show up at a restaurant unannounced. The maitre d' will most certainly ask:

Une table pour combien de personnes?
ewn tahbl poor kohN-byaN duh pehr-sohn?
A table for how many?

Your response should contain all the necessary information:

Une table pour quatre personnes, s'il vous plaît.
ewn tahbl poor kahtr pehr-sohn seel voo pleh
A table for four, please.

Let's say that you've now been seated, and you look around and are delighted with the fine china, the crystal, the linen napkins, and the crisp white table cloth. But wait! Madam's place has not been properly set. Table 17.1 gives you the vocabulary you need when asking the waiter for cutlery, as well as other terms that will come in handy.

Table 17.1 A Table Setting

bowl	le bol	*luh bohl*
carafe	le carafe	*luh kah-rahf*
cup	la tasse	*lah tahss*
dinner plate	l'assiette (f.)	*lah-syeht*
fork	la fourchette	*lah foor-sheht*
glass	le verre	*luh vehr*
knife	le couteau	*luh koo-to*
menu	le menu, la carte	*luh muh-new, lah kahrt*
napkin	la serviette	*lah sehr-vyeht*
pepper shaker	la poivrière	*lah pwah-vree-yehr*
place setting	le couvert	*luh koo-vehr*
salt shaker	la salière	*lah sahl-yehr*
saucer	la soucoupe	*lah soo-koop*
soup dish	l'assiette à soupe(f.)	*lah-syeht ah soop*
tablecloth	la nappe	*lah nahp*
teaspoon	la cuiller	*lah kwee-yehr*
waiter	le garçon	*luh gahr-sohN*
waitress	la serveuse	*lah sehr-vuhz*
wine glass	le verre à vin	*luh vehr ah vaN*

Cultural Tidbits

In France, most restaurants offer a *prix fixe* (price fixed) menu or *menu touristique,* which consists of an appetizer, soup, main course, salad, dessert, and drink for a pre-determined price. While your choice of dishes may be restricted, this still offers an excellent value for the money. Ordering *à la carte* is, without exception, a more expensive option.

If you find that something is missing from your table, or if you need to make a request of the staff, the following phrases will help you get want you want.

➤ Use an indirect object pronoun:

Il me faut...	*eel muh foh*	I need
Il lui faut...	*eel lui foh*	He/She needs
Il nous faut...	*eel noo foh*	We need
Il leur faut...	*eel leur foh*	They need

➤ Use the expression *avoir besoin de*—to need:

J'ai besoin de...	*zhay buh-zwaN duh*	I need
Il a besoin de...	*eel ah buh-zwaN duh*	He needs
Elle a besoin de...	*ehl ah buh-zwaN duh*	She needs
Nous avons besoin de...	*noo zah-vohN buh-zwaN duh*	We need
Ils ont besoin de...	*eel zohN buh-zwaN duh*	They need
Elles ont besoin de...	*ehl zohN buh-zwaN duh*	They need

Now, use what you've learned to tell your server that you need: a salt shaker, a napkin, a fork, a knife, a plate, or a spoon.

Garçon, What Do You Recommend?

The waiter has come to give you a menu and see if you'd like a drink before dinner. You may use the following expressing for ordering both your drinks and your food:

I would like...	I'll have...	Please bring me...
Je voudrais...	Je prendrai...	Apportez-moi, s'il vous plaît
zhuh voo-dreh	*zhuh prahN-dray*	*ah-pohr-tay mwah seel voo pleh*
before-dinner drink	cocktail	Nothing for me.
un apéritif	un cocktail	Rien pour moi.
uhN nah-pay-ree-teef	*uhN kohk-tehl*	*ryaN poor mwah*

Cultural Tidbits

It is customary for the French to enjoy *un apéritif* before dinner. Although these drinks are touted as being an appetite stimulant, a real Frenchman will tell you that having an apéritif is just an excuse for enjoying a before dinner drink. Among the more popular varieties are: Vermouth (a wine made from red or white grapes—Martini and Cinzano are the all-time favorites), Pernod and Ricard (licorice-flavored drinks made from anise), Cynar (made from artichoke hearts), and Dubonnet et Byrrh (wine and brandy flavored with herbs and bitters).

This Menu Is Greek to Me

A French menu can be confusing and overwhelming unless you know certain culinary terms. And if you are a novice to the French language, you might feel that it is too embarrassing or pointless to ask about a dish because you know that you probably won't understand the waiter's explanation! Table 17.2 gives you the terms you need to interpret sauce names and other items on a French menu.

Table 17.2 What's on the Menu?

Dishes Served		Contain
aïoli	*ah-yoh-lee*	mayonnaise flavored with garlic
à la bonne femme	*ah lah bohn fahm*	a white wine sauce with vegetables
béarnaise	*bay-ahr-nehz*	a butter-egg sauce flavored with wine, shallots, and tarragon
bercy	*behr-see*	a meat or fish sauce
blanquette	*blahN-keht*	a creamy egg and white wine sauce usually served with stew
crécy	*kray-see*	carrots
daube	*dohb*	a stew, usually beef, with red wine, onions, and garlic
farci(e)	*fahr-see*	a stuffing
florentine	*floh-rahN-teen*	spinach
forestière	*foh-rehs-tyehr*	wild mushrooms
hollandaise	*oh-lahN-dehz*	an egg yolk, butter sauce with lemon juice or vinegar
jardinière	*zhahr-dee-nyehr*	vegetables
maître d'hôtel	*mehtr do-tehl*	a butter sauce with parsley and lemon juice
mornay	*mohr-nay*	a white sauce with cheese
parmentier	*pahr-mahN-tyay*	potatoes
périgourdine	*pay-ree-goor-deen*	mushrooms (truffles)
provençale	*proh-vahN-sahl*	a vegetable garnish
rémoulade	*ray-moo-lahd*	mayonnaise flavored with mustard
véronique	*vay-rohN-neek*	grapes
vol-au-vent	*vohl-o-vahN*	puff pastry with creamed meat

Now you should feel somewhat confident to order. Tables 17.3 through 17.5 will help you get from the appetizer through the main course. If you have any problems with the names of various types of meat or fish, refer back to Chapter 16.

Table 17.3 Appetizers (les hors-d'oeuvre—lay zohr-duhvr)

crudités variées	*krew-dee-tay vah-ryay*	sliced raw vegetable usually in a vinaigrette sauce
escargots à la bourguignonne	*ehs-kahr-go ah lah boor-gee-nyohn*	snails in garlic sauce
foie gras	*fwah grah*	fresh, sometimes uncooked goose liver, served with toasted French bread
pâté	*pah-tay*	pureed liver or other meat served in a loaf
quiche lorraine	*keesh loh-rehn*	egg custard tart served with meat (bacon or ham)
quenelles	*kuh-nehl*	dumplings
rillettes	*ree-yeht*	pork mixture served as a spread

Table 17.4 Soups (les soupes—lay soop)

la bisque	*lah beesk*	creamy soup made with crayfish
la bouillabaisee	*lah boo-yah-behs*	seafood stew
le consommé	*luh kohN-soh-may*	clear broth
la petite marmite	*lah puh-teet mahr-meet*	rich consommé served with vegetables and meat
le potage	*luh poh-tahzh*	thick soup made of pureed vegetables
la soupe à l'oignon	*lah soop ah loh-nyohN*	onion soup served with bread and cheese
velouté	*vuh-loo-tay*	creamy soup

Table 17.5   Meats (les viandes—lay vyahnd)

le bifteck	*luh beef-tehk*	steak
l'entrecôte (f.)	*lahNtr-koht*	sirloin steak
l'escalope (f.)	*leh-skah-lohp*	scallopine, cutlet
la côte de boeuf	*lah koht duh buhf*	prime rib
la poitrine de...	*lah pwah-treen duh*	breast of...
le carré d'agneau	*luh kah-ray dah-nyo*	rack of lamb
le chateaubriand	*luh shah-to-bree-yahN*	a porterhouse steak
le foie	*luh foie*	liver
le gigot d'agneau	*luh zhee-go dah-nyo*	leg of lamb
le pot-au-feu	*luh poh-to-fuh*	boiled beef
le rosbif	*luh rohs-beef*	roastbeef
le tournedos	*luh toor-nuh-do*	small fillets of beef
les côtes de porc (f.)	*lay koht duh pohr*	pork chops
les côtes de veau (f.)	*lay koht duh vo*	veal chops
les médaillons de...(m)	*lay may-dah-yohN duh*	small rounds of
les saucisses (f.)	*lay so-sees*	sausages
le hamburger	*luh ahm-bewr-gehr*	hamburger

That's the Way I Like It

Even if you know how to order your hamburger or veal chops, you want to be certain that your entree is cooked to your specifications. The waiter might ask:

> Vous le (la, les) voulez comment?
>
> *voo luh (lah, lay) voo-lay koh-mahN*
>
> How do you want it (them)?

Table 17. 6 will help you to express your wants and needs.

As a Rule
Remember to use the appropriate direct object pronoun to refer to the noun you are using.

Vous recommandez le gigot? Vous le recommandez?

Vous prenez l'escalope?

Vous la prenez?

Table 17.6 How Would You Like It Prepared?

Meats and Vegetables

baked	cuit au four	*kwee to foor*	broiled	rôti	*ro-tee*
boiled	bouilli	*boo-yee*	browned	gratiné	*grah-tee-nay*
breaded	au gratin	*o grah-taN*	chopped	hâché	*ah-shay*
fried	frit	*free*	sauteed	sauté	*so-tay*
grilled	grillé	*gree-yay*	steamed	à la vapeur	*ah lah vah-puhr*
in its natural juices	au jus	*o zhew*	stewed	en cocotte	*ahN koh-koht*
mashed	en purée	*ahN pew-ray*	very rare	bleu	*bluh*
poached	poché	*poh-shay*	rare	saignant	*seh-nyahN*
pureed	en purée	*ahN pew-ray*	medium	à point	*ah pwaN*
roasted	rôti	*ro-tee*	well-done	bien cuit	*byaN kwee*
with sauce	en sauce	*ahN sos*			

Eggs	**des oeufs**	**day zuh**
fried	au plat	*o plah*
hard-boiled	durs	*dewr*
medium-boiled	mollets	*moh-leh*
poached	pochés	*poh-shay*
scrambled	brouillés	*broo-yay*
soft-boiled	à la coque	*ah lah kohk*
omelette	une omelette	*ewn nohm-leht*
plain omelette	une omelette nature	*ewn nohm-leht nah-tewr*

Cultural Tidbits

Keep in mind that French chefs have a different interpretation of the terms rare, medium, and well-done. To him (or her), rare means almost alive, medium is a tiny bit more than our rare, and well done is a bit more than our medium. What the chef thinks is burned is what we mean by well-done. He may prepare it well-done, but don't expect a smile when it is served.

Spice It Up

The French use a lot of herbs, spices, seasonings, and condiments to flavor their foods. Knowing the words in Table 17.7 will help you determine the ingredients of your dish or enable you to ask for a seasoning you prefer:

Table 17.7   Herbs, Spices, and Condiments

basil	le basilic	*luh bah-zee-leek*
bay leaf	la feuille de laurier	*lah fuhy duh loh-ryay*
butter	le beurre	*luh buhr*
capers	les câpres (m.)	*lay kahpr*
chives	la ciboulette	*lah see-boo-leht*
dill	l'aneth (m.)	*lah-neht*
garlic	l'ail (m.)	*lahy*
ginger	le gingembre	*luh zhaN-zhahNbr*
honey	le miel	*luh myehl*
horseradish	le raifort	*luh reh-fohr*
jam, jelly	la confiture	*lah kohN-fee-tewr*
ketchup	le ketchup	*luh keht-chuhp*
lemon	le citron	*luh see-trohN*
maple syrup	le sirop d'érable	*luh see-roh day-rahbl*
mayonnaise	la mayonnaise	*lah mah-yoh-nehz*
mint	la menthe	*lah mahNt*
mustard	la moutarde	*lah moo-tahrd*
oil	l'huile (f.)	*lweel*
oregano	l'origan (m.)	*loh-ree-gahN*
parsley	le persil	*luh pehr-seel*
pepper	le poivre	*luh pwahvr*
salt	le sel	*luh sehl*
sugar	le sucre	*luh sewkr*
tarragon	l'estragon (m.)	*lehs-trah-gohN*
vinegar	le vinaigre	*luh vee-nehgr*

Cultural Tidbits

It is unnecessary to specify that you do not want m.s.g. in your food, since this flavor enhancer is not used in France. The acronym m.s.g. is completely foreign to the average French person and to those who prepare other types of cuisine in French-speaking countries.

Special Diets

If you have certain likes and dislikes, or dietary restrictions that you would like to make known, keep the following phrases handy:

I am on a diet.	Je suis au régime.	*zhuh swee zo ray-zheem*
I'm a vegetarian.	Je suis végétarien(ne.)	*zhuh swee vay-zhay-tah-ryaN (ryen)*
I can't eat anything made with...	Je ne peux rien manger de cuisiné au (à la)...	*zhuh nuh puh ryaN mahN-zhay duh kwee-zee-nay o (ah lah)...*
I can't have...	Je ne tolère...	*zhuh nuh toh-lehr*
any dairy products	aucun produit laitier	*o-kuhN proh-dwee leh-tyay*
any alcohol	aucun produit alcoolique	*o-kuhN proh-dwee ahl-koh-leek*
any saturated fats	aucune matière grasse animale	*o-kewn mah-tyehr grahs ah-nee-mahl*
any shellfish	aucun fruit de mer	*o-kuhN frweed mehr*
I'm looking for a dish...	Je cherche un plat...	*zhuh shehrsh uhN plah*
high in fiber	riche en fibre	*reesh ahN feebr*
low in cholesterol	léger en cholestérol	*lay-zhay ahN koh-lehs-tay-rohl*
low in fat	léger en matières grasses	*lay-zhay ahN mah-tyehr grahs*
low in sodium	léger en sodium	*lay-zhay ahN sohd-yuhm*
non-dairy	non-laitier	*nohN-leh-tyay*
salt-free	sans sel	*sahN sehl*
sugar-free	sans sucre	*sahN sewkr*
without artificial coloring	sans colorant	*sahN koh-loh-rahN*
without preservatives	sans conservateurs	*sahN kohN-sehr-vah-tuhr*

Send It Back Please

Certainly there are times, even in France, when the cooking or table setting is just not up to your standards. Table 17.8 presents some problems you might run into.

Table 17.8   Possible Problems

...is cold	...est froid(e)	*eh frwahd*
...is too rare	...n'est pas assez cuit(e)	*neh pah zah-say kwee(t)*
...is over-cooked	...est trop cuit(e)	*tro kwee(t)*
...is tough	...est dur(e)	*eh dewr*
...is burned	...est brûlé(e)	*eh brew-lay*
...is too salty	...est trop salé(e)	*eh tro sah-lay*
...is too sweet	...est trop sucré(e)	*eh tro sew-kray*
...is too spicy	...est trop épicé(e)	*eh tro ay-pee-say*
...is spoiled	...est tourné(e)	*eh toor-nay*
...is bitter	...est aigre	*eh tehgr*
...tastes like...	...a le goût de...	*ah luh goo duh*
...is dirty	...est sale	*eh sahl*

Fancy Endings

In France, it is traditional to have *une salade* (ewn sah-lahd) followed by *des fromages variés* (day froh-mahzh vah-ryay—cheeses). Popular cheeses include: boursin, brie, camembert, chèvre, munster, port-salut, and roquefort. When choosing a cheese you might want to ask:

Is it...	Est-il...	eh-teel
mild	maigre	*mehgr*
sharp	piquant	*pee-kahN*
hard	fermenté	*fehr-mahN-tay*
soft	à pâte molle	*ah paht mohl*

Finally, it's time for dessert, and there are so many French specialties from which to choose. Table 17.9 will help you make a decision.

Table 17.9 Divine Desserts

une bavaroise	*ewn bah-vahr-wahz*	bavarian cream
des beignets	*day beh-nyeh*	fruit doughnuts
une bombe	*ewn bohNb*	ice cream with many flavors
une charlotte	*ewn shahr-loht*	sponge cake and pudding
une crème caramel	*ewn krehm kah-rah-mehl*	egg custard served with caramel sauce
une gaufre	*ewn gohfr*	waffle
des oeufs à la neige	*day zuh ah lah nehzh*	meringues in a custard sauce
une omelette norvégienne	*ewn nohm-leht nohr-vay-zhyehn*	baked Alaska
des poires hélène	*day pwahr ay-lehn*	poached pears with vanilla ice cream and chocolate sauce
des profiteroles	*day proh-fee-trohl*	cream puffs with chocolate sauce

If you are ordering ice cream, the following terms will help you get the type and flavor (*le parfum*—luh pahr-fuhN) you prefer:

an ice cream	une glace	*ewn glahs*
a yogurt	un yaourt	*uhN yah-oort*
cone	un cornet	*uhN kohr-neh*
cup	une coupe	*ewn koop*
chocolate	au chocolat	*o shoh-koh-lah*
vanilla	à la vanille	*ah lah vah-nee-y*
strawberry	aux fraises	*o frehz*

Drink to Me Only

The French usually drink wine with dinner. The wines you might order include the following:

red wine	le vin rouge	*luh vaN roozh*
rosé wine	le vin rosé	*luh vaN ro-zay*

white wine	le vin blanc	*luh vaN blahN*
sparkling wine	le vin mousseux	*luh vaN moo-suh*
champagne	le champagne	*luh shahN-pah-nyuh*

Cultural Tidbits

Some popular French after-dinner drinks include: Cognac (brandy), Armagnac (unblended brandy), Bénédictine (a blend of 150 plants and herbs), Chambord (raspberry-flavored liqueur), Cointreau (cognac blended with sweet and bitter orange peels), and Grand Marnier (orange-flavored liqueur). Generally, French men prefer brandies (which are made by distilling wine or fermented fruit mash that has been aged in wooden casks), while French women opt for the sweeter tasting liqueurs (which are made by combining a spirit, such as brandy, with sugar and fruit or mint and other plant extracts).

The French do not load their drinks with ice cubes (*des glaçons*—day glah-sohN) the way many Americans do. In fact, "on the rocks" is not even an option in some places. You might even pay extra for ice since it's a rare commodity.

Perhaps you do not indulge in alcohol or prefer something else to drink with your meal. During the course of a meal, you might even wish to have several different drinks: juice, water, soda, coffee, or tea. Other beverages you might enjoy during or after dinner are presented in Table 17.10.

Table 17.10 Beverages

coffee	un café	*uhN kah-fay*
with milk (morning)	au lait	*o leh*
espresso	-express	*ehks-prehs*
with cream	-crème	*krehm*
black	noir	*nwahr*
iced	glacé	*glah-say*
decaffeinated	décaféiné	*day-kah-fay-ee-nay*
tea	un thé	*uhN tay*
with lemon	au citron	*o see-trohN*

continues

Table 17.10   Continued

with sugar	sucré	*sew-kray*
herbal	aux fines herbes	*o feen zehrb*
mineral water	de l'eau minérale	*duh lo mee-nay-rahl*
carbonated	gazeuse	*gah-zuhz*
non-carbonated	plate	*plaht*

I'm Thirsty

You've spent a long and tiring day sightseeing and you feel that it's time to stop and pause for a moment. You'd like to rest your weary feet and you need a quick pick-me up. You see a French café and realize that it's the perfect place to stop, grab a nice cool drink, and people-watch. If you're thirsty, learning the irregular verb *boire* (to drink) in Table 17.11 will help you order what you like. *Boire* is similar to a "shoe verb" in that the nous and vous forms change. They do not, however, look like the infinitive. The forms for the other subject pronouns do.

Table 17.11   The Verb boire (to drink)

je bois	*zhuh bwah*	I drink
tu bois	*tew bwah*	you drink
il, elle, on boit	*eel (ehl, ohN) bwah*	he, she, one drinks
nous buvons	*noo bew-vohN*	we drink
vous buvez	*voo bew-vay*	you drink
ils, elles boivent	*eel (ehl) bwahv*	they drink

Cultural Tidbits

The cost of a drink or meal in a French café depends upon where it is consumed. The same soft drink is cheapest if purchased at the indoor counter (because you have to stand), more expensive at an indoor table (because the scenery isn't terribly exciting), and most expensive at a table on the outside terrace (where you can take in everything that is going on). Don't be surprised to pay $3 for a 6 oz. bottle of coke!

You Only Want Some, Not All?

The food is delicious, even better than you expected. *Pâtisseries* beckon on every corner. Temptations lurk everywhere. You do not, however, want to return from vacation 20 pounds heavier. Don't eat it all, share some with a companion.

The partitive is used in French to express part of a whole, or an indefinite quantity and is equivalent to the English *some* or *any*.

Partitive	Used Before
du (de + le)	masculine singular nouns beginning with a consonant
de la	feminine singular nouns beginning with a consonant
de l'	any singular noun beginning with a vowel
des (de + les)	all plural nouns

Although *some* or *any* may be omitted in English, the partitive must always be used in French and must be repeated before each noun:

> Apportez-moi *de la* mousse et *du* café, s'il vous plaît.
>
> *ah-pohr-tay-mwah duh lah moos ay dew kah-fay seel voo pleh*
>
> Bring me some moussse and some coffee, please.

> Avez-vous *de l'*orangeade?
>
> *ah-vay-voo duh loh-rahN-zhahd*
>
> Do you have any orangeade?

> Je préfère manger *des* fruits de mer.
>
> *zhuh pray-fehr mahN-zhay day frweed mehr*
>
> I prefer eating seafood.

As a Rule

The partitives *(du, de la, de l', des)* express some or part of a whole. The definite articles *(le, la, l', les)* are used in a general sense to express the entire class of things:

J'aime le chocolat. (I like chocolate [in general].)

Donne-moi du chocolat, s'il te plaît. (Give me *some* chocolate.)

Use the partitive when you want to express the concept *some* or *any*.

In a negative sentence, or before an adjective preceding a plural noun, the partitive is expressed by *de* (no definite article is used).

As a Rule
Remember to use *un* or *une* when speaking about one portion or serving.

De (d') is used after nouns of quantity:

un bol de chocolat	a bowl of hot chocolate
un verre de lait	a glass of milk
une tasse de café	a cup of coffee
une bouteille d'eau	a bottle of water

Nous n'avons pas *de* ragoût.

noo nah-vohN pah duh rah-goo

We don't have (any) stew.

Je ne mange pas *de* fruits.

zhuh nuh mahNzh pah duh frwee

I don't eat fruit.

Elle prépare de bons gâteaux.

ehl pray-pahr duh bohN gah-to

She prepares good cakes.

Room Service

Did you ever just feel like lounging around your hotel room and being lazy, perhaps after several days of intensive work or sightseeing? Why not spend a leisurely morning in your room and order in room service? See how well you do by selecting the breakfast of your choice.

N° de Chambre ☐	Nombre de personnes ☐
Heure de service désirée entre 7 h et 11 h	☐

PETIT-DÉJEUNER CONTINENTAL

Corbeille de notre boulanger :
Petit pain, croissant, pain au chocolat, beurre et confiture

☐ Café au lait	☐ Café noir	☐ Chocolat
☐ Thé au lait	☐ Thé nature	☐ Thé citron
☐ Lait chaud	☐ Lait froid	☐ Verveine Tilleul

SUPPLEMENTS

☐ Œuf coque	15 F	☐ Œufs brouillés	20 F
☐ Œufs au plat	20 F	☐ Œufs au plat jambon	25 F
☐ Omelette	20 F	☐ Omelette au jambon	25 F
☐ Jus d'Orange Pamplemousse	15 F	☐ Perrier, Evian, Vittel	10 F

Taxes et service compris

The Pronoun en

Imagine that you've spent the whole day out on the town with a friend and now you'd like to go eat. You reach into your pocket and lo and behold you find that you've exhausted your cash supply. You turn to your companion and ask the logical question: Do you have any money? He wants to answer you in French and say: "Yes, I do." He can't use the verb *faire* (to do) because faire can't stand alone. If he said: "Je fais de l'argent." that would mean that he is making money, not something he'd want to admit to doing.

The way around this predicament is to use the pronoun en, a handy word, that, when used properly, will prove to be extremely helpful.

The pronoun *en* refers to previously mentioned things or places. *En* usually replaces *de* + noun and may mean some or any (of it/them), of it/them, about it/them, from it/them, or from there:

Il veut *des biscuits*.	Je ne veux pas *de salade*.
Il *en* veut.	Je n'*en* veux pas.
eel ahN vuh	*zhuh nahN vuh pah*
He wants some (of them).	I don't want any (of it).
Nous parlons *du restaurant*.	Elles sortent *du café*.
Nous *en* parlons.	Elles *en* sortent.
noo zahN pahr-lohN	*ehl zahN sohrt*
We speak about it.	They leave (it) from there.

En is always expressed in French even though it may have no English equivalent or is not expressed in English:

As-tu *de l'argent*?	Do you have any money?
Oui, j'*en* ai.	Yes, I do.

En is used with idiomatic expressions requiring *de*:

J'ai besoin *d'un couteau*.	I need a knife.
J'*en* ai besoin.	I need one.

En is used to replace a noun (de + noun) after a number or a noun or adverb of quantity:

Il prépare dix *sandwiches*.	He is preparing ten sandwiches.
Il *en* prépare dix.	He is preparing ten (of them).
Il prépare une tasse *de thé*.	He is preparing a cup of tea.
Il *en* prépare une tasse.	He is preparing a cup of it.
Il prépare beaucoup *de tartes*.	He is preparing a lot of pies.
Il *en* prépare beaucoup.	He is preparing a lot (of them).

En is placed before the verb to which its meaning is tied, usually before the conjugated verb. When there are two verbs, *en* is placed before the infinitive:

J'*en* prends.	I take (eat) some.
Je n'*en* prends pas.	I don't take (eat) any.
Je désire *en* prendre.	I want to take (eat) some.
N'*en* prends pas.	Don't take (eat) any.

In an affirmative command *en* changes position and is placed immediately after the verb and is joined to it by a hyphen. The familiar command forms of *er* verbs (regular and irregular) retain their final *s* before *en*. This is to prevent the clash of two vowel sounds together. Remember to put a liaison (linking) between the final consonant and *en*.

Prends-*en*! (*prahN zahN*)   Take (eat) some! (Familiar)

Prenez-*en*! (*pruh-nay zahN*)   Take (eat) some! (Polite)

Using en

We all have our own peculiar eating habits, sometimes choosing things to eat that make others stare at us in disbelief. Here are some questions about your culinary preferences. Answer them by using the pronoun *en*. Then try changing all your affirmative answers to the negative and vice versa.

1. Vous mangez des légumes?

2. Vous prenez du café?

3. Vous parlez des restaurants français?

4. Vous désirez manger un dessert délicieux?

5. Vous aimez préparer de la mousse au chocolat?

6. Vous allez essayer des plats français?

Should I or Shouldn't I?

You've returned from a fabulous trip only to discover that you can't buckle your belt and you ripped your jeans as you bent over. You want to lose weight but temptations abound everywhere. What does your conscience dictate?

Je mange du chocolat? des fruits?

Du chocolat? N'en mange pas. Des fruits? Manges-en.

1. Je mange des bonbons? des légumes?

2. Je prépare de la salade? de la mousse?

3. Je prends du poisson? des saucisses?

4. Je choisis de la glace? du yaourt?

5. J'achète de l'eau minérale? du soda?

It Was Delicious

I'm interested in your opinion. What did you think of your meal? Was it just average or did you give it rave reviews? If you thought it was truly exceptional, you might want to exclaim your pleasure by using the adjective *quel* in Table 17.12 to express *what a!*

Table 17.12 Quel and Quelle

	Masculine	Feminine
Singular	quel	quelle
Plural	quels	quelles

Make sure to put the adjective in its proper position:

Quel repas formidable!   Quels desserts délicieux!

kehl ruh-pah fohr-mee-dahbl   *kehl deh-sehr day-lee-syuh*

What a great meal!   What delicious desserts!

Quelle mousse excellente!   Quelles bonnes omelettes!

kehl moos ehk-seh-lahNt   *kehl bohn zohm-leht*

What an excellent mousse!   What good omelettes!

How Was It?

I knew you'd love French food. Now you want to tell me just how much you enjoyed it. Use the correct form of *quel* to express how you felt about what you ate and drank: soups, steak, wine, salad, cheeses, mousse.

Don't forget to ask for the check at the end of your meal:

L'addition, s'il vous plaît.

lah-dee-syohN seel voo pleh

The check please.

Cultural Tidbits

In many restaurants *le service est compris*—the service is included (usually 15 percent). You might want to leave a little more if your server was excellent. The word for *tip* is *un pourboire* (uhN poor-bwahr).

The Least You Need to Know

➤ You can read a French menu if you know the right terms.

➤ Use the partitive *(de, du, de la, de l', des)* to express *some*.

➤ The pronoun *en* expresses *some* and may replace the partitive.

Chapter 18

Let's Have Fun

In This Chapter

➤ Ways to have fun

➤ All about *vouloir* (to want) and *pouvoir* (to be able to)

➤ Extending invitations

➤ Using adverbs to describe abilities

You've seen the sights, collected mementos, and purchased souvenirs and designer clothing. You feel much better, too, now that you have eaten. It's time to have fun and enjoy yourself, or simply to take a pause and relax.

Are you off to the sea to engage in water sports, up to the mountains for skiing or hiking, onto the links for a round of golf, or onto the courts for a brisk tennis match? Are you a film buff or a theater-goer? Do you enjoy a lively opera or an elegant ballet? Perhaps the game's the thing and you'll spend some time with a one-armed bandit in a luxurious casino. This chapter will help you do it all, invite someone to accompany you, and describe your abilities.

Are You a Sports Fan?

As a Rule
Use the verb *faire* when talking about engaging in a sport.

Je fais du volleyball. (I play volleyball.)

On fait de la natation? (How about going swimming?)

My husband loves to golf and his clubs have seen nearly as many countries as we have! I adore the beach and like nothing better than to feel the sand between my toes as I gaze out at the ocean. Whether you're a beach lover or a sports fanatic, you'll need some specific phrases and terms to make your preferences known. Table 18.1 provides a list of sports and outdoor activities.

Table 18.1 Sports

One Plays	On fait	OhN feh
aerobics	de l'aérobic (m.)	*duh lahy-roh-beek*
baseball	du base-ball	*dew bays-bohl*
basketball	du basket-ball	*dew bahs-keht bohl*
bicycling	du vélo	*dew vay-lo*
boating	du canotage	*dew kah-noh-tahzh*
canoeing	du canoë	*dew kah-noh-ay*
cycling	du cyclisme	*dew see-kleez-muh*
deep-sea fishing	de la pêche sous-marine	*duh la pehsh soo-mah-reen*
diving	du plongeon	*dew plohN-zhohN*
fishing	de la pêche	*duh lah pehsh*
football	du football américain	*dew foot-bohl ah-may-ree-kaN*
golf	du golf	*dew gohlf*
hockey	du hockey	*dew oh-kee*
horseback riding	de l'équitation (f.)	*duh lay-kee-tah-syohN*
hunting	de la chasse	*duh lah shahs*
jai alai	de la pelote (basque)	*duh lah puh-loht (bahsk)*
jogging	du jogging	*dew zhoh-geeng*
mountain climbing	de l'alpinisme (m.), de l'escalade (f.)	*duh lahl-pee-neez-muh, duh lehs-kah-lahd*

One Plays	On fait	OhN feh
parasailing	du parachutisme	*dew pah-rah-shew-teez-muh*
ping-pong	du ping-pong	*dew peeng-pohNg*
sailing	du bateau à voiles	*dew bah-to ah vwahl*
scuba (skin) diving	de la plongée sous-marine	*duh lah plohN-zhay soo-mah-reen*
skating	du patin	*dew pah-taN*
ski	du ski	*dew skee*
soccer	du football	*dew foot-bohl*
surfing	du surf	*dew sewrf*
swimming	de la natation	*duh lah nah-tah-syohN*
tennis	du tennis	*dew teh-nees*
volleyball	du volley-ball	*dew voh-lee bohl*
waterskiing	du ski nautique	*dew skee no-teek*

Cultural Tidbits

Cycling is one of the most popular sports in France. In June and July the longest bicycle race (la course, *lah koors*) in the world, the Tour de France (also known by Frenchmen as La Grande Boucle, *lah grahNd bookl*), captures the attention of sports fans all over France and the world. This spectacular event covers approximately 2,500 kilometers (over 1,500 miles) in 22 laps (étapes, *ay tahp*) over different terrains—mountains as well as flatlands. The competition begins in a different city each year but always finishes in Paris. It is considered a great honor to be chosen as *une ville étape*, a city where a lap ends. Work and school end early so that everyone can go out and watch the arrival of the racers and scramble to receive a free cap (une casquette, *ewn kahs-keht*) distributed by the sponsors of the event. Approximately 100–150 cyclists come from France and other countries to compete for the coveted *maillot jaune* (yellow T-shirt) and the various cash prizes awarded to the winner, the cyclist with the best cumulative time. The race is actually a team effort where helpers, known as *lièvres* (*lee-ehvr*), take turns helping their best member pace and push himself to victory.

229

Would You Like to Join Me?

It really isn't much fun to play alone. Why not ask someone to join you? To extend an invitation you may use the irregular verbs *vouloir* (to want) and *pouvoir* (to be able to) in Tables 18.2 and 18.3. Both verbs have similar conjugations. They are similar to "shoe verbs" in that their nous and vous forms begin like the infinitive, while their other forms undergo a change.

Table 18.2 The Verb vouloir (to want)

je veux	*zhuh vuh*	I want
tu veux	*tew vuh*	you want
il, elle, on veut	*eel, (ehl, ohN) vuh*	he (she, one) wants
nous voulons	*noo voo-lohN*	we want
vous voulez	*voo voo-lay*	you want
ils, elles veulent	*eel (ehl) vuhl*	they want

Table 18.3 The Verb pouvoir (to be able to [can])

je peux	*zhuh puh*	I am able to (can)
tu peux	*tew puh*	you are able to (can)
il, elle, on peut	*eel, ehl, ohN puh*	he, she, one is able to (can)
nous pouvons	*noo poo-vohN*	we can
vous pouvez	*voo poo-vay*	you can
ils, elles peuvent	*eel, (ehl) puhv*	they can

To invite someone to do something you would ask:

> Vous voulez (Tu veux) + infinitive of the verb (Do you want to...?)

> Vous voulez (Tu veux) faire du ski? Do you want to go skiing?

or

> Vous pouvez (Tu peux) + infinitive of the verb (Can you...?)

> Vous pouvez (Tu peux) aller à la pêche? Can you go fishing?

Each sport has its own particular playing field or milieu. When you're ready for some exercise refer to Table 18.4 to choose the place where you would go to participate in the sport or activity:

Table 18.4 Where to Go

beach	la plage	*lah plahzh*
course (golf)	le parcours	*luh pahr-koor*
court	le court	*luh koort*
court (jai alai)	le fronton	*luh frohN-tohN*
field	le terrain	*luh teh-raN*
gymnasium	le gymnase	*luh zheem-nahz*
mountain	la montagne	*lah mohN-tah-nyuh*
ocean	l'océan (m.)	*loh-see-ahN*
park	le parc	*luh pahrk*
path	le sentier	*luh sahN-tyay*
pool	la piscine	*lah pee-seen*
rink	la patinoire	*lah pah-tee-nwahr*
sea	la mer	*lah mehr*
slope	la piste	*lah peest*
stadium	le stade	*luh stahd*
track	la piste	*lah peest*

Extend an Invitation

Tomorrow's forecast is perfect for the sports-minded. Pick up the phone and invite someone to go with you to the proper place so that you can go: hiking, skiing, jogging, skating, mountain-climbing, or diving.

Accepting an Invitation

Whether you've been invited to participate in a sport or an outing, visit a museum, or just stay at someone's home these phrases will allow you to graciously accept any invitation extended to you:

Avec plaisir.	*ah-vehk pleh-zeer*	With pleasure.
Bien entendu.	*byaN nahN-tahN-dew*	Of course.
Bien sûr.	*byaN sewr*	Of course.
C'est une bonne idée.	*seh tewn bohn ee-day*	That's a good idea.
Chouette!	*shoo-eht*	Great!
D'accord.	*dah-kohr*	O.K. (I agree)

Et comment!	*ay koh-mahN*	And how! You bet!
Il n'y a pas d'erreur.	*eel nyah pah deh-ruhr*	There's no doubt about it.
Pourquoi pas?	*poor-kwah pah*	Why not?
Si tu veux (vous voulez)	*see tew vuh (voo voo-lay)*	If you want to.
Volontiers!	*voh-lohN-tyay*	Gladly.

Refusing an Invitation—Making Excuses

What if you really can't go to an event because of some prior engagement or commitment? Or, perhaps you just feel like being alone. You can cordially refuse any invitation without hurting anyone's feelings by expressing your regrets or giving an excuse. You might say:

C'est impossible.	*seh taN-poh-seebl*	It's impossible.
Encore!	*ahN-kohr*	Not again!
Je n'ai pas envie.	*zhuh nay pah zahN-vee*	I don't feel like it.
Je ne peux pas.	*zhuh nuh puh pah*	I can't.
Je ne suis pas libre.	*zhuh nuh swee pah leebr*	I'm not free.
Je ne veux pas.	*zhuh nuh vuh pah*	I don't want to.
Je regrette.	*zhuh ruh-greht*	I'm sorry.
Je suis désolé(e).	*zhuh swee day-zoh-lay*	I'm sorry.
Je suis fatigué(e).	*zhuh swee fah-tee-gay*	I'm tired.
Je suis occupé(e).	*zhuh swee zoh-kew-pay*	I'm busy.

Showing Indecision and Indifference

We all have our days when we're very wishy-washy. One minute we're gung-ho about an idea, and the next moment we wouldn't even contemplate the same notion. If you can't make up your mind, or if you are indifferent to an idea, you might use one of these phrases:

Ça dépend.	*sah day-pahN*	It depends.
Ça m'est égal.	*sah meh tay-gahl*	It's all the same to me.
Ce que tu préfères (vous préférez).	*suh kuh tew pray-fehr (voo pray-fay-ray)*	Whatever you want.

Comme tu veux (vous voulez).	*kohm tew vuh (voo voo-lay)*	Whatever you want.
Je n'ai pas de préférence.	*zhuh nay pas duh pray-fay-rahNs*	I don't have any preference.
Je ne sais pas trop.	*zhuh nuh seh pah tro*	I really don't know.
Peut-être.	*puh-tehtr*	Perhaps. Maybe.

Let's Do Something Else

Perhaps sports aren't part of your agenda. There are plenty of other activities you can pursue to have a good time. The phrases in Table 18.5 will give you the tools to make many other intriguing suggestions. Should you delight in going to the opera, ballet, theater, or a concert, don't forget to bring along *les jumelles* (lay zhew-mehl)(f.)—binoculars.

Table 18.5 Places to Go and Things to Do

Le Lieu (*luh lyuh*), the place	L'Activité (*lahk-tee-vee-tay*), the activity
aller à l'opéra (*oh-pay rah*)	écouter les chanteurs/listen to the singers
aller à la plage (*plahzh*)	nager/swim, prendre un bain de soleil/sunbathe
aller à une discothèque (*dees-koh-tehk*)	danser/dance
aller au ballet (*bah-leh*)	voir les danseurs/see the dancers
aller au casino (*kah-zee-no*)	jouer/gamble
aller au centre commercial/mall (*sahNtr koh-mehr-syahl*)	faire du lèche-vitrines/go window shopping
aller au cinéma (*see-nay mah*)	voir un film/see a film
aller au concert (*kohN-sehr*)	écouter l'orchestre/listen to the orchestra
aller au théâtre (*tay-ahtr*)	voir une pièce/see a play
faire une randonnée/hike (*rahN-doh-nay*)	voir les sites pittoresques/see the sights
rester dans sa chambre (à la maison)/ stay in one's room, at home	jouer aux cartes/play cards, jouer aux dames/play checkers, jouer aux échecs/play chess, lire un roman/read a novel

Do You Accept or Refuse?

Let's say you've received a ton of invitations; one friend would like you to go window shopping, while another is urging you to go parasailing. You also have conflicting plans for the evening: your husband would like to go to the movies, but your daughter is eager to go to a disco. And if that isn't enough, business colleagues have even asked you to spend the evening at the opera! Fashion a reply to all these invitations using the phrases you've learned so far.

By the Sea

Did you ever arrive at the pool or beach only to realize that you forgot to bring your suntan lotion or some other essential item? Your day could be ruined unnecessarily. Remember to pack these items for a pleasant day in the sun:

beach ball	un ballon de plage	*uhN bah-lohN duh plahzh*
beach chair	une chaise longue	*ewn shehz lohNg*
beach towel	un drap de bain	*uhN drah dbaN*
sunglasses	des lunettes de soleil (f.)	*day lew-neht duh soh-lehy*
suntan lotion	la lotion solaire	*lah loh-syohN soh-lehr*
	la creme solaire	*lah krehm soh-lehr*
suntan oil	l'huile solaire	*lweel soh-lehr*

Cultural Tidbits

In France and on some of the French islands of the Caribbean, it is not uncommon to see women sunbathing topless, or to see men (and women) in very thin string (*ficelle*) and thong bikinis. Don't gawk! The French attitude toward sunbathing is much more relaxed than the American—to blend in, you might have to join in.

At the Movies and on T.V.

Do you crave some quiet relaxation? Is the weather bad? Do you feel like getting away from everyone and everything? There's always a movie or T.V. It seems that cable has invaded the planet and can accommodate anyone who needs a few carefree hours in the room. So if you want to be entertained, consult Table 18.6 for the possibilities.

On passe quel genre de film?	Qu'est-ce qu'il y a à la télé?
ohN pahs kehl zhahNr duh feelm	*kehs keel yah ah lah tay-lay*
What kind of film are they showing?	What's on T.V.?

Table 18.6   Movies and Television Programs

adventure film	un film d'aventure	*uhN feelm dah-vahN-tewr*
cartoon	un dessin animé	*uhN deh-saN ah-nee-may*
comedy	un film comique	*uhN feelm koh-meek*
documentary	un documentaire	*uhN doh-kew-mahN-tehr*
drama	un drame	*uhN drahm*
game show	un jeu	*uhN zhuh*
horror movie	un film d'horreur	*uhN feelm doh-ruhr*
love story	un film d'amour	*uhN feelm dah-moor*
mystery	un mystère	*uhN mees-tehr*
news	les informations (f.)	*lay zaN-fohr-mah-syohN*
police story	un film policier	*uhN feelm poh-lee-syay*
science-fiction film	un film de science-fiction	*uhN feelm duh see-ahNs-feek-syohN*
soap opera	un feuilleton (mélodramatique)	*uhN fuhy-tohN (may-loh-drah-mah-teek)*
spy movie	un film d'espionnage	*uhN feelm dehs-pee-yoh-nazh*
talk show	une causerie	*ewn koz-ree*
weather	la météo	*lay may-tay-o*
western	un western	*uhN wehs-tehrn*

Cultural Tidbits

In French movie theaters, an usher, usually a young woman (une ouvreuse—*ewn noo-vruhz*) will show you to your seat and expect a tip (un pourboire—*uhN poor-bwahr*). Commercials are often shown for at least 15 minutes before the main feature. During that time the usher comes around with a selection of candy and ice cream. Do you crave popcorn? Sorry, it's not sold! The following abbreviations will help you when choosing a movie or theater:

INT-18 ans	Interdit aux moins de 18 ans	Forbidden for those under 18
V.O.	Version originale	Original version, subtitled
V.F.	Version française	Dubbed in French
T.R.	Tarif réduit	Reduced rate
C.V.	Carte vermeille	"Red" senior citizens' card
Pl.	Prix des places	Price of a seat

Expressing Your Opinion

Use the following phrases to express your enjoyment of a film or program.

I love it!	J'adore!	*zhah-dohr*
It's a good movie.	C'est un bon film.	*seh tuhN bohN feelm*
It's amusing!	C'est amusant!	*seh tah-mew-zahN*
It's great!	C'est génial!	*seh zhay-nyahl*
It's moving!	C'est émouvant!	*seh tay-moo-vahN*
It's original!	C'est original!	*seh toh-ree-zhee-nahl*

If you are less than thrilled with the show, try these phrases:

I hate it!	Je déteste!	*zhuh day-tehst*
It's a bad movie!	C'est un mauvais film.	*seh tuhN mo-veh feelm*
It's a loser!	C'est un navet!	*seh tuhN nah-veh*
It's garbage!	C'est bidon!	*seh bee-dohN*
It's the same old thing!	C'est toujours la même chose!	*seh too-zhoor lah mehm shohz*
It's too violent!	C'est trop violent!	*seh tro vee-oh-lahN*

I Think...

Using the phrases you've learned, give your opinion of the following types of movies: love story, science fiction, horror, police film, mystery, and animated film.

At a Concert

A friend has invited you to the Opéra in Paris, but you feel a little hesistant about going. Although you're familiar with some French composers and their works (*Carmen,* by Bizet is your personal favorite), you're afraid you won't be able to hold up your end of the conversation. The names of the instruments in Table 18.7 should assist you in expressing your ideas.

Table 18.7   Musical Instruments

accordeon	l'accordéon	*lah-kohr-day-ohN*
cello	le violoncelle	*luh vee-oh-lohN-sehl*
clarinet	la clarinette	*lah klah-ree-neht*
drum	le tambour	*luh tahN-boor*
drums	la batterie	*lah bah-tree*
flute	la flûte	*lah flewt*
guitar	la guitare	*lah gee-tahr*
harp	la harpe	*lah ahrp*
horn	le cor	*luh kohr*
oboe	le hautbois	*luh o-bwah*
piano	le piano	*luh pyah-no*
piccolo	le piccolo	*luh pee-koh-lo*
saxophone	le saxophone	*luh sahk-soh-fohn*
trombone	le trombone	*luh trohN-bohn*
trumpet	la trompette	*lah trohN-peht*
violin	le violon	*luh vee-oh-lohN*

Jouer à vs. Jouer de

In English, we use the verb *to play* whether we are referring to the playing of an instrument or the playing of a sport. The French, however, make a distinction. The verb *jouer* means to play. When followed by the preposition *de* + definite article *(du, de la, de l', des)* *jouer* refers to the playing of musical instruments:

Il joue du piano.
eel zhoo dew pyah-no
He plays the piano.

Elle joue de la clarinette.
ehl zhoo duh lah klah-ree-neht
She plays the clarinet.

When referring to sports or to games (such as card or board games) *jouer* is followed by *à* + definite article *(au, à la, à l', aux)*:

Ils jouent au tennis.
eel zhoo o teh-nees
They play tennis.

Elles jouent aux cartes.
ehl zhoo o kahrt
They play cards.

How Well Do You Do Things?

Adverbs are often used to describe how well you do something, such as "he plays the cello beautifully" (in English most adverbs end in *ly*). In French, adverbs are used for the same purpose, and they generally end in *ment*.

Adverbs are formed by adding *ment* to the masculine, singular form of adjectives that end in a vowel. If the masculine form of the adjective ends in a consonant, first change it to the feminine form and then add *ment*. This works quite well as long as you look for the proper letter at the end of the adjective and remember the feminine forms. Tables 18.8 and 18.9 show you just how easy this is.

Table 18.8   Adverbs Formed from Masculine Adjectives

Masculine—Adj.	Adverb	Meaning
facile (*fah-seel*)	facilement (*fah-seel-mahN*)	easily
passionné (*pah-syoh-nay*)	passionnément (*pah-syoh-nay-mahN*)	enthusiastically
probable (*proh-bahbl*)	probablement (*proh-bahbl-mahN*)	probably
rapide (*rah-peed*)	rapidement (*rah-peed-mahN*)	rapidly, quickly
sincère (*saN-sehr*)	sincèrement (*saN-sehr-mahN*)	sincerely
vrai (*vreh*)	vraiment (*vreh-mahN*)	truly, really

Table 18.9 Adverbs Formed from Feminine Adjectives

Masculine—Adj.	Feminine—Adj.	Adverb	Meaning
lent (*lahN*)	lente (*lahNt*)	lentement (*lahNt-mahN*)	slowly
certain (*sehr-taN*)	certaine (*sehr-tehn*)	certainement (*sehr-tehn-mahN*)	certainly

Masculine—Adj.	Feminine—Adj.	Adverb	Meaning
seul (*suhl*)	seule (*suhl*)	seulement (*suhl-mahN*)	only
actif (*ahk-teef*)	active (*ahk-teev*)	activement (*ahk-teev-mahN*)	actively
complet (*kohN-pleh*)	complète (*kohN-pleht*)	complètement (*kohN-pleht-mahN*)	completely
continuel (*kohN-tee-new-ehl*)	continuelle (*kohN-tee-new-ehl*)	continuellement (*kohN-tee-new-ehl-mahN*)	continuously
doux (*doo*)	douce (*doos*)	doucement (*doos-mahN*)	gently
fier (*fyehr*)	fière (*fyehr*)	fièrement (*fyehr-mahN*)	proudly
franc (*frahN*)	franche (*frahNsh*)	franchement (*frahNsh-mahN*)	frankly
sérieux (*say-ree-yuh*)	sérieuse (*say-ree-uhz*)	sérieusement (*say-ree-uhz-mahN*)	seriously

Two irregular formations are:

Masculine—Adj.	Feminine—Adj.	Adverb	Meaning
bref (*brehf*)	brève (*brehv*)	brièvement (*bree-ehv-mahN*)	briefly
gentil (*zhahN-tee*)	gentille (*zhahN-tee*)	gentiment (*zhahN-tee-mahN*)	gently

Exceptions to the Rule

Life would be so easy if there were no exceptions to the rules. This, however, is not the case with French adverbs. Fortunately, the irregularities are easy to understand and should present no difficulties in adverb formation.

Some adverbs are formed by changing a silent *e* from the adjective to *é* before the adverbial *ment* ending:

énorme (*ay-nohrm*)	énormément (*ay-nohr-may-mahN*)	enormously
intense (*aN-tahNs*)	intensément (*aN-tahN-say-mahN*)	intensely
précis (*pray-see*)	précisément (*pray-see-zay-mahN*)	precisely
profond (*proh-fohN*)	profondément (*proh-fohN-day-mahN*)	profoundly

Adjectives ending in *ant* and *ent* have adverbs ending in *amment* and *emment* respectively:

constant (*kohN-stahN*)	constamment (*kohN-stah-mahN*)	constantly
courant (*koo-rahN*)	couramment (*koo-rah-mahN*)	fluently
différent (*dee-fay-rahN*)	différemment (*dee-fay-reh-mahN*)	differently
évident (*ay-vee-dahN*)	évidemment (*ay-vee-deh-mahN*)	evidently
récent (*ray-sahN*)	récemment (*ray-seh-mahN*)	recently

Be careful with these adverbs that have distinct forms from adjectives:

Adjective	Adverb
bon (*bohN*)/good	bien (*byaN*)/well
mauvais (*moh-veh*)/bad	mal (*mahl*)/badly
meilleur (*meh-yuhr*)/better	mieux (*myuh*)/better
petit (*puh-tee*)/little	peu (*puh*)/little

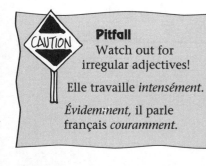

Pitfall
Watch out for irregular adjectives!

Elle travaille *intensément*.

Évidemment, il parle français *couramment*.

Elle est petite et elle mange peu.

ehl eh puh-teet ay ehl mahNzh puh

She is little and she eats little.

Ils sont de bons musiciens et ils jouent bien de la guitare.

eel sohN duh bohN mew-zee-syaN ay eel zhoo byaN duh lah gee-tahr

They are good musicians and they play the guitar well.

Some adverbs and adverbial expressions are not formed from adjectives at all and, therefore, do not end in *ment*. Table 18.10 gives the most common adverbs that follow this rule. These familiar, high-frequency words are extremely useful in everyday conversation.

Table 18.10 Adverbs and Adverbial Expressions not Formed from Adjectives

alors	*ah-lohrs*	then
après	*ah-preh*	afterward
aussi	*o-see*	also, too
beaucoup	*bo-koo*	much
bientôt	*byaN-to*	soon
comme	*kohm*	as
d'habitude	*dah-bee-tewd*	usually, generally
déjà	*day-zhah*	already
encore	*ahN-kohr*	still, yet, again
enfin	*ahN-faN*	finally, at last
ensemble	*ahN-sahNbl*	together
ensuite	*ahN-sweet*	then, afterwards
ici	*ee-see*	here
là	*lah*	there
loin	*lwaN*	far
longtemps	*lohN-tahN*	a long time
maintenant	*maNt-nahN*	now
même	*mehm*	even
moins	*mwaN*	less
parfois	*pahr-fwah*	sometimes
plus	*plew*	more
près	*preh*	near
presque	*prehsk*	almost
puis	*pwee*	then
quelquefois	*kehl-kuh-fwah*	sometimes
si	*see*	so
souvent	*soo-vahN*	often

continues

Table 18.10 Continued

tard	*tahr*	late
tôt	*to*	soon, early
toujours	*too-zhoor*	always, still
tout	*too*	quite, entirely
tout à coup	*too tah koo*	suddenly
tout à fait	*too tah feh*	entirely
tout de suite	*toot sweet*	immediately
très	*treh*	very
trop	*tro*	too much
vite	*veet*	quickly

Position of Adverbs

Adverbs are generally placed after the verb they modify. Sometimes, however, the position of the adverb is variable and is usually placed where we would logically put an English adverb.

D'habitude il joue bien au football.

dah-bee-tewd eel zhoo byaN o foot-bohl.

Usually he play soccer well.

Il joue très bien au football.

eel zhoo treh byaN o foot-ball

He plays soccer very well.

How Well Do You Do?

How's your cooking? Can you carry a tune? Are you light on your feet or do you stomp on your partner's toes on the dance floor? We each perform according to our own individual abilities. Express how you feel you fare at these activities by using adverbs:

Example: parler anglais   Je parle anglais couramment.

    parler français

    jouer du piano

    jouer au golf

    cuisiner (cook)

    penser (think)

    travailler

voyager

chanter

danser

nager

The Least You Need to Know

➤ The verb *faire* is used to express participation in a sport.

➤ *Vouloir* and *pouvoir* + a verb infinitive can be used to propose, accept, and refuse invitations.

➤ Adverbs are formed by adding *ment* to many adjectives ending in a vowel.

As a Rule

If you can't think of the adverb, or if one does not exist, use the phrases *d'une façon* (*dewn fah-sohN*) or *d'une manière* (*dewn mah-nyehr*), which both express *in a way*, *in a manner*, or *in a fashion*.

He plays intelligently.

Il joue d'une façon (d'une manière) intelligent.

eel zhoo dewn fah-sohN (dewn mah-nyehr) aN-teh-lee-zhahN

Part 4

Problems

Chapter 19

Dealing with a Bad Hair Day and Getting Other Personal Services

In This Chapter

➤ Personal services

➤ Problems and solutions

➤ Using stress pronouns

➤ Making comparisons

You've been traveling and having a wonderful time. All of a sudden there is a problem that just can't wait: your roots have surfaced in record time, you've spilled mustard on your new white silk shirt, your contact lens has torn, you've broken a heel on your shoe, or your five-year-old has dropped your camera, smashing the lens. You're not home, and you're very hesitant about what to do. Ask the concierge of your hotel or consult *les pages jaunes* (*lay pahzh zhon*), the yellow pages. Don't worry, the French have competent, expert technicians, and all you have to do is know what to say to get the job done. This chapter will make that task easy.

My Hair Needs Help, Now!

You're on vacation, you're feeling quite carefree and the sky's the limit. You pass by a salon and you're struck by a sudden whim to return home with a brand new look. Why not be daring? You're in Paris, the world-famous center of *haute couture* (high style and fashion). You want a more tantalizing "you" and this is the place to get it.

In the past, men went *chez le coiffeur* (to the barber's) while women were accustomed to going *au salon de beauté* (to the beauty parlor). Today these establishments have become more or less unisex with men and women demanding more or less the same services. To get what you want simply ask:

Could you give me...	I would like...	please
Pourriez-vous me donner...	Je voudrais...	s'il vous plaît
poo-ryay voo muh doh-nay	*zhuh voo-dreh*	*seel voo pleh*

Today's salons provide the services listed in Table 19.1

Table 19.1   Hair Care

a blunt cut	une coupe en carré	*ewn koop ahN kah-ray*
a coloring (vegetable)	une teinture (végétale)	*ewn taN-tewr (vay-zhay-tahl)*
a facial	un massage facial	*uhN mah-sahzh fah-syahl*
a haircut	une coupe de cheveux	*ewn koop duh shuh-vuh*
a manicure	une manucure	*ewn mah-new-kewr*
a pedicure	une pédicurie	*ewn pay-dee-kew-ree*
a permanent	une permanente	*ewn pehr-mah-nahNt*
a set	une mise en plis	*ewn mee-zohN plee*
a shampoo	un shampooing	*uhN shahN-pwaN*
a trim	une coupe	*ewn koop*
a waxing	une épilation	*ewn ay-pee-lah-syohN*
highlights	des reflets	*day ruh-fleh*
layers	une coupe dégradée	*ewn koop day-grah-day*

Table 19.2 gives you the phrases you need to get other services. Use the following phrase to preface your request:

Could you please...?
Pourriez-vous...s'il vous plaît?
poo-ryay voo...seel voo pleh

Table 19.2   Other Services

blow dry my hair	me donner un brushing	*muh doh-nay uhN bruh-sheeng*
curl my hair	me friser les cheveux	*muh free-zay lay shuh-vuh*
shave my beard (my mustache)	me raser la barbe (la moustache)	*muh rah-zay lah bahrb (lah moo-stahsh)*
straighten my hair	me défriser les cheveux	*muh day-free-zay lay shuh-vuh*
trim my bangs	me rafraîchir la frange	*muh rah-freh-sheer lah frahNzh*
trim my beard (mustache, sideburns)	me rafraîchir la barbe (la moustache, les pattes)	*muh rah-freh-sheer lah bahrb (lah moo-stahsh, lay paht)*

Expressing Your Preferences

It is hard enough getting the haircut and style you want when there is no language barrier—imagine the disasters that could befall your poor head in a foreign country? The following phrases will help you make your styling and coloring preferences clear.

Je préfère mes cheveux…
zhuh pray-fehr may shuh-vuh
I prefer my hair…

long	longs	*lohN*
medium	mi-longs	*mee-lohN*
short	courts	*koor*
wavy	frisés	*free-zay*
curly	bouclés	*boo-klay*
straight	raides (lissés)	*rehd (lee-say)*
auburn	auburn, châtain clair	*oh-bewrn, shah-taN klehr*
black	noir	*nwahr*
blond	blond	*blohN*
brunette	brun	*bruhN*
chestnut brown	châtain	*shah-taN*
red	roux	*roo*
a darker color	une teinte plus foncée	*ewn taNt plew fohN-say*

| a lighter color | une teinte plus claire | *ewn taNt plew klehr* |
| the same color | la même couleur | *lah mehm koo-luhr* |

Are you allergic to any products or specific chemicals? Are you sensitive to smells? Do you hate it when your hair feels like cardboard? If you don't like certain hair care products, don't be shy, tell the hairdresser:

Ne mettez pas de (d')… s'il vous plaît.
nuh meh-tay pah duh … seel voo pleh
Don't put any…please

conditioner	après-shampooing	*ah-preh shahN-pwaN*
	shampooing démelant	*shahN-pwaN day-muh- lahN*
gel	gel coiffant (m.)	*zhehl kwah-fahN*
hairspray	laque (f.)	*lahk*
lotion	lotion (f.)	*loh-syohN*
mousse	mousse coiffante (f.)	*moos kwah-fahN*
shampoo	shampooing (m.)	*shahN-pwaN*

Cultural Tidbits

Do you want to cover that gray with a natural looking color? Why not allow a student at L'Oréal headquarters in Clichy, a suburb of Paris, to work miracles on you? After all, it was Eugène Schueller, a Parisian hairdresser who, in the early 1900s, developed the first permanent hair color using an oxidation process. Needless to say, women who were unsatisfied with the results of crude dyes and herbal compounds were ecstatic. Mr. Schueller, elated with his success, continued to do extensive research in the hair care field, created many new products (shampoos, setting lotions, conditioners, mousse) and lauched the company that is today L'Oréal. If you're interested, why not pick up a copy of *La Coiffure de Paris,* a technical magazine that has become the professional hairdresser's bible in Europe?

I'm Having Problems

There are phrases that will come in handy when you are seeking certain services or are trying to have something repaired. Use the following phrases at the dry cleaner, the shoemaker, the optometrist, the jeweler, or the camera store.

At what time do you open?
Vous êtes ouvert à quelle heure?
voo zeh too-vehr ah kehl uhr

At what time do you close?
Vous fermez à quelle heure?
voo fehr-may ah kehl uhr

What days are you open? Closed?
Vous êtes ouvert (vous fermez) quels jours?
voo zeht oo-vehr (voo fehr-may) kehl zhoor

Can you fix… for me?
Pouvez-vous me réparer…?
poo-vay voo muh ray-pah-ray

Can you fix it (them) today?
Pouvez-vous le (la, l', les) réparer aujourd'hui?
poo-vay voo luh (lah, lay) ray-pah-ray o-zhoor-dwee

May I have a receipt?
Puis-je avoir un reçu?
pweezh ah-vwahr uhN ruh-sew

Can you fix it (them) temporarily (while I wait)?
Pouvez-vous le (la, l', les) réparer provisoirement (pendant que j'attends)?
poo-vay voo luh (lah, lay) ray-pah-ray proh-vee-zwahr-mahN (pahN-dahN kuh zhah-tahN)

At the Dry Cleaner's—à la Teinturerie

You've unpacked. Your blue pants look like you slept in them and your tan jacket has an ugly stain on the sleeve that you hadn't noticed when you packed it. Don't fret. Your stains, spots, tears, and wrinkles can be taken care of if you know how to explain your problem and ask for the necessary service.

What's the problem?	There is (are)…	
Quel est le problème?	*Il y a…*	
kehl eh luh proh-blehm	*eel yah*	
a hole	un trou	*uhN troo*
a missing button	un bouton qui manque	*uhN boo-tohN kee mahNk*
a spot	une tache	*ewn tahsh*
a tear	une déchirure	*ewn day-shee-rewr*

Cultural Tidbits

Don't expect to find as many laundromats in France as in the United States. And don't expect the quick same-day service that has spoiled so many of us. Although French laundries are very good, they are slow. Plan on waiting a few days to get your stains removed and your clothes cleaned. If you're lucky, in big cities you might find a dry cleaner who can have your laundry ready in a day. Your best bet is to travel with as many permanent press clothes as possible. You may do your wash in the sink. Enjoy the bidet, but it's definitely not for washing your clothes.

Now that you've explained the problem, state what you'd like done about it:

Can you (dry) clean this (these)...for me?
Vous pouvez me nettoyer (à sec) ce (cette, cet, ces)...?
voo poo-vay muh neh-twah-yay ah sehk suh (seht, seht, say)...

Can you please mend this (these)...for me?
Vous pouvez me faire recoudre ce (cette, cet, ces)...?
voo poo-vay muh fehr ruh-koodr suh (seht, seht, say)...

Can you please press this (these)...for me?
Vous pouvez me repasser (réparer) ce (cette, cet, ces)...?
voo poo-vay muh ruh-pah-say (ray-pah-ray) suh (seht, seht, say)

Can you please starch this (these)...for me?
Vous pouvez m'amidonner ce (cette, cet, ces)...?
voo poo-vay mah-mee-doh-nay suh (seht, seht, say)...

Do you do invisible mending?
Vous faites le stoppage?
voo feht luh stoh-pahzh

As a Rule
If you'd like a service performed for someone else, use the appropriate indirect object: *te* (for you), *lui* (for him, her), *nous* (for us), *vous* (for you), *leur* (for them).

Can you please weave this coat for him (her)?

Vous pouvez *lui* tisser ce manteau?

Can you please weave this (these)...for me?
Vous pouvez me tisser ce (cette, cet, ces)...?
voo poo-vay muh tee-say suh (seht, seht, say)...

As a Rule
The verb *faire* (to make, do) can be used before an infinitive when you want to express that you are having something done for yourself (such as a personal service):

I would like to have my suit dry cleaned.

Je voudrais faire nettoyer à sec mon costume.

zhuh voo-dreh fehr neh-twah-yay ah sehk mohN kohs-tewm

At the Laundry—à la Blanchisserie or à la Laverie Automatique

If your laundry has piled up and you don't mind doing it yourself, you might try to seek out a laundromat. Use the following phrases to get the information you need.

I have a lot of dirty laundry.
J'ai beaucoup de lessive.
zhay bo-koo duh leh-seev

I'd like to wash my clothes.
Je voudrais laver mes vêtements.
zhuh voo-dreh lah-vay may veht-mahN

I'd like to have my clothes washed.
Je voudrais faire laver mes vêtements.
zhuh voo-dreh fehr lah-vay may veht-mahN

So you're embarrassed to have anyone see your dirty laundry. Or perhaps you're afraid that your beautiful new silk shirt will get ruined by an amateur. If you want to do the job yourself, the following phrases might serve you well:

Is there a free washing machine (dryer)?
Y a-t-il une machine à laver (un séchoir) libre?
ee ah-tee ewn mah-sheen ah lah-vay (uhN saysh-wahr) leebr

Where can I buy soap powder?
Où puis-je acheter de la lessive en poudre?
oo pweezh ahsh-tay duh lah leh-seev ahN poodr

At the Shoemaker's—Chez le Cordonnier

Let's say that you've walked so much that you've worn your soles down, or you've broken a shoelace on your dress shoes, or perhaps you would just like a shine. The following phrases will help you describe your problem.

Can you repair … for me?
Pouvez-vous me réparer …?
poo-vay voo muh ray-pah-ray

these shoes, these boots, this heel, this sole
ces chaussures, ces bottes, ce talon, cette semelle
say sho-sewr, say boht, suh tah-lohN, seht suh-mehl

Do you sell shoelaces?
Vendez-vous des lacets?
vahN-day-voo day lah-seh?

I'd like a shoe shine.
Je voudrais un cirage.
zhuh voo-dreh zuhN see-rage

I Need These Shoes

You've got an unexpected, important business meeting to attend and your walking shoes are inappropriate attire. Your dress shoes are in need of repair and you need them in a hurry. What service does this shoemaker provide?

CV, CORDONNERIE, VARTAN

Prend et Livre à domicile

83, r. de Longchamp

765016 PARIS

At the Optometrist's—Chez l'Opticien

What could be more annoying than losing or tearing a contact lens, or breaking or losing a pair of glasses while away from home? For those of us who depend on these optical necessities the following phrases could one day prove useful.

Can you repair these glasses for me?
Pouvez-vous me réparer ces lunettes?
poo-vay voo muh ray-pah-ray say lew-neht

The lens (the frame) is broken.
Le verre (La monture) est cassé(e).
Luh vehr (lah mohN-tewr) eh kah-say

Can you replace this contact lens?
Pouvez-vous remplacer cette lentille (ce verre) de contact?
poo-vay voo rahN-plah-say seht lahN-tee-y (suh vehr) duh kohN-tahkt

Do you have progressive lenses?
Avez-vous des verres progressifs?
ah-vay-voo day vehr proh-greh-seef

Do you sell sunglasses?
Vendez-vous des lunettes de soleil?
vahN-day voo day lew-neht duh soh-lehy

Cultural Tidbits

Varilux, or progressive eyeglass lenses, are now being used by many individuals to replace bifocals. These lenses, developed and perfected in France, contain several different increasing or decreasing strength presciptions in just one lens. They allow near-sighted and far-sighted alike to have excellent near, mid-range, and distant vision without having to look through annoying lines that cut across the visual field.

I Need Them Now

Individuals with very poor vision may have eyeglasses with lenses as thick as coke bottles, that distort the size and shape of their eyes. And because of the strength of their prescription, these same people may have trouble finding replacement lenses in an emergency. What two services are being offered below?

OPTIQUE, **ANTOINE**

S.O.S. LUNETTES, EN 1 HEURE, RENSEIGNEZ-VOUS, SPÉCIAL MYOPES

verres, de fortes correction, ne déformant, plus le visage

37 bd St Germain, 75005 PARIS

At the Jeweler's—Chez le Bijoutier

If your watch has stopped, or isn't working as it should, you might find it necessary to have it repaired before returning home:

Can you repair this watch?	My watch doesn't work.
Pouvez-vous réparer cette montre?	Ma montre ne marche pas.
poo-vay voo ray-pah-ray seht mohNtr	*mah mohNtr nuh mahrsh pah*
My watch is fast (slow).	Do you sell bands (batteries)?
Ma montre avance (retarde).	Vendez-vous des bandes (des piles)?
ma mohNtr ah-vahNs (ruh-tahrd)	*vahN-day voo day bahnd (day peel)*

It's My Watch

You have to meet a friend at a specific time. You look at your watch and realize that it isn't working properly. You pass by a jewelry store and decide to stop in for a quick repair. Explain your problem and the service you want.

At the Camera Shop—au Magasin de Photographie

For many people, a vacation is not a vacation unless they capture it on film. If you need to visit a camera shop or film store in a French speaking country, the following words and phrases will come in handy.

a camera	un appareil-photo	*uhN nah-pah-rahy foh-to*
a video camera	un appareil vidéo	*uhN nah-pah-rahy vee-day-o*

If you have special needs, you might ask:

Do you sell rolls of 20 (36) exposure film in color (black and white)?
Vendez-vous des pellicules de vingt (trente-six) en couleur (noir et blanc)?
vahN-day voo day peh-lee-kewl duh vaN (trahNt-sees) ahN koo-luhr (nwahr ay blahN)

Do you sell film for slides?
Vendez-vous des pellicules pour diapositives?
vahN-day voo day peh-lee-kewl poor dee-ah-poh-zee-teev

I would like to have this film developed.
Je voudrais faire développer ce film.
zhuh voo-dreh fehr day-vloh-pay suh feelm

255

I Need a New Camera

Are you dissatisfied with the pictures you've been taking? Perhaps you just want something a bit more modern that's easier to use. What services would you expect to receive at this photo store supply?

PHOTO-EXPERT, TOUTES LES GRANDES MARQUES

Vente-Achat-Echange, Réparation

Vente au plus bas prix, Achat au plus haut cours

Other Services

In addition to the shoemaker, the camera store, and the hairdresser, you may need other special services from time to time. For instance, you may need to find your consulate to report a lost passport. Or perhaps your handbag has been stolen and you'd like to file a police report. You may even want a translator to make sure you don't get into deeper trouble. The following phrases should help.

Where is...	the police station?
Où est...	le commissariat de police?
oo eh	*luh koh-mee-sah-ryah duh poh-lees*
the American consulate?	the American embassy?
le consulat américain?	l'ambassade américaine?
luh kohN-sew-lah ah-may-ree-kaN	*lahN-bah-sahd ah-may-ree-kehn*
I lost...	my passport.
J'ai perdu...	mon passeport.
zhay pehr-dew	*mohN pahs-pohr*
my wallet.	Help me, please.
mon portefeuille.	Aidez-moi, s'il vous plaît.
mohN pohr-tuh-fuhy	*eh-day mwah seel voo pleh*
I need an interpreter.	Does anyone here speak English?
Il me faut un interprète.	Y a-t-il quelqu'un qui parle anglais?
eel muh fo tuhN naN-tehr-preht	*ee ah teel kehl kuhN kee pahrl ahN-gleh*

More Stress

Stress pronouns are so-named because you will use them when you need to emphasize a certain fact. Sress pronouns may highlight or replace certain nouns or pronouns and they are used after prepositions. This concept sounds more confusing than it is. Table 19.3 shows subject pronouns with their corresponding stress pronouns.

Table 19.3   Stress Pronouns

	Singular			Plural	
subject	*stress pronoun*	*meaning*	*subject*	*stress pronoun*	*meaning*
(je)	moi (mwah)	I, me	(nous)	nous (noo)	we, us
(tu)	toi (twah)	you (fam.)	(vous)	vous (voo)	you (pl. pol.)
(il)	lui(lwee)	he, him	(ils)	eux (uh)	they, them
(elle)	elle (ehl)	she, her	(elles)	elles (ehl)	they, them
(on)	soi (soi)	oneself			

Using Stress Pronouns

Stress pronouns can be used in situations where you want to emphasize the subject.

Moi, je veux parler au propriétaire.
mwah zhuh vuh pahr-lay o proh-pree-ay-tehr
Me, I want to speak to the owner.

Lui, il a fait une faute.
lwee eel ah feh tewn foht
He made a mistake.

Stress pronouns are used after *ce + être* (it is):

Qui est-ce? C'est moi.
kee ehs? seh mwah
Who is it? It is I.

C'est lui qui répare les montres.
seh lwee kee ray-pahr lay mohNtr
He (It is he who) repairs watches.

Stress pronouns are used when the pronoun has no verb:

Qui est la propriétaire? Elle.
kee eh lah proh-pree-ay-tehr ehl
Who is the owner? She (is).

Stress pronouns are used in compound subjects:

Anne et eux vont chez le coiffeur.
ahn ay uh vohN shay luh kwah-fuhr
Anne and they are going to the hairdresser.

If one of the stress pronouns is *moi*, the subject pronoun *nous* is used in summary (because *someone + me* = we) but does not have to appear in the sentence:

Henri et moi, nous allons chez l'opticien.
Henri et moi allons chez l'opticien.
Henry and I go to the optometrist.

257

If one of the stress pronouns is *toi*, the subject *vous* is used in summary (because *someone +* *you* [singular] = you [plural]) but does not have to appear in the sentence:

> Guy et toi, vous allez chez le cordonnier?
> Guy et toi allez chez le cordonnier.
> Guy and you go to the shoemaker.

Stress pronouns are used after a preposition when referring to a person or persons:

Je vais chez toi.	Ne pars pas sans lui.
zhuh veh shay twah	*nuh pahr pah sahN lwee*
I'm going to your house.	Don't leave without him.

Stress pronouns are used after certain verbs that do not use a direct object:

avoir affaire à	*ah-vwahr ah-fehr ah*	to have business with
être à	*ehtr ah*	to belong to
penser à	*pahN-say ah*	to think about (of)
se fier à	*suh fee-ay ah*	to trust
s'intéresser à	*saN-tay-reh-say ah*	to be interested in

J'ai affaire à lui.	Cette montre est à moi.
zhay ah-fehr ah lwee	*seht mohNtr eh tah mwah*
I have business with him.	That watch is mine.

Relieve My Stress

If you want to speak like a native, make sure that you use stress pronouns correctly. Here are some examples of the different types of sentences requiring them. Fill in the appropriate pronoun:

1. (us) Il a affaire à _____.

2. (he, I) _____ et _____ allons à l'ambassade.

3. (you fam.) _____, tu vas chez le coiffeur?

4. (she) _____, elle répare bien les vêtements.

5. (they masc.) Je ne peux pas partir sans _____

6. (you pol.) C'est _____ qui allez m'accompagner.

Comparison Shopping

Which shop offers the least expensive merchandise? Which merchant is the most honest? Who is the most reliable? When shopping for goods or services, we often compare cost, reputation, and the goods or services themselves before making a choice. The following table gives you the phrases and adjectives you need when making comparisons.

As a Rule

The comparative and superlative forms of the adjectives used must agree in gender and number with the nouns they describe.

Jeanne est moins grande que son frère.

Les boutiques de Paris sont les plus élégantes.

Table 19.4 Comparison of Adjectives—Inequality

Positive	honnête (*oh-neht*)	honest
Comparative	plus honnête (*plew zoh-neht*), moins honnête (*mwaN zoh-neht*)	more honest, less honest
Superlative	le (la, les) plus honnête(s), le (la, les) moins honnête(s)	the most honest, the least honest

Que may or may not be used after the comparative. When used, *que* expresses *than*. *Que* becomes *qu'* before a vowel or vowel sound.

> Qui est plus charmant(e)?
>
> Roger est plus charmant (que Lucien).
>
> Sylvie est plus chamante (qu'Anne).

The preposition *de* + definite article *(du, de la, de l', des)* may be used to express *in (of) the*.

> Ce cordonnier est honnête.
>
> Ce cordonnier est plus honnête que lui.
>
> Ce cordonnier est le plus honnête (de la ville).
>
> Ces coiffeuses sont aimables.
>
> Ces coiffeuses sont les plus aimables.
>
> Ces coiffeuses sont les moins aimables (du salon).

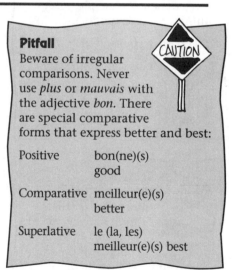

Pitfall

Beware of irregular comparisons. Never use *plus* or *mauvais* with the adjective *bon*. There are special comparative forms that express better and best:

Positive	bon(ne)(s) good
Comparative	meilleur(e)(s) better
Superlative	le (la, les) meilleur(e)(s) best

When I prepare my special recipe for French pot roast, everyone gathers around the table in eager anticipation. My son Eric eats the slowest and savors every morsel. My husband eats with gusto. But my son Michael, he eats the fastest of all. His reasoning is: "More for me!" Whether it's eating, working, or running, the different ways in which people do things may be compared. Table 19.5 shows how to make comparisons using adverbs.

259

Table 19.5 Comparison of Adverbs—Inequality

Positive	rapidement	*rah-peed-mahN*	rapidly
Comparative	plus rapidement,	*plew rah-peed-mahN,*	more rapidly,
	moins rapidement	*mwaN rah-peed-mahN*	
less rapidly			
Superlative	le plus rapidement,		the most
	le moins rapidement		rapidly, the least rapidly

As a Rule
There is no agreement of the definite article in the superlative with any word in the sentence. *Le* is always used. That's because we're using adverbs to describe actions (verbs) and agreement occurs only when we are using adjectives to describe people, places, things, or ideas (nouns).

Elle parle franchement.

Elle parle plus franchement que moi.

Elle parle le plus franchement du groupe.

As a Rule
The tags *-ci* (this, these) and *-la* (that, those) may be joined to nouns to help differentiate between two things being compared.

Ce coiffeur-*ci* est plus sympathique que ce coiffeur-*là*.

suh kwah-fuhr-see eh plew saN-pah-teek kuh suh kwah-fuhr-lah

This hairdresser is nicer than that hairdresser.

You've spent the day visiting museums in Paris. The Louvre is vast and contains treasures from antiquity, while the Picasso museum is very modern. Did you find these museums equally appealing, or did you prefer one over the other? Did you spend equal amounts of time in each, or did one visit last longer than the other? If everything were equal, then you may express this equality by using:

aussi + adjective or adverb + *que*

(as…as)

Il est aussi charmant qu'eux.
eel eh to-see shahr-mahN kuh
He is as charming as they.

Elle travaille aussi dur que nous.
ehl trah-vahy o-see dewr kuh noo
She works as hard as we do.

Make a Comparison

How do you compare to those you know? Are you shorter? Thinner? More charming? Do you dance better? Work more seriously? Listen more patiently? Use what you've learned above to compare yourself to friends or family members.

The Least You Need to Know

➤ Your problems can be solved and you can get the services you need in a foreign country with a few simple key phrases.

➤ Stress pronouns are used for emphasis after *c'est* and *ce sont,* in compound subjects, after prepositions and certain verbs, or alone when there is no verb.

➤ Use *plus* (more) or *moins* (less) before adjectives or adverbs to make comparions or state the superlative.

➤ Use *aussi* (as) before adjectives and adverbs to express that things are equal.

Pitfall

Beware of irregular comparisons. Never use *plus* or *mauvais* with the adverbs *bien, beaucoup,* and *peu.* There are special comparative and superlative forms for these words:

Positive
bien/well	peu/little
beaucoup/more	

Comparative
mieux/better	plus/more
moins/less	

Superlative
le mieux/best	le plus/
le moins/	(the) most
(the) least	

Chapter 20

Is There a Doctor in the House?

In This Chapter

➤ Your body

➤ Symptoms, complaints, and illnesses

➤ Expressing *how long*

➤ All about *dire* (to say, tell)

➤ How to use reflexive verbs

In the last chapter you learned how to take care of minor problems and repairs. With just a few simple sentences you can readily deal with life's petty annoyances. In this chapter, you'll learn the key words and phrases you'll need should you become sick while abroad.

Falling ill while you're away from home is hard enough, and the situation is even tougher if you can't communicate what is wrong. In this chapter you will learn how to explain your ailments and how long you've been experiencing the symptoms.

Where Does It Hurt?

I feel especially well-suited to writing this chapter, since our family seems to have spent an inordinate amount of time in foreign hospitals while we were supposed to be on vacation! For instance, one year my uncle arrived in France for a holiday only to be hit with a gall bladder attack. He spent the rest of his vacation flat on his back recovering from surgery for gallstones. Or take my son, who while vacationing in the Dominican Republic, was rushed to a hospital after he smashed his tooth against a toilet bowl. And then there was the year that my husband and I were nearly leveled by jet lag while backpacking through Europe. After going without sleep for 10 days we finally got sleeping suppositories from a Parisian doctor. But by the end of our trip, I wound up in a hospital in Leeds, England, with severe gastroenteritis.

While I hope your luck isn't like ours, it pays to be prepared if illness strikes. To begin with, familiarize yourself with the parts of the body in Table 20.1.

Table 20.1 Parts of the Body

ankle	la cheville	*lah shuh-vee-y*
arm	le bras	*luh brah*
back	le dos	*luh do*
body	le corps	*luh koor*
brain	le cerveau, la cervelle	*luh sehr-vo, lah sehr-vehl*
chest	la poitrine	*lah pwah-treen*
ear	l'oreille (f.)	*loh-rehy*
eye	l'oeil (m.)	*luhy*
eyes	les yeux	*lay zyuh*
face	la figure, le visage	*lah fee-gewr, luh vee-zahzh*
finger	le doigt	*luh dwah*
foot	le pied	*luh pyay*
hand	la main	*lah maN*
head	la tête	*lah teht*
heart	le coeur	*luh kuhr*
knee	le genou	*luh zhuh-noo*
leg	la jambe	*lah zhahNb*
mouth	la bouche	*lah boosh*

nail	l'ongle (m.)	*lohNgl*
neck	le cou	*luh koo*
nose	le nez	*luh nay*
skin	la peau	*lah po*
shoulder	l'épaule	*lay-pohl*
spine	l'épine dorsale, la colonne vertébrale	*lay-peen dohr-sahl, lah koh-lohn vehr-tay-brahl*
stomach	l'estomac (m.), le ventre	*leh-stoh-mah, lun vahNtr*
throat	la gorge	*lah gohrzh*
toe	l'orteil (m.)	*lohr-tehy*
tongue	la langue	*lah lahNg*
tooth	la dent	*lah dahN*
wrist	le poignet	*luh pwah-nyeh*

You Give Me a Pain in the...

Do you want to avoid a trip to the doctor while on vacation? The soundest piece of advice anyone can give you is, if you don't have a cast-iron stomach, don't drink the tap water when you travel. But let's say you forgot this warning and ate salad greens that were washed with tap water. Or, you ordered a drink on the rocks, ignorant of the future gastrointestinal effects of the ice cubes. You've spent too much time in *les toilettes* and now you find it necessary to go to the doctor. The obvious first question will be: "What's the matter with you? Qu'est-ce que vous avez (*kehs-kuh voo zah-vay*)?" To say what hurts or bothers you, the expression avoir mal à + definite article is used:

> J'ai mal au ventre.
> *zhay mahl o vahNtr*
> I have a stomach ache.

> Ils ont mal aux pieds.
> *eel zohN mahl o pyay*
> Their feet hurt.

As a Rule

Remember that when you say what ails you or anyone else, you must conjugate the verb *avoir* so that it agrees with the subject. Although the French use *avoir* to express what's bothering them, our English may not include the word *have*.

Elle a mal aux yeux.
Her eyes hurt.

If you have to go to the dentist, use the expression: *avoir mal aux dents* (to have a toothache) or *avoir une rage* (ewn rahzh) *de dents* (to have a very bad toothache).

J'ai mal aux dents.
I've got a toothache.

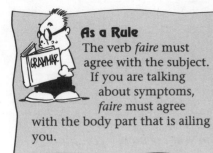

As a Rule
The verb *faire* must agree with the subject. If you are talking about symptoms, *faire* must agree with the body part that is ailing you.

Another way of talking about your symptoms is to use the expression *faire mal à*—to hurt (which requires an indirect object for *à* + person). Use the appropriate indirect object pronoun to refer to those who might be in pain (*me* [to me], *te* [to you], *lui* [to him/her], *nous* [to us], *vous* [to you], *leur* [to them]). Remember, too, to use the correct form of the possessive adjective that refers to the person in question (*mon, ma, mes; ton, ta, tes; son, sa, ses; notre, nos; votre, vos; leur, leurs*).

Mon ventre me fait mal.

mohN vahNtr muh feh mahl

My stomach hurts (me).

Ses pieds lui font mal.

say pyay lwee fohN mahl

His (Her) feet hurt (him, her).

Let's say that your symptoms are more specific than a vague ache or pain. Table 20.2 gives a list of possible symptoms, which will come in handy if you need to describe a problem. Use the phrase *J'ai* (zhay)—I have—to preface your complaint.

Table 20.2   Other Symptoms

abscess	un abscès	*uhN nahb-seh*
blister	une ampoule	*ewn nahN-pool*
broken bone	une fracture	*ewn frahk-tewr*
bruise	une contusion	*ewn kohN-tew-zyohN*
bump	une bosse	*ewn bohs*
burn	une brûlure	*ewn brew-lewr*
chills	des frissons	*day free-sohN*
cough	une toux	*ewn too*
cramps	des crampes	*day krahNp*
diarrhea	de la diarrhée	*dun lah dee-ah-ray*
fever	de la fièvre	*duh lah fyehvr*
indigestion	une indigestion	*ewn naN-dee-zhehs-tyohN*
lump	une grosseur	*ewn groh-sewr*
migraine	une migraine	*ewn mee-grehn*
pain	une douleur	*ewn doo-luhr*

rash	une éruption	*ewn nay-rewp-syohN*
sprain	une foulure	*ewn foo-lewr*
swelling	une enflure	*ewn nahN-flewr*
wound	une blessure	*ewn bleh-sewr*

Other useful phrases include:

Je tousse.
zhuh toos
I'm coughing.

J'éternue.
zay-tehr-new
I'm sneezing.

Je saigne.
zhuh seh-nyuh
I'm bleeding.

Je suis constipé(e).
zhuh swee kohN-stee-pay
I'm constipated.

J'ai des nausées.
zhay day no-zay
I'm nauseous.

J'ai du mal à dormir.
zhay dew mahl ah dohr-meer
I have trouble sleeping.

Je me sens mal.
zhuh muh sahN mahl
I feel bad.

J'ai mal partout.
zhay mahl pahr-too
I hurt everywhere.

Je n'en peux plus.
zhuh nahN puh plew
I'm exhausted.

I Don't Feel So Hot

Now use all that you've learned so far to describe your symptoms and complaints to a doctor. Pretend you have flu-like symptoms, an allergy, a sprained ankle, and finally a migraine.

This Is What You Have

Obviously, you won't be the only one doing the talking when you visit the doctor. You will also be asked to fill out forms, tell about any medications you are taking, and answer other questions about your symptoms and general health. The doctor or nurse may ask you:

Avez-vous subi (eu)...?	Souffrez-vous de (d')...?	
ah-vay voo sew-bee(ew)	*soo-fray voo duh...*	
Have you had...?	Do you suffer from...?	
allergic reaction	une réaction allergique	*ewn ray-ahk-syohN ah-lehr-zheek*
angina	une angine	*ewn nahN-zheen*
appendicitis	l'appendicite (f.)	*lah-pahN-dee-seet*
asthma	l'asthme (m.)	*lahz-muh*
bronchitis	la bronchite	*lah brohN-sheet*
cancer	le cancer	*luh kahN-sehr*
cold	un rhume	*uhN rewm*
diabetes	le diabète	*luh dee-ah-beht*
dizziness	le vertige	*luh vehr-teezh*
dysentery	la dysenterie	*lah dee-sahN-tree*
exhaustion	l'épuisement (m.)	*lay-pweez-mahN*
flu	la grippe	*lah greep*
gout	la goutte	*lah goot*
heart attack	une crise cardiaque	*ewn kreez kahr-dyahk*
hepatitis	l'hépatite	*lay-pah-teet*
measles	la rougeole	*lah roo-zhohl*
mumps	les oreillons (m.)	*lay zoh-reh-yohN*
pneumonia	la pneumonie	*lah pnuh-moh-nee*
polio	la poliomyélite	*lah poh-lyoh-myay-leet*
smallpox	la variole	*lah vah-ryohl*
stroke	une attaque d'apoplexie	*ewn nah-tahk dah-poh-plehk-see*
sunstroke	une insolation	*ewn naN-soh-lah-syohN*
tetanus	le tétanos	*luh tay-tah-no*
tuberculosis	la tuberculose	*lah tew-behr-kew-lohz*

How Long Have You Felt This Way?

Your doctor will probably ask how long you've been experiencing your symptoms. The phrases in Table 20.4 suggest the number of ways you may hear the question posed and the ways in which to answer the question. The phrases vary in difficulty but they all mean the same thing. If you need to ask *how long*, the first expression is the easiest one to use.

As a Rule
Remember that *de* contracts with *le* to become *du* and with *les* to become *des*.

Table 20.3 How Long Have Your Symptoms Lasted?

Question		Answer	
Depuis quand… (*duh-pwee kahN…*)	Since when…	Depuis… (*duh-pwee*)	since
Depuis combien de temps (*duh-pwee kohN-byaN duh tahN*)	How long has (have)…been	Depuis… (*duh-pwee*)	for…
Combien de temps y a-t-il que… (*kohN-byaN duh tahN ee ah-teel kuh…*)	How long has (have)…been	Il y a + time + que… (*eel yah + time + kuh*)	for…
Ça fait combien de temps que… (*sah feh kohN-byaN duh tahN kuh*)	How long has (have)…been	Ça fait + time + que… (*sah feh + time + kuh*), Voilà + time + que (*vwah-lah + time + que*)	for…

Depuis combien de temps souffrez-vous?
duh-pwee kohN-byaN duh tahN soo-fray voo
How long have you been suffering?

Depuis deux jours.
duh-pwee duh zhoor
For two days.

Depuis quand souffrez-vous?
duh-pwee kahN soo-fray voo
Since when have you been suffering?

Depuis hier.
duh-pwee yehr
Since yesterday.

Combien de temps y a-t-il que vous souffrez?
kohN-byaN duh tahN ee ah-teel kuh voo soo-fray
How long have you been suffering?

Il y a un jour.
eel yah uhN zhoor
For one day.

Ça fait combien de temps que vous souffrez?

sah feh kohN-byaN duh tahN kuh voo soo-fray

How long have you been suffering?

Ça fait une semaine. / Voilà une semaine.
sah feh tewn suh-mehn / vwah-lah ewn suh-mehn
It's been a week. / For a week.

269

I'm Suffering

Now use all the variations to explain how long you've been suffering. Talk about a cough you've had for two weeks, a headache that has hung on for three days, or the stomach ache that has been bugging you for nearly a month.

Tell the Truth

What do you say when someone asks how you are? Do you say that you are fine or do you describe every little ache and pain you've been experiencing? When you want to express what you say or tell someone, use the irregular verb *dire* (to tell, say) in Table 20.4:

Table 20.4   The verb dire (to say, tell)

je dis	*zhuh dee*	I say, tell
tu dis	*tew dee*	you say, tell
il, elle, on dit	*eel (ehl, ohN) dee*	he (she, one) says, tells
nous disons	*noo dee-zohN*	we say, tell
vous dites	*voo deet*	you say, tell
ils, elles disent	*eel (ehl) deez*	they say, tell

As a Rule
To express *that* after *dire* use *que*:

On dit que je ne suis pas gravement malade.

ohN dee kuh zhuhn swee pah grahv-mahN mah-lahd

They say that I'm not very sick.

What Are You Doing to Yourself?

If you want to express how you feel, you can use the irregular verb *se sentir*. As you can see, *se sentir* is not just an ordinary verb because it has a special pronoun before it. This pronoun, which can act as either a direct or indirect object pronoun, is called a reflexive pronoun. A reflexive pronoun shows that the subject is performing an action upon itself. The subject and the reflexive pronoun refer to the same person(s) or thing(s): *She* hurt *herself. They* enjoy *themselves.* Sometimes, as with the verb *se sentir*, it is unclear from the English, that the verb is reflexive. Table 20.6 demonstrates how to conjugate a reflexive verb using the correct reflexive pronouns:

Table 20.5 The verb se sentir (to feel)

je **me** sens	*zhuh muh sahN*	I feel
tu **te** sens	*tew tuh sahN*	you feel
il, elle, on **se** sent	*eel, ehl, ohN suh sahN*	he, she, one feels
nous **nous** sentons	*noo noo sahN-tohN*	we feel
vous **vous** sentez	*voo voo sahN-tay*	you feel
ils, elles **se** sentent	*eel, ehl suh sahNt*	they feel

Now you can express how you feel:

I feel well.
Je me sens bien.
zhuh muh sahN byaN

I feel bad.
Je me sens mal.
zhuh muh sahN mahl

I feel better.
Je me sens mieux.
zhuh muh sahN myuh

I feel worse.
Je me sens pire.
zhuh muh sahN peer

> **As a Rule**
> Reflexive verbs can always be identified by the *se* that precedes the infinitive.

Now you're on your way out the door, but not before paying the bill (*sa note*—sah noht) and asking the following question:

> May I please have a receipt for my medical insurance?
>
> Puis-je avoir une quittance pour mon assurance maladie, s'il vous plaît?
>
> *pweezh ah-vwahr ewn kee-tahNs poor mohN nah-sew-rahNs mah-lah-dee seel voo pleh?*

Reflexive or Not?

Of course you know the feeling of returning home from a trip with a suitcase packed with gifts for family members and friends. But do you treat yourself right, too? Do you cast aside all financial concerns and treat yourself to that special souvenir you wanted? In French, when you perfom an action *upon* or *for* yourself, that action (verb) is reflexive and requires a reflexive pronoun. In many instances, you can use the same verb, without the reflexive pronoun and perform the action *upon* or *for* someone else. In these cases, an object pronoun (direct or indirect) is used.

Je *me* lave.

I wash myself.

Je lave mon chien.

I wash my dog.

Je *le* lave.

I wash him.

In the last example, the direct object pronoun *le* expresses *him*.

Je *m'*achète un sac.	J'achète un sac à Anne.	Je *lui* achète un sac.
I buy myself a bag.	I buy a bag for Ann.	I buy (for) her a bag.

In the last example, the indirect object pronoun *lui* expresses *for her*.

There are some verbs that are usually or always used reflexively. Table 20.7 provides a list of the most common reflexive verbs:

Table 20.6   Common Reflexive Verbs

s'appeler *	*sah-play*	to be named, called
s'approcher de	*sah-proh-shay duh*	to approach
s'arrêter de	*sah-ruh-tay duh*	to stop
se baigner	*suh beh-nyay*	to bathe
se blesser	*suh bleh-say*	to hurt oneself
se brosser	*suh broh-say*	to brush
se casser	*suh kah-say*	to break
se coiffer	*suh kwah-fay*	to do one's hair
se coucher	*suh koo-shay*	to go to bed
se demander	*suh duh-mahN-day*	to wonder
se dépêcher	*suh day-peh-shay*	to hurry
se déshabiller	*suh day-zah-bee-yay*	to undress
s'endormir	*sahN-dohr-meer*	to go to sleep
se fâcher (contre)	*suh fah-shay kohNtr*	to get angry (with)
s'habiller	*sah-bee-yay*	to dress
s'inquiéter de *	*saN-kee-ay-tay duh*	to worry about
se laver	*suh lah-vay*	to wash
se lever *	*suh luh-vay*	to get up
se maquiller	*suh mah-kee-yay*	to apply make-up
se mettre à	*suh mehtr ah*	to begin
s'occuper de	*soh-kew-pay duh*	to take care of
se peigner	*suh peh-nyay*	to comb

se promener *	*suh proh-mnay*	to take a walk
se rappeler *	*suh rah-play*	to recall
se raser	*suh rah-zay*	to shave
se reposer	*suh ruh-poh-zay*	to rest
se réveiller	*suh ray-veh-yay*	to wake up
se tromper	*suh trohN-pay*	to make a mistake

* These verbs all have spelling changes and must be conjugated accordingly. Refer back to Chapter 12.

Suppose you are telling someone all the things you do in the morning to prepare yourself for work or school. You might say: "I brush my teeth. I shave my mustache. I wash my hair." Since you use the word *my*, you don't have to finish the sentence with "for my-self." It's understood. In French, however, the opposite is done. The reflexive pronoun *me* (for myself) is used. It then becomes unnecessary to use the possessive adjective *my* (*mon, ma, mes*) when referring to parts of the body, since the action is obviously being performed on the subject. And so, the definite article is used instead.

Je me brosse les dents.   Il se rase la barbe.
zhuh muh brohs lay dahN   *eel suh rahz lah bahrb*
I brush my teeth.   He shaves his beard.

Position of the Reflexive Pronoun

No matter what language you study, it is not uncommon to find that word orders differ from one language to the next. In English, we generally put reflexive pronouns after verbs. You might tell a friend: "I always look at myself in the mirror before I go out." In French, this is not the case. The reflexive pronoun is placed in the same position as the other pronouns you have studied (direct, indirect, *y* and *en*)—that is, before the verb to which their meaning is tied (usually the conjugated verb). When there are two verbs, the pronoun is placed before the infinitive.

Je *me* lave.   Je ne *me lave* pas.   Je vais *me* laver.   Ne *te* lave pas!

In an affirmative command, reflexive pronouns change position and are placed immediately after the verb and are joined to it by a hyphen. *Te* becomes *toi* when it follows the verb:

Lave-*toi!*   Lavez-*vous!*

Using Reflexive Verbs

Use what you've learned so far to describe all the things you do before leaving the house in the morning. *(Je me lave.)* Then, talk about the things you do before going to bed at night. *(Je vais me laver.)*

Commanding Reflexively

You're traveling in a group and sharing a room with a few friends. You're all getting ready to go out on the town. Practice using reflexives by telling a friend (and then a group of friends) to do and not to do the following: take bath, hurry up, shave, get dressed, brush teeth, have fun.

> Example: brush hair
> Brosse-toi les cheveux!   Ne te brosse pas les cheveux!
> Brossez-vous les cheveux!   Ne vous brossez pas les cheveux!

The Least You Need to Know

> ➤ If you fall ill in another country, at the very least you'll be able to tell the doctor where you hurt.

> ➤ To express *how long* something has lasted use *depuis quand…, depuis combien de temps…, combien de temps y a-t-il que…,* or *ça fait combien de temps que….*

> ➤ Reflexive verbs, identified by the reflexive pronouns that accompany them, are used to show that the subject is acting upon itself.

Chapter 21

Oops, I Forgot...

In This Chapter

➤ Drugstore and medical items—large and small

➤ All about *venir* (to come)

➤ Speaking in the past

Chapter 20 helped express how you feel. You learned to communicate your good health as well as your aches and pains, signs and symptoms, and complaints and problems. Whether you just need a few aspirins or a prescription drug to help you feel like your good old self again, you'll want to take a trip to the drugstore. When you get there, you'll be amazed at all the other things you can purchase.

On the last trip we took, both my husband and I forgot to pack our toothbrushes, tooth-paste, and a hair brush. Imagine our dismay when we realized our blunder. However, we laughed it off and simply went to the nearest drugstore. In France, we had the choice of going to *une pharmacie* (*ewn fahr-mah-see*), *une droguerie* (*ewn drohg-ree*), or *un drugstore* (*uhN druhg-stohr*). Confused? Don't worry, this chapter will guide you to the correct spot where you can find all of your toiletry needs as well as any medication you need to take. In addition, you'll also learn how to express yourself in the past tense.

From Finding Drugs to Finding Toothpaste

Whether you are trying to obtain medication or a bottle of shampoo, you want to be sure you're in the right place in France.

A *pharmacie*, which is easily identified by a green cross above the door, sells presciption drugs, over-the-counter medications, items intended for personal hygiene, and some cosmetics. If the pharmacy is closed, there will usually be a sign on the door telling customers where they can locate a neighboring pharmacy that is open all night *(une pharmacie de garde)*.

A *droguerie* sells chemical products, paints, household cleansers and accessories (mops, brooms, buckets), and some hygiene and beauty products, but does not dispense prescriptions.

A *drugstore* resembles a small department store. You would expect to find varied sections selling personal hygiene items, books, magazines, newspapers, records, maps, guides, gifts and souvenirs, but no prescription medicine. Additionally, you may also find fast-food restaurants, a bar, and even a movie theater.

If you are indeed trying to fill a prescription, you can say to the druggist:

> I need medication.
> Il me faut des médicaments.
> *eel muh fo day may-dee-kah-mahN*

> Could you please fill this prescription (immediately)?
> Pourriez-vous exécuter (tout de suite) cette ordonnance, s'il vous plaît?
> *poo-ryay voo ehg-zay-kew-tay (toot sweet) seht ohr-doh-nahNs seel voo pleh*

If you're simply looking for something over-the-counter, Table 21.1 will help you find it. Begin by saying to a clerk: *Je cherche...* (zhuh shersh)—I'm looking for...

Table 21.1   Drugstore Items

For Men and Women		
alcohol	de l'alcool	*duh lahl-kohl*
antacid	un anti-acide	*uhN nahN-tee ah-seed*
antihistamine	un antihistaminique	*uhN nahn-tee-ees-tah-mee-neek*
antiseptic	un antiseptique	*uhN nahN-tee-sehp-teek*
aspirins	des aspirines	*day zah-spee-reen*
bandages (wound)	des pansements (m.)	*day pahNs-mahN*
brush	une brosse	*ewn brohs*
condoms	des préservatifs (m.)	*day pray-zehr-vah-teef*
cotton (absorbent)	du coton de l'ouate	*dew koh-tohN duh lwaht*

cough drops	des pastilles (f.)	*day pah-stee-y*
cough syrup	le sirop contre la toux	*luh see-roh kohNtr lah too*
deodorant	du déodorant	*dew day-oh-doh-rahN*
depilatory	un dépilatoire	*uhN day-pee-lah-twahr*
eye drops	les gouttes pour les yeux, du collyre	*lay goot poor lay zyuh, dew koh-leer*
first-aid kit	un paquet de pansement	*uhN pah-keh duh pahNs-mahN*
gauze pads	des bandes de gaze(f.)	*day bahnd duh gahz*
heating pad	un thermoplasme	*uhN tehr-moh-plahz-muh*
ice pack	une vessie de glace	*ewn veh-see duh glahs*
laxative (mild)	un laxatif (léger)	*uhN lahk-sah-teef (lay-zhay)*
mirror	un miroir	*uhN meer-whahr*
moisturizer	de la crème hydratante	*duh lah krehm ee-drah-tahNt*
mouthwash	un dentifrice	*uhN dahN-tee-frees*
nail file	une lime à ongles	*ewn leem ah ohNgl*
nose drops	des gouttes nasales (f.)	*day goot nah-zahl*
razor (electric)	un rasoir (électrique)	*uhN rah-zwahr (ay-lehk-treek)*
razor blades	des lames de rasoir (f.)	*day lahm duh rah-zwahr*
safety pins	des épingles de sûreté (f.)	*day zay-paNgl duh sewr-tay*
scissors	des ciseaux (m.)	*day see-zo*
shampoo	du shampooing	*dew shahN-pwaN*
anti-dandruff	anti-pellicules	*ahN-tee peh-lee-kewl*
shaving cream	de la crème à raser	*duh lah krehm ah rah-zay*
sleeping pills	des somnifères (m.)	*day sohm-nee-fehr*
soap (bar)	une savonette	*ewn sah-voh-neht*
talcum powder	du talc	*dew tahlk*
thermometer	un thermomètre	*uhN tehr-mo-mehtr*
tissues	des mouchoirs en papier (m.)	*day moosh-wahr ahN pah-pyay*
toothbrush	une brosse à dents	*ewn brohs ah dahN*
toothpaste	de la pâte dentifrice	*duh lah paht dahN-tee-frees*
tweezers	une pince à épiler	*ewn paNs ah ay-pee-lay*
vitamins	des vitamines (f.)	*day vee-tah-meen*

continues

Table 21.1 Continued

For Babies		
bottle	un biberon	*uhN beeb-rohN*
diapers (disposable)	des couches (disponibles) (m.)	*day koosh dees-poh-neebl*
pacifier	une sucette	*ewn sew-seht*

Special Needs

A pharmacy that specializes in *la location d'appareils médiaux* (lah loh-kah-syohn dah-pah-rehy may-dee-ko)—the rental of medical appliances—would either sell or have information concerning the items for the physically challenged featured in Table 21.2:

Où puis-je obtenir…
oo pweezh ohb-tuh-neer
Where can I get…

Table 21.2 Special Needs

cane	une canne	*ewn kahn*
crutches	des béquilles	*day bay-kee*
hearing aid	un audiophone	*uhN no-dyoh-fohn*
seeing-eye dog	un chien d'aveugle	*uhN shyaN dah-vuhgl*
walker	un déambulateur	*uhN day-ahN-bew-lah-tuhr*
wheel chair	un fauteuil roulant	*uhN fo-tuhy roo-lahN*

Have It On Hand

You've rented an apartment in Nice for the summer and you want to ensure that you have a well-stocked medicine cabinet. Using what you've learned, what should you pick up at the local *pharmacie*?

Come with Me

If you called a pharmacy to locate a certain product, you would use the verb *venir* to inform the pharmacist of when you would be *coming* to pick it up. Table 21.3 provides the forms of this irregular verb, which is similar to a shoe verb in that the *nous* and *vous* forms look like the infinitive while the forms for the other subject pronouns do not.

Table 21.3 The Verb venir (to come)

je viens	*zhuh vyaN*	I come
tu viens	*tew vyaN*	you come
il, elle, on vient	*eel (ehl, ohN) vyaN*	he, she, one comes
nous venons	*noo vuh-nohN*	we come
vous venez	*voo vuh-nay*	you come
ils, elles viennent	*eel (ehl) vyehn*	they come

Are You Living in the Past?

"Oh, no!" you exclaim to yourself. It seems you've misplaced your eye drops or you can't find your shaving cream. One reason you might go to a *pharmacie* or a *droguerie* is because you forgot something at home that you really need. In order to express what you did or did not do, you must use the past tense. In French this tense is called the *passé composé*—the compound past. The word compound is a key word because it implies that the past tense is made up of more than one part. Two elements are needed to form the *passé composé*—a helping verb, which expresses that something **has** taken place, and a past participle, which expresses exactly what the action was. In English we most often use only the past participle and not the helping verb, although it is implied. We'd say: "Oh, no! I forgot my toothbrush." (not, "Oh no! I have forgotten my toothbrush.") In French, the helping verb must be used: "Zut! J'ai oublié ma brosse à dents."

Forming the Passé Composé

The *passé composé* is formed as follows:

subject (noun or pronoun) + helping verb + past participle

As a Rule
The third person singular form *il vient* is pronounced with a nasal sound whereas the plural form *ils viennent* is not.

Il vient du Canada.
Ils viennent vite.

As a Rule
Venir + *de* (d' before a vowel or vowel sound) + infinitive can be used to express that something has just happened:

Je viens d'arriver.
I just arrived.

Nous venons de lui téléphoner.
We just called him.

The Helping Verb Avoir

Since *avoir* means to have, it is quite logical that it would serve as a helping verb. Because it is the first verb to follow the subject, the verb *avoir* must be conjugated. Refresh your memory:

j'ai	nous avons
tu as	vous avez
il, elle, on a	ils, elles ont

To this, you must now add a past participle.

Forming the Past Participle of Regular Verbs

All regular *er, ir,* and *re* verbs form their past participles differently as shown in Table 21.4. There are no changes made to the past participles of shoe verbs (*-cer, -ger, -yer, e +* consonant *+ er,* and *é +* consonant *+ er* verbs). The past participle remains the same for every subject: Jái dansé, Tu as dansé, etc.

Table 21.4   Past Participle Formation

er Verbs	*ir* Verbs	*re* Verbs
voya**ger** voya**gé**	choi**sir** choi**si**	répon**dre** répon**du**

Tu as oublié les aspirines.
tew ah oo-blee-yay lay zah-spee-reen
You forgot the aspirins.

Ils ont rendu le rasoir.
eel zohN rahN-dew luh rah-zwahr.
They returned the razor.

Le docteur a réfléchi avant d'agir.
luh dohk-tuhr ah ray-flay-shee ah-vahN dah-zheer
The doctor thought before acting.

Saying No in the Past

Since the helping verb is conjugated, this is the verb that is used to form the negative and questions. *Ne* and *pas* are placed around it:

Tu *n'*as *pas* oublié les aspirines.
tew nah pah zoo-bee-yay lay zah-spee-reen
You didn't forget (You haven't forgotten) the aspirins.

Le docteur *n'*a *pas* réfléchi avant d'agir.
luh dohk-tuhr nah pas ray-flay-shee ah-vahN dah-zheer
The doctor didn't think before acting.

Ils *n'*ont *pas* rendu le rasoir.

eel nohN pah rahN-dew luh rah-zwahr

They didn't return (They haven't returned) the razor.

Did You or Didn't You?

A trip to the doctor is often necessary and rarely pleasant when one isn't feeling up to par. In order to get well, one should cooperate. Some patients, as we all know, are very stubborn. Tell what each person did and didn't do in the past:

Example: je/parler à l'infirmière

J'ai parlé à l'infirmière.

Je n'ai pas parlé à l'infirmière.

je/remplir le formulaire   nous/acheter nos médicaments

tu/répondre franchement   elle/chercher ses pilules

tu/obéir au docteur   ils/attendre le pharmacien

Forming a Question in the Past

A question may very easily be formed by using *intonation, est-ce que,* or *n'est-ce pas:*

Ils ont rendu le rasoir?

Eel zohN rahN-dew luh rah-zwahr

Est-ce qu'ils ont rendu le rasoir?

ehs-keel zohN rahN-dew luh rah-zwahr

Ils ont rendu le rasoir, *n'est-ce pas*?

eel zohn rahN-dew luh rah-zwahr nehs pah

As a Rule
Avoid inverting with *je*. Remember to add *-t-* when inverting *il a (a-t-il)* and *elle a (a-t-elle)* in order to avoid a clash between the two pronounced vowels.

To use inversion, simply invert the *subject pronoun* and the conjugated helping verb.

As-tu oublié les aspirines?

ah-tew oo-blee-yay lay zah-spee-reen

Did you forget (Have you forgotten) the aspirins?

Le docteur, a-t-il réfléchi avant d'agir?

luh dohk-tuhr ah-teel ray-flay-shee ah-vahN dah-zheer

Did the doctor think before acting?

A-t-il rendu le rasoir?

ah-teel rahN-dew luh rah-zwahr

Did he return (Have they returned) the razor?

As a Rule
Some short adverbs may be placed before the past participle:

Elle a trop mangé.

Il a déjà répondu à la question.

Asking a Negative Question in the Past

This is a relatively easy task when not using inversion:

Ils *n'ont pas* rendu le rasoir?

eel nohN pah rahN-dew luh rah-zwahr

Pitfall
A negative construc-
tion doesn't work with
n'est-ce pas because we
cannot use a double
negative in French.

Est-ce qu'ils *n'ont pas* rendu le rasoir?

ehs-keel nohN pah rahN-dew luh rah-zwahr

Haven't they returned (Didn't they return) the razor?

Forming a negative question with inversion is a bit trickier. *Ne* and *pas* are placed around the inverted pronoun and verb:

N'as-tu pas oublié les aspirines?
nah-tew pah zoo-blee-yay lay zah-spee-reen
Did*n't* you forget (Have*n't* you forgotten) the aspirins?

As a Rule
Phrases joined by
hyphens can not be
separated.

N'a-t-elle pas acheté
ses médicaments?

Didn't she buy her medicine?

Le docteur, *n'a-t-il pas* réfléchi avant d'agir?
luh dohk-turh nah-teel pah ray-flay-shee ay-vahN dah-zheer
Did*n't* the doctor think before acting?

N'ont-ils pas rendu le rasoir?
nohN-teel pah rahN-dew luh rah-zwahr
Did*n't* they return (Have*n't* they returned) the razor?

Ask Questions

What makes a person get sick? Eating too much? Working too hard? Not following the doctor's orders? Ask both affirmative and negative questions in the past about each of these subjects:

Example: il/trop crier   A-t-il trop crié?   N'a-t-il pas trop crié?

1. nous/travailler trop dur   3. ils/perdre conscience   5. tu/trop manger

2. elle/obéir au docteur   4. vous/trop maigrir   6. il/attendre dehors longtemps

Past Participles of Irregular Verbs

Those verbs not belonging to the *er, ir,* or *re* family have irregular past participles shown in Table 21.5. We have studied some of these verbs in depth in previous chapters; others will appear in subsequent chapters as noted.

Table 21.5   Irregular Past Participles

Infinitive	Past Participle	
avoir (to have)	eu	*ew*
boire (to drink)	bu	*bew*
connaître (to be acquainted with *Chap.23)	connu	*koh-new*
devoir (to have to *Chap. 22)	dû	*dew*
dire (to say, tell)	dit	*dee*
écrire (to write *Chap. 23)	écrit	*ay-kree*
être (to be)	été	*ay-tay*
faire (to make, do)	fait	*feh*
lire (to read *Chap. 23)	lu	*lew*
mettre (to put [on])	mis	*mee*
pouvoir (to be able to)	pu	*pew*
prendre (to take)	pris	*pree*
recevoir (to receive)	reçu	*ruh-sew*
savoir (to know *Chap. 23)	su	*sew*
voir (to see)	vu	*vew*
vouloir (to want)	voulu	*voo-lew*

These verbs form the *passé composé* in the same way as regular verbs.

> Il a été au cinéma.
>
> Il n'a pas été au cinéma.
>
> A-t-il été au cinéma?
>
> N'a-t-il pas été au cinéma?

The Helping Verb être

A few common verbs use *être* instead of *avoir* as the helping verb. Most of these verbs show some kind of motion either involving going up, down, in, out, or staying at rest. To help remember which verbs use *être*, think of a house whose inhabitants are *DR. & MRS. VANDERTRAMPP*:

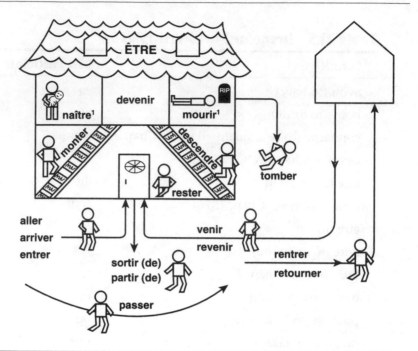

	Infinitive	Past Participle	
D	devenir (to become)	devenu*	*duh-vuh-new*
R	revenir (to come back)	revenu*	*ruh-vuh-new*
M	mourir (to die)	mort*	*mohr*
R	retourner (to return)	retourné	*ruh-toor-nay*
S	sortir (to go out)	sorti	*sohr-tee*
V	venir (to come)	venu*	*vuh-new*
A	arriver (to arrive)	arrivé	*ah-ree-vay*
N	naître (to be born)	né*	*nay*
D	descendre (to descend, go down)	descendu	*deh-sahN-dew*
E	entrer (to enter)	entré	*ahN-tray*
R	rentrer (to return)	rentré	*rahN-tray*
T	tomber (to fall)	tombé	*tohN-bay*
R	rester (to remain, stay)	resté	*rehs-tay*
A	aller (to go)	allé	*ah-lay*
M	monter (to go up, mount)	monté	*mohN-tay*

	Infinitive	Past Participle	
P	partir (to leave)	parti	*pahr-tee*
P	passer (to pass by [without a direct object])	passé	*pah-say*

All * past participles are irregular and must be memorized. All reflexive verbs use être as their helping verb. They will be discussed in the next chapter.

Of course, just like *avoir*, *être* must be conjugated. Refresh your memory:

je suis	nous sommes
tu es	vous êtes
il, elle, on est	ils, elles sont

Notice what happens, however, when we add the past participle in Table 21.6. (The * indicates that the subject may be singular or plural.)

Table 21.6   The Past Tense with être

Masculine Subjects	Feminine Subjects
je suis allé	je suis allée
tu es allé	tu es allée
il est allé	elle est allée
nous sommes allés	nous sommes allées
vous êtes allé(s)*	vous êtes allée(s)*
ils sont allés	elles sont allées

As you can see, the past participles of all verbs conjugated with *être* agree in gender (masculine or feminine [add *e*]) and number (singular or plural [add *s*]) with the subject. For a mixed group, always use the masculine forms. If the masculine past participle ends in an unpronounced consonant, the consonant will be pronounced for the feminine singular and plural forms.

Il est resté.	Elle est restée.	Ils sont restés.
eel eh reh-stay	*ehl eh reh-stay*	*eel sohN reh-stay*
He stayed.	She stayed.	They stayed.
Il est parti.	Elle est partie.	Elles sont parties.
eel eh pahr-tee	*ehl eh pahr-tee*	*ehl sohN pahr-tee*
He left.	She left.	They (f.) left.

Il est venu tôt.	Elle est venue tôt.	Ils sont venus tôt.
eel eh vuh-new to	*ehl eh vun-new to*	*eel sohN vuh-new to*
He came early.	She came early.	They came early.
Il est mort.	Elle est morte.	Elles sont mortes.
eel eh mohr	*ehl eh mohrt*	*ehl sohN mohrt*
He died.	She died.	They died.

Negatives and questions are formed in the same way with *être* as the helping verb as with *avoir*:

Elle est arrivée.

Elle *n'*est *pas* arrivée.

Est-elle arrivée?

*N'*est-elle *pas* arrivée?

What Did They Do?

Yesterday was Saturday and most people were free to do as they wished. Did they go out or hang out around the house? Tell what each person did using the correct helping verb (*avoir* or *être*) and the past participle:

1. il/faire du football
2. nous/être en ville
3. tu/voir ce film
4. je/pouvoir finir le travail
5. elles/prendre une grand décision
6. vous/lire un livre
7. ils/avoir un rendez-vous
8. elle/faire des courses
9. je (f.)/arriver chez un ami
10. nous (m.)/revenir du Canada
11. ils/rester à la maison
12. tu (f.)/partir à la campagne
13. vous (m. pl.)/aller à la plage
14. elle/sortir avec des amies
15. ils/descendre en ville
16. elles/rentrer tard

What Didn't You Do Today?

Did you ever make a list of chores, only to find at the end of the day that your list was totally unrealistic? Let's say you made a list for today and now your day has come to an end. Tell what you did and did not accomplish.

The Least You Need to Know

➤ To get prescription drugs you must go to *une pharmacie* not *un drugstore*.

➤ The past tense in French is made up of two parts: a helping verb (*avoir* or *être*) and a past participle.

Chapter 22

I Have to Make an Important Phone Call

In This Chapter

➤ How to make a phone call

➤ Proper phone etiquette

➤ What to say if there's a problem

➤ How to use reflexive verbs in the past tense

Your medicinal problems and toiletry needs were taken care of in the last chapter. You feel great and would like to let your family and friends know that everything is all right. It's time to phone home.

Placing a phone call from a foreign country to your home is always a bit of a challenge. It is often necessary to speak with an operator and most people don't realize how difficult it is to communicate by telephone with someone who speaks a different language. The luxury of relying on reading someone's body language or watching his lips for clues disappears once a telephone is introduced. This chapter will help you place a call within or outside the country you are visiting; prepare you for dealing with busy signals, wrong numbers, and other phone mishaps; and teach you how to use reflexive verbs in the past.

How Do I Use This Thing?

If you plan to call long distance from a foreign country, expect that someone will have to explain to you how to use the phone system. It is also likely that the procedures for making local calls will be different than the ones you are used to back home. One thing you will want to make sure to do is correctly express the type of call you wish to make. Table 22.1 provides you your options.

Table 22.1   Types of Phone Calls

collect call	la communication en P.C.V. *lah koh-mew-nee-kah-syohN ahN pay-say-vay*
credit card call	la communication par carte de crédit *lah koh-mew-nee-kah-syohN pahr kahrt duh kray-dee*
local call	la communication locale *lah koh-mew-nee-kah-syohN loh-kahl*
long-distance call	la communication interurbaine *lah koh-mew-nee-kah-syohN aN-tehr-ewr-behn*
out of the country call	la communication à l'étranger *lah koh-mew-nee-kah-syohN ah lay-trahN-zhay*
person-to-person call	la communication avec préavis *lah koh-mew-nee-kah-syohN ah-vehk pray-ah-vee*

To facilitate your understanding of using a telephone, you should familiarize yourself with the different parts of the phone featured in Table 22.2.

Table 22.2   The Telephone

booth	la cabine téléphonique	*lah kah-been tay-lay-foh-neek*
button	le bouton	*luh boo-tohN*
coin return button	le bouton de remboursement	*luh boo-tohN duh rahN-boors-mahN*
cordless phone	le poste sans cordon	*luh pohst sahN kohr- dohN*
portable phone	le téléphone portatif	*luh tay-lay-fohn pohr- tah-teef*
dial	le cadran	*luh kah-drahN*
keypad	le clavier à touches	*luh klah-vyay ah toosh*
phone card	la télécarte	*lah tay-lay-kahrt*
public phone	le téléphone public	*luh tay-lay-fohn pew-bleek*
receiver	le combiné, le récepteur	*luh kohN-bee-nay, luh ray-sehp-tuhr*

slot	la fente	*lah fahNt*
speaker telephone	le poste mains libres	*luh pohst maN leebr*
telephone	le téléphone	*luh tay-lay-fohn*
telephone book	l'annuaire	*lahn-wehr*
telephone number	le numéro de téléphone	*luh new-may-ro duh tay-lay-fohn*
token	le jeton	*luh zheh-tohN*
touch-tone phone	le poste à clavier (à touches)	*luh pohst ah klah-vyay (ah toosh)*

Cultural Tidbits

The telephone system in France, France Télécom, is controlled by the government agency P. T. T. (postes, télégraphes et téléphones) and provides many services to its *abonné(e)s* (ah-boh-nay)—subscribers. Almost the entire phone system is automatic (you don't need operator assistance to place local or long distance calls) and is connected to the international dialing system. Public pay phones are available in post offices, cafés, in some convenience stores, and on the streets of larger cities.

You are now ready to place a call. Be prepared for your hotel to charge exorbitant rates; that's usually the case. In France, it's an excellent idea to purchase a *Télécarte* (available at the places listed above), which enables you to buy 50 or 120 message units of calls. The number of message units required for the call depends on the total speaking time and the area phoned. More message units would be necessary to call a farther distance or to speak for longer periods of time. A magnetic strip on the Télécarte, similar to the one on a credit card, allows you to use French phones. Since the pictures on these cards vary and change over time, some of the Télécartes will one day be collector's items. Table 22.3 explains how to complete your call using a Télécarte.

Table 22.3 How to Make a Phone Call

| to call back | rappeler, retéléphoner | *rah-play (ruh-tay-lay-fohn-nay)* |
| to dial | composer (faire) le numéro | *kohN-po-zay (fehr) luh new-may-ro* |

continues

Table 22.3 Continued

to hang up (the receiver)	raccrocher, quitter	*rah-kroh-shay (kee-tay)*
to insert the card	introduire la carte	*aN-troh-dweer lah kahrt*
to know the area code	savoir l'indicatif, du pays (country), de la ville (city)	*sah-vwahr laN-dee-kah-teef dew pay-ee duh lah veel*
to leave a message	laisser un message	*leh-say uhN meh-sahzh*
to listen for the dial tone	attendre la tonalité	*ah-tahNdr lah toh-nah-lee-tay*
to pick up (the receiver)	décrocher	*day-kroh-shay*
to telephone	téléphoner, appeler par téléphone, donner un coup de fil	*tay-lay-foh-nay, ah-play pahr tay-lay-fohn, doh-nay uhN koo duh feel*

Phone Home

The front of the French yellow pages (*les pages jaunes—lay pahzh zhon*) provides a tremendous amount of information. What choices are given if you want to phone home?

Special Needs

Many telephone products are available for those with limited visual, auditory, and motor skills. Read the following description of items available to the physically challenged. Can you figure out what kinds of products can be obtained?

Pour aider les personnes handicapées qui ont des difficultés à utiliser le téléphone, cinq produits de base concernant les déficients auditifs, visuels et moteurs, sont proposés:

—le combiné téléphonique à écoute amplifiée réglable

—l'avertisseur lumineux d'appel téléphonique

—le poste téléphonique simplifié à 2 numéros préenregistrés

—la bobine (reel) magnétique pour capsule téléphonique

—les couronnes (rings, rims) à gros chiffres, à repères (with marks) ou en braille adaptables sur un poste téléphonique à cadran.

Did you say an adjustable, amplified receiver? A special light informing the user that a call was made? A simplified phone with two preregistered numbers? A close-captioned telephone? An outer ring with large numbers? A telephone dial written in braille? Good for you!

Hello? Who's This?

Telephone dialogues are a lot more difficult to conduct than face-to-face conversations, since you're not able to observe a person's facial expressions and gestures. In addition, telephones tend to distort voices and sounds. Therefore it would be wise for you to familiarize yourself with the expressions used when making and answering a phone call. Table 22.4 will show you how to begin a telephone conversation.

Table 22.4 Making a Phone Call

Calling		Answering	
allô (*ah-lo*)	hello	allô (*ah-lo*)	hello
Je suis bien...chez? (*zhuh swee byaN... shay*)	Is this the... residence?	Qui est à l'appareil? (*kee eh tah lah-pah-rehy*)	Who's calling?
C'est... (*seh...*)	It's...	Ici... (*ee-see...*)	This is...
...est là? (*... eh lah?*)	Is... in (*there*)?		
Je voudrais parler à... (*zhuh voo-dreh pahr-lay ah*)	I would like to speak to...	Ne quittez (quitte) pas. (*nuh kee-tay (keet) pah*),	Hold on,
		Un moment (*uhN moh-mahN*),	Just a moment,
		Il (Elle) n'est pas là (*eel [ehl] neh pah lah*)	He (She) is not in.

continues

Table 22.4 Continued

Calling		Answering	
Quand sera-t-il (elle) de retour? (kahN suh-rah-teel [tehl] duh ruh-toor)	When will he (she) be back?	Voulez-vous (veux-tu) laisser un message? (*voo-lay voo [vuh-tew] leh-say uhN meh-sahzh*)	Do you want to leave a message?
Je vais rappeler plus tard. (*zhuh veh rah-play plew tahr*)	I'll call back later.		

Whoops, I'm Having a Problem

There are many problems you can run into when making a phone call: a wrong number, a busy signal, a hang up. Here are some examples of phrases you may say or hear should you run into any difficulties:

As a Rule
Allô is only used on the telephone in France. To greet someone in person use *bonjour, bonsoir* (in the evening only), or *salut* to be more friendly.

Vous demandez quel numéro?
voo duh-mahN-day kehl new-may-ro?
What number are you calling?

C'est une erreur. (J'ai) Vous avez le mauvais numéro.
seh tewn eh-ruhr (zhay) voo zah-vay luh moh-veh new-may-ro
It's a mistake. (I have) You have the wrong number.

On nous a coupés.
ohN noo zah koo-pay.
We got cut off (disconnected).

Recomposez le numéro, s'il vous plaît.
ruh-kohN-poh-zay luh new-may-ro seel voo pleh
Please redial the number.

Le téléphone est en panne (hors de service).
luh tay-lay-fohn eh tahN pahn (tohr dsehr-vees)
The telephone is out of order.

J'entends mal.
zhahN-tahN mahl
I can't hear you.

Je ne peux pas vous (t') entendre.
zhuh nuh puh pah voo zahN-tahNdr (tahN-tahNdr)
I can't hear you.

Rappelez-moi (Rappelle-moi) plus tard.
rah-play (rah-pehl)-mwah plew tahr
Call me back later.

What Do You Have to Do?

Perhaps you are very busy and do not have the time to talk on the phone today. The irregular verb *devoir*, in Table 22.5, enables you to express what you have to do instead. This verb resembles a shoe verb in that the *nous* and *vous* forms look like the infinitive, while the other forms do not.

Table 22.5   The Verb devoir (to have to)

je dois	*zhuh dwah*	I have to
tu dois	*tew dwah*	you have to
il, elle, on doit	*eel (ehl, ohN) dwah*	he (she, one) has to
nous devons	*noo duh-vohN*	we have to
vous devez	*voo duh-vay*	you have to
ils, elles doivent	*eel (ehl) dwahv*	they have to

Since the verb *devoir* is followed by another verb, *devoir* is conjugated while the second verb remains in the infinitive:

Je dois raccrocher.   Ils doivent se reposer.
zhuh dwah rah-kroh-shay   *eel dwahv suh ruh-po-zay*
I have to hang up.   They have to rest.

Nous devons téléphoner à notre famille.
noo duh-vohN tay-lay-foh-nay ah nohtr fah-mee-y
We have to call our family.

I Can't Talk Now

We've all had experiences where the phone has started ringing just as we've gotten one foot out the door, or when we're up to our elbows in grease. Sometimes we're in too much of a hurry to turn around and pick it up. Tell why each of these people can't speak on the phone right now by using devoir (conjugated) + infinitive.

1. elle/réparer sa voiture   2. nous/aller en ville   3. tu/sortir

4. vous/faire des courses   5. ils/travailler   6. je/partir tout de suite

What Did You Do to Yourself

Other reasons why you didn't have time to talk on the phone may involve the use of a reflexive verb in the past. All reflexive verbs use *être* as a helping verb in the *passé composé*:

Je me suis endormi(e).   Nous nous sommes endormi(e)s.

Tu t'es endormi(e).   Vous vous êtes endormi(e)(s).

Il s'est endormi.	Ils se sont endormis.
Elle s'est endormie.	Elles se sont endormies.

In the negative and in questions the reflexive pronoun stays before the conjugated helping verb:

Elle ne *s'est* pas réveillée à temps.

S'est-elle réveillée à temps?

Ne *s'est*-elle pas réveillée à temps?

There is no agreement of the past participle if the reflexive pronoun is used as an indirect object. This happens only rarely:

Elle *s'*est lavée.

She washed *herself.*

Herself is the direct object. Since *s'* is a preceding direct object, the past participle *lavée* must agree with the preceding feminine direct object pronoun *s'.*

Elle *s'*est lavé les cheveux.

She washed her hair *herself.*

The implied *(for) herself* is the indirect object. *Hair* is the direct object. Since *s'* is a preceding indirect object and the direct object (*les cheveux*) comes after the verb, there is no agreement of the past participle *lavé* with the preceding indirect object pronoun *s'.*

Excuses

Tell why each person didn't get to make the phone call he or she was supposed to make:

1. je (f.)/se casser le bras
2. elle/se réveiller tard
3. nous(m.)/s'occuper d'autre chose
4. ils/se mettre à travailler
5. vous (f. pl.)/se lever à midi
6. tu (f.)/se coucher tôt

The Least You Need to Know

➤ Use the information in the front of the French yellow pages to guide you on how to make most of your telephone calls.

➤ A Télécarte will allow you to use most French phones.

➤ In the past tense, reflexive verbs use *être* as their helping verb.

Chapter 23

Where's the Nearest Post Office?

> **In This Chapter**
>
> ➤ Dealing with your mail
>
> ➤ All about *écrire* (to write) and *lire* (to read)
>
> ➤ The difference between *savoir* and *connaître*
>
> ➤ The imperfect and the *passé composé*

In the previous chapter you learned how to make a phone call, begin a telephone conversation, explain any difficulties with the line, and use proper phone etiquette. You also learned that public telephones are readily available in French post offices—and that's where we are off to next.

Chances are that you won't go to a post office to make a phone call, but you will visit one to send letters, postcards, and packages to family and friends. You'll learn how to send registered and special delivery letters as well as letters via air mail so that you can be assured your mail gets to its destination—and gets there fast. In your correspondence you'll be able to express facts you learned and people you became acquainted with as well as describe all the activities you participated in from the time of your arrival.

Will My Letter Get There?

You've just visited the Musée du Louvre, dined at La Tour d'Argent, and shopped at Chanel, and now you can't wait to share your experiences with your friends and family. Usually any letter sent through the mail arrives at its destination. The real question is how soon it will get there. If it's speed you want, postage rates will be higher. It costs 2.80F to send a first-class, local letter in France. At an exchange rate of 5F=\$1, American postage is a bargain. Of course no letter or package can be mailed unless you have a few mail essentials such as envelopes and stamps. Table 23.1 provides you the vocabulary you need to send your mail.

Table 23.1 Mail and Post Office Terms

address	l'addresse (f.)	*lah-drehs*
addressee	le destinataire	*luh dehs-tee-nah-tehr*
air letter	l'aérogramme (m.)	*lahy-roh-grahm*
commemorative stamp	le timbre commémoratif	*luh taNbr koh-may-moh-rah-teef*
envelope	l'enveloppe (f.)	*lahN-vlohp*
letter	la lettre	*lah lehtr*
mailbox	la boîte aux lettres	*lah bwaht o lehtr*
money order	le mandat-poste	*luh mahN-dah pohst*
package	le paquet	*luh pah-keh*
parcel	le colis	*luh koh-lee*
postcard	la carte postale	*lah kahrt pohs-tahl*
postage	l'affranchissement(m.)	*lah-frahN-shees-mahN*
postal code	le code postal (régional)	*luh kohd pohs-tahl (ray-zhoh-nahl)*
postal meter	la machine à affranchir	*lah mah-sheen ah ah-frahN-sheer*
postal worker	le facteur (m.), la factrice (f.)	*luh fahk-tuhr, lah fahk-trees*
postmark	le cachet de la poste	*luh kah-sheh duh lah pohst*
rate	le tarif	*luh tah-reef*
sender	l'expéditeur, l'expéditrice	*lehks-pay-dee-tuhr, lehks-pay-dee-trees*
sheet of stamps	la feuille de timbres	*lah fuhy duh taNbr*
slot	la fente	*lah fahNt*
stamp	le timbre	*luh taNbr*
window	le guichet	*luh gee-sheh*

Getting Service

So you've written your letter, folded it, and sealed it in an envelope. Now all you need to do is find a post office or a mailbox. If you don't know where one is located, simply ask:

Où se trouve (est) le bureau de poste le plus proche (la boîte aux lettres la plus proche)?

oo suh troov (eh) luh bew-ro duh pohst luh plew prohsh (lah bwaht o lehtr lah plew prohsh)

Where is the nearest post office (mailbox)?

Different types of letters and packages require special forms, paperwork, and special postage rates. It is important to know how to ask for the type of service you need:

Quel est le tarif de l'affranchissement...?

kehl eh luh tah-reef duh lah-frahN-shees-mahN

What is the postage rate...?

for foreign country (for overseas)	pour l'étranger	*poor lay-trahN-zhay*
for the United States	pour les États-Unis	*poor lay zay-tah zew-nee*
for an air mail letter	pour une lettre envoyée par avion	*poor ewn lehtr ahN-vwah-yay pahr ah-vyohN*
for a registered letter	pour une lettre recommandée	*poor ewn lehtr ruh-koh-mahN-day*
for a special delivery letter	pour une lettre par exprès	*poor ewn lehtr pahr ehks-preh*

Je voudrais envoyer cette lettre (ce paquet) par courrier régulier (par avion, par exprès).

zhuh voo-dreh zahN-vwah-yay seht lehtr (suh pah-keh) pahr koo-ryay ray-gew-lyay | (pahr ah-vyohN, pahr ehks-preh)

I would like to send this letter (this package) by regular mail (by air mail, special delivery).

Je voudrais envoyer ce paquet livrable contre remboursement (payable à l'arrivée).

zhuh voo-dreh zahN-vwah-yay suh pah-keh lee-vrahbl kohNtr rahN-boors-mahN (peh-yahbl ah lah-ree-vay)

I would like to send this package C.O.D.

As a Rule

Remember to put the correct form of the demonstrative adjective (*ce, cet, cette,* or *ces*) before the noun you are using.

Combien coûtent *ces* cartes postales?

Combien pèse cette lettre (ce paquet)?

kohN-byaN pehz seht lehtr (suh pah-keh)

How much does this letter (package) weigh?

Quand arrivera-t-il (elle)? Quand arriveront-ils (elles)?

kahN tah-ree-vrah teel (tehl) kahN tah-ree-vrohN teel (tehl)

When will it arrive? When will they arrive?

At the Post Office

So you finally found a post office. You walk in and immediately notice the following sign:

Les P. T. T. annonce une nouvelle série de timbres du Chunnel pour commémorer son premier anniversaire. La série sera émise en timbres de 5F et de 10F. Les timbres seront disponible dès le 3 mai dans les bureaux de poste.

You can't help it; you're an incorrigible collector. What is the post office offering? What is it celebrating? When is it available?

I Want to Send a Telegram

There's wonderful news—your daughter just had a bouncing baby boy. There's a great business deal—a big French firm wants to market your line of clothing. There's a reason to celebrate—your book of poems has been published. There's a surprise—you're getting married after a whirlwind courtship and you want to send a telegram:

Je voudrais envoyer un télégramme (en P.C.V.)
zhuh voo-dreh zahN-vwah-yay uhN tay-lay-grahm (ahN pay-say-vay)
I would like to send a telegram (collect).

Quel est le tarif par mot?
kehl eh luh tah-reef pahr mo
What is the rate per word?

Puis-je avoir un formulaire, s'il vous plaît?
pweezh ah-vwahr uhN fohr-mew-lehr seel voo pleh
May I please have a form?

Où sont les formulaires?
oo sohN lay fohr-mew-lehr
Where are the forms?

What Should I Write?

As you fill out different kinds of paperwork, you will be asked to write down a variety of information. Familiarize yourself with the irregular verb *écrire* (to write) in Table 23.2. Notice that it is necessary to add a *v* before the ending in all the plural forms. The past participle of *écrire* is *écrit* (ay-kree).

Table 23.2   The Verb écrire (to write)

j'écris	*zhay-kree*	I write
tu écris	*tew ay-kree*	you write
il, elle, on écrit	*eel(ehl, ohNn) ay-kree*	he (she, one) writes
nous écrivons	*noo zay-kree-vohN*	we write
vous écrivez	*voo zay-kree-vay*	you write
ils, elles écrivent	*eel (ehlz) ay-kreev*	they write

Can You Read This?

You will be doing a lot of reading in French whether it be forms and signs, menus, magazines, or newspapers. The irregular verb *lire* (to read) is presented in Table 23.3. It is necessary to add an *s* before the ending in all the plural forms. The past participle of *lire* is *lu* (lew).

Table 23.3   The Verb lire (to read)

je lis	*zhuh lee*	I read
tu lis	*tew lee*	you read
il , elle, on lit	*eel (ehl, ohN) lee*	he (she, one) reads
nous lisons	*noo lee-zohN*	we read
vous lisez	*voo lee-zay*	you read
ils, elles lisent	*eel (ehl) leez*	they read

Do French magazines intrigue you? Are you interested in catching up on the news? Is there a sign you don't understand? I'll never forget the time I saw a sign that read "EAU NON-POTABLE." Although I was a French major, I had never come across this phrase and "potable" was an unfamiliar English cognate to me. I knew that *eau* was water, but that was all I understood. It's a good thing I didn't take a drink. When I later looked up the phrase, I found that it meant that the water was unfit to drink. Table 23.4 features items that you may read while in France.

299

Table 23.4   Things to Read

ad	une annonce publicitaire	*ewn nah-nohNs pew-blee-see-tehr*
book	un livre	*uhN leevr*
magazine	un magazine, une revue	*uhN mah-gah-zeen, ewn ruh-vew*
menu	la carte, le menu	*lah kahrt, luh muh-new*
newspaper	un journal	*uhN zhoor-nahl*
novel	un roman	*uhN roh-mahN*
pamphlet	une brochure	*ewn broh-shewr*
receipt	le reçu, la quittance	*luh ruh-sew, lah kee-tahNs*
sign	un écriteau	*uhN nay-kree-to*
warning	un avertissement	*uhN nah-vehr-tees-mahN*

What Do You Know about This?

Do you know the name of a great French restaurant? You do? Do you know where it's located? How about the phone number? You know the owner too? He's your second cousin and he really knows how to prepare a mean bouillabaisse? That's great. To express certain facts, information, relationships, and abilities you will need the two French verbs that express *to know*—*savoir* in Table 23.5 and *connaître* in Table 23.6.

Table 23.5   The Verb savoir (to know)

je sais	*zhuh seh*	I know
tu sais	*tew seh*	you know
il, elle, on sait	*eel (ehl, ohN) seh*	he (she, one) knows
nous savons	*noo sah-vohN*	we know
vous savez	*voo sah-vez*	you know
ils, elles savent	*eel (ehl) sahv*	they know

Table 23.6   The Verb connaître (to know)

je connais	*zhuh koh-neh*	I know
tu connais	*tew koh-neh*	you know
il, elle, on connaît	*eel (ehl, ohN) koh-neh*	he (she, one) knows

nous connaissons	*noo koh-neh-sohN*	we know
vous connaissez	*voo koh-neh-say*	you know
ils connaissent	*eel koh-nehs*	they know

What's the Difference?

If there are two ways to express *to know*, how are you supposed to know when to use each one? The important thing to remember is that the French differentiate between knowing facts and how to do things (*savoir*) and knowing (being acquainted with) people, places, things, and ideas (*connaître*).

Savez-vous l'adresse?	Sait-il faire du ski?
sah-vay voo lah-drehs	*seh-teel fehr dew skee*
Do you know the address?	Does he know how to ski?

The verb *connaître* shows familiarity with a person, a place, or thing. If you can replace *to know* with *to be acquainted with* then you know to use the verb *connaître*.

Connaissez-vous Marie?	Connais-tu cette chanson?
koh-neh-say-voo mah-ree	*koh-neh-tew seht shahN-sohN*

Do you know Marie? (Are you acquainted with her?) Do you know that song? (Have you heard it? But you don't know the words?)

Notice the difference between:

Je sais ce poème.	I know this poem (by heart).
Je connais ce poème.	I know this poem. (I'm familiar with it.)

Savoir or Connaître?

Keep the differences between the two verbs in mind and you will quickly learn to use them properly. Show that you've gotten the hang of it by filling in the blanks with the correct form of *savoir* or *connaître*.

1. Ils _____ où se trouve le bureau de poste.
2. Je ne _____ pas son nom.
3. _____-vous les Dupont?
4. Nous _____ parler français.
5. _____-tu cet homme?
6. Elle _____ Paris.
7. _____-vous que je suis de Nice?
8. Nous _____ ce monument.

301

What Were You Doing?

I **was sitting** idly at a club on the boulevard St. Germain, sipping a Cointreau and watching everyone else have a good time. **I didn't know** anyone and **I was getting bored.** All of a sudden, the music *started up* and I *became* intrigued by a sexy Frenchman who **could dance** up a storm. I'm not shy so I *went over* to him and *asked* him for the next dance. I **couldn't** believe he *said* yes. We *danced* and *talked* all night and I *wound up* having a very pleasant evening. He even *asked me* for my number.

It happened recently but, nonetheless, in the past. In English, we speak or write easily in the past without giving much thought to what we are saying. In French, however, it's not that simple because there are two different past tenses: the *passé composé* and the *imperfect* (*l'imparfait*) as shown in the preceding paragraph. This tends to make speaking in the past a bit confusing. If you mistake one for the other, you'll still be understood. Sometimes either tense is correct. What's the difference? The *passé composé* expresses specific actions or events that were completed in the past whereas the *imperfect* expresses an uncompleted action or a continuing state in the past.

Formation of the Imperfect

Before going into a more detailed explanation, let's see how the imperfect is formed. For regular and irregular verbs this is done by dropping the *ons* ending from the *nous* form of the present tense and adding the following endings. Table 23.7 shows how easy this is.

je	*ais*	nous	*ions*
tu	*ais*	vous	*iez*
il, elle, on	*ait*	ils, elles	*aient*

Table 23.7   The Imperfect

er Verbs	*ir* Verbs	*re* Verbs
nous parl**ons**	nous finiss**ons**	nous répond**ons**
je parlais *(zhuh pahr-leh)*	je finissais *(zhuh fee-nee-seh)*	je répondais *(zhuh ray-pohN-deh)*
tu parlais *(tew pahr-leh)*	tu finissais *(tew fee-nee-seh)*	tu répondais *(tew ray-pohN-deh)*
il, elle, on parlait *(eel [ehl,ohN] pahr-leh)*	il, elle, on finissait *(eel [ehl, ohN] fee-nee-seh)*	il, elle, on répondait *(eel [ehl, ohN] ray-pohN-deh)*
nous parlions *(noo pahr-lyohN)*	nous finissions *(noo fee-nee-syohN)*	nous répondions *(noo ray-pohN-dyohN)*

er Verbs	*ir* Verbs	*re* Verbs
vous parliez *(voo pahr-lyay)*	vous finissiez *(voo fee-nee-syay)*	vous répondiez *(voo ray-pohN-dyay)*
ils, elles parlaient *(eel [ehl] pahr-leh)*	ils, elles finissaient *(eel [ehl] fee-nee-seh)*	ils, elles répondaient *(eel [ehl] ray-pohN-deh)*

The only verb that is irregular in the imperfect is *être:*

j'étais *(zay-teh)*   nous étions *(noo zay-tyohN)*

tu étais *(tew ay-teh)*   vous étiez *(voo zay-tyay)*

il, elle, on *(eel,ehl,ohN ay-teh)*   ils, elles *étaient (eel, ehl zay-teh)*

As a Rule
Verbs ending in *ions* in the present have an *i* before the *ions* and *iez* imperfect endings:

Example: vérifier (to check)

present   imperfect
nous vérif*ions*   nous vérif*iions*
vous vérif*iez*   vous vérif*iiez*

For all other irregular verbs in the present tense, you must know the correct *nous* form in order to form the imperfect. How good is your memory? Fill in the *nous* form for the irregular verbs in Table 23.8 and then supply the correct form of the imperfect for the subject given.

Table 23.8 The Imperfect of Irregular Verbs

avoir (to have)	nous _____	elle _____
boire (to drink)	nous _____	je _____
connaître (to be acquainted with)	nous _____	vous _____
devoir (to have to)	nous _____	tu _____
dire (to say, tell)	nous _____	ils _____
dormir (to sleep)	nous _____	nous _____
écrire (to write)	nous _____	elles _____
faire (to make, do)	nous _____	vous _____
lire (to read)	nous _____	je _____
mettre (to put [on])	nous _____	nous _____
partir (to leave)	nous _____	tu _____
pouvoir (to be able to)	nous _____	elle _____
prendre (to take)	nous _____	ils _____

continues

Table 23.8   Continued

recevoir (to receive)	nous _____	vous _____
savoir (to know)	nous _____	elles _____
sentir (to feel, smell)	nous _____	il _____
servir (to serve)	nous _____	elle _____
sortir (to go out)	nous _____	tu _____
voir (to see)	nous _____	elles _____
vouloir (to want)	nous _____	je _____

There are spelling changes in certain shoe verbs:

➤ *cer* verbs

Verbs ending in *cer* change *c* to *ç* before a or o to maintain the soft c sound. These changes occur within the shoe.

j'avançais	nous avancions
tu avançais	vous avanciez
il, elle on avançait	ils, elles avançaient

➤ *ger* verbs

Verbs ending in *ger* insert a silent *e* between g and a or o to keep the soft g sound. These changes occur within the shoe.

je mangeais	nous mangions
tu mangeais	vous mangiez
il, elle on mangeait	ils, elles mangeaient

The Passé Composé vs the Imperfect

Which should you use? And when? The *passé composé* expresses an action that was completed at a specific time in the past. Think of a camera. The *passé composé* represents an action that could be captured by an instamatic—the action happened and was completed.

The *imperfect* expresses an action that continued in the past over an indefinite period of time. Think again of a camera. The *imperfect* represents an action that could be captured by a video camera—the action continued to flow, it *was* happening, *used to* happen, or *would* (meaning *used to*) happen. The *imperfect* is a descriptive tense. Table 23.9 provides a more in-depth look at the differences between the two tenses.

Table 23.9 Comparison of the Passé Composé and the Imperfect

Passé Composé	Imperfect
1. Expresses specific actions or events that were started and completed at a definite time in the past (even if the time isn't mentioned): J'ai parlé au directeur. (I spoke to the director.)	**1.** Describes ongoing or continuous actions in the past (which may or may not have been completed): Je parlais au directeur. (I was speaking to the director.)
2. Expresses a specific action or event that occurred at a specific point in time: Hier il est sorti à midi. (Yesterday he went out at noon.)	**2.** Describes repeated or habitual actions that took place in the past: D'habitude il sortait à midi. (He usually went out at noon.)
3. Expresses a specific action or event that was repeated a stated number of times: Ils sont allés au cinéma six fois. (They went to the movies six times.)	**3.** Describes a person, place, thing, or state of mind: Nous étions contents. (We were happy.) La mer était calme. (The sea was calm.) La porte était ouverte. (The door was open.) Je voulais partir. (I wanted to leave.)

Passé Composé or Imparfait?

The weather was beautiful and I went on a picnic with a friend. Something unforeseen happened that almost ruined our day. Complete our story with the correct form of the verb in the *passé composé* or in the imperfect:

C'(être)_____ une belle journeé de printemps. Le ciel (être)_____ bleu et les oiseaux (chanter)_____. Je ne (faire)_____ pas grand'chose quand tout à coup le téléphone (sonner)_____. C'(être)_____ mon amie Barbara. Elle me (m') (demander) _____ si je (vouloir) _____ faire un pique-nique dans les bois. Je (J') (dire) _____ "Oui, volontiers!" Alors je (partir) _____ la chercher à 10 h chez elle et nous (aller) _____ au parc en voiture. En route, nous (s'arrêter) _____ à la charcuterie acheter des sandwiches et des boissons. À 11 h nous (arriver) _____ au parc. Le soleil (briller) _____ et il (faire) _____ si beau. Nous (trouver) _____ vite un endroit pour nous installer. Nous (commencer) _____ à manger nos sandwiches quand tout à coup une abeille (attaquer) _____ Barbara. Elle (crier) _____ mais elle (s'échapper) _____. Nous (passer) _____ le reste de la journée à parler de nos amis et à nous amuser. L'après-midi (être) _____ magnifique.

The Least You Need to Know

➤ *Savoir* means to know a fact or how to do something. *Connaiître* means to be acquainted with a person, place, or thing.

➤ The imperfect is usually formed by adding appropriate endings to the *nous* form (minus the *ons* ending) of the verb.

➤ The imperfect is used to describe what the subject *was* doing. The *passé composé* states what the subject *did*.

Part 5

Let's Get Down to Business

Chapter 24

I Want to Rent a Château

In This Chapter

➤ Apartments and houses

➤ Creature comforts

➤ The conditional

Although you love the luxury of a well-appointed hotel, this might not prove to be cost-efficient in the long run. You could be better off purchasing or renting an apartment, a house, a condominium, or even buying time in a time-sharing property. This chapter will teach you how to get the facilities you want and need and how to express what you would do in certain circumstances. You'll also learn how to express your plans for the future.

I Want to Rent a Château

Renting a château might be a stretch to the pocketbook but renting or buying a piece of property in a French-speaking country is not at all uncommon today. If you're even considering such a move, read Peter Mayle's *A Year in Provence*. Not only is the book an enjoyable, light read, but it may convince you that you might love to live in the south of France. So if you've decided that it's time to get daring and buy a home of your own, you will want to be able to read and understand the ads in the papers and be able to ask an agent or seller what is being offered. Whether it be a fireplace, huge closets, or central heating, Table 24.1 will help you decipher what features a house or apartment contains. Use *Il me faut* (eel muh fo)—I need—to express what you want.

Table 24.1 The House, the Apartment, the Rooms

air conditioning (central)	la climatisation (centrale)	*lah klee-mah-tee-zah-syohN (sahN-trahl)*
apartment	l'appartement (m.)	*lah-par-tuh-mahN*
attic	le grenier	*luh gruh-nyay*
backyard	le jardin	*luh zhahr-daN*
balcony	le balcon	*luh bahl-kohN*
basement	le sous-sol	*luh soo-sohl*
bathroom	la salle de bains, le W.C., la toilette	*lah sahl duh baN, luh doobl vay say, lah twah-leht*
bedroom	la chambre (à coucher)	*lah shahNbr ah koo-shay*
cathedral ceiling	le vide cathédrale	*luh veed kah-tay-drahl*
ceiling	le plafond	*luh plah-fohN*
closet	la penderie, la garde-robe	*lah pahN-dree, lah gahrd-rohb*
courtyard	la cour	*lah koor*
den	la salle de séjour, le living	*lah sahl duh say-zhoor, luh lee-veeng*
dining room	la salle à manger	*lah sahl ah mahN-zhay*
door	la porte	*lah pohrt*
elevator	l'ascenseur (m.)	*lah-sahN-suhr*
fireplace	la cheminée	*lah shuh-mee-nay*
floor	le plancher	*luh plahN-shay*
floor (story)	l'étage (m.)	*lay-tahzh*
garage	le garage	*luh gah-rahzh*
ground floor	le rez-de-chaussée	*luh rayd-sho-say*

hallway	le couloir, le vestibule	*luh koo-lwahr, luh vehs-tee-bewl*
heating	le chauffage	*luh sho-fahzh*
electric	électrique	*ay-lehk-treek*
gas	au gaz	*o gahz*
house	la maison	*lah meh-zohN*
kitchen	la cuisine	*lah kwee-zeen*
laundry room	la buanderie	*lah bwahN-dree*
lease	le bail	*luh bahy*
living room	le salon	*luh sah-lohN*
maintenance	l'entretien (m.)	*lahNtr-tyaN*
owner	le propriétaire	*luh proh-pree-yay-tehr*
private road	l'allée privée (f.)	*lah-lay pree-vay*
rent	le loyer	*luh lwah-yay*
roof	le toit	*luh twah*
room	la pièce, la salle	*lah pyehs, lah sahl*
security deposit	la caution	*lah ko-syohN*
shower	la douche	*lah doosh*
stairs	l'escalier (m.)	*lehs-kah-lyay*
storage room	le débarras	*luh day-bah-rah*
tenant	le locataire	*luh loh-kah-tehr*
terrace	la terrasse	*lah teh-rahs*
window	la fenêtre	*lah fuh-nehtr*

Cultural Tidbits

France has always enjoyed a renowned, gastronomical reputation. Surprising as it may seem, older French kitchens were somber, dark rooms hidden away in the rear of the house, almost as if they were an embarrassment. In today's French home, however, the kitchen, with its sleek, ultra-modern and dynamic design, holds a place of honor. And what do many American women pay top dollar for in their kitchens? French cabinets that contain shelves, turntables, and compartments to please and thrill even the most demanding gourmet cook.

All the Comforts of Home

You simply must have a double oven so that you can impress your French business associates with your repertoire of *nouvelle cuisine*. A microwave oven is a must and how about a dishwasher? What about furniture, a television, and a clothes washer and dryer? Just what furniture and appliances come with the property you have purchased or rented? Consult Table 24.2 for a complete list of just about everything there is. Use: *y a-t-il...?* (*ee ah-teel*, Is [Are] there...?) to ask your questions.

Table 24.2   Furniture and Accessories

armchair	un fauteuil	*uhN fo-tuhy*
bed	un lit	*uhN lee*
bookcase	une étagère	*ewn nay-tah-zhehr*
carpet	un tapis	*uhN tah-pee*
chair	une chaise, un siège	*ewn shehz, uhN syehzh*
clock	une pendule	*ewn pahN-dewl*
curtains	des rideaux (m.)	*day ree-do*
dishwasher	un lave-vaisselle	*uhN lahv veh-sehl*
dresser	une commode	*ewn koh-mohd*
dryer	un séchoir, un sèche-linge	*uhN say-shwahr, uhN sehsh-laNzh*
food processor	un robot multifunctions (m.)	*uhN roh-bo mewl-tee-fuhNk-syohN*
freezer	un congélateur	*uhN kohN-zhay-lah-tuhr*
furniture	des meubles (m.)	*day muhbl*
home appliances	des appareils-électro-ménagers (m.)	*day zah-pah-rehy ay-lehk-tro-may-nah-zhay*
lamp	une lampe	*ewn lahNp*
microwave oven	un four à micro-ondes	*uhN foor ah mee-kro ohNd*
oven	un four	*uhN foor*
refrigerator	un réfrigérateur	*uhN ray-free-zhee-rah-tuhr*
rug	un tapis	*uhN tah-pee*
shades	des stores	*day stohr*
sofa	un canapé, un divan	*uhN kah-nah-pay, uhN dee-vahN*

stereo	une chaîne stéréo	*ewn shehn stay-ray-o*
stove	une cuisinière	*ewn kwee-zee-nyehr*
table	une table	*ewn tahbl*
night	de nuit	* duh nwee*
television	une télévision	*ewn tay-lay-vee-zyohN*
large screen	à grand écran	* ah grahN day-krahN*
VCR	un magnétoscope	*uhN mah-nyay-toh-skohp*
wardrobe	une armoire (f.)	*ewn nahr-mwahr*
washing machine	une machine à laver	*ewn mah-sheen ah lah-vay*

Let's Buy Furniture

Suppose you've rented or purchased an unfurnished place. What are some services you'd expect a furniture store to provide?

Read the ad on the following page to find out what attractive offers you could expect from the company.

Mobilier de Cannes

Une valuer sûre

Nous vous garantissons gratuitement (free) vos meubles pendant 5 ans et le revêtement de sièges pendant 2 ans contre tout défaut de fabrication

Nous nous déplaçons gratuitement chez vous pour prendre des mesures, établir des devis (estimates), vous conseiller.

Nous vous offrons une garantie tous risques, gratuitement, pendant un an.

Nous reprenons vos vieux meubles lors de l'achat de meubles neufs.

Nous assurons ces services et garanties, sans supplément de prix, dans tous nos magasins, partout en France continentale.

Buying or Renting

Whether you buy or rent there are bound to be certain preferences you'd like to express or particular questions you have. Use the following phrases and expressions to help you get exactly what you want:

I'm looking for...   the classified ads, the real estate advertising section
Je cherche...   les petites annonces, la publicité immobilière
zhuh shersh   *lay puh-tee tah-nohNs, lah pew-blee-see-tay ee-moh-bee-lyehr*

a real estate agency   I would like to rent (buy)...
une agence immobilière   Je voudrais louer (acheter)...
ewn nah-zhahNs ee-moh-bee-lyehr   *zhuh voo-dreh loo-ay (ahsh-tay)*

an apartment, a condominium, a house
un appartement, un condominium, une maison
uhN nah-pahr-tuh-mahN, uhN kohN-doh-mee-nyuhm, ewn meh-zohN

Is it luxurious?   Are there break-ins?
Est-ce de haute prestation?   Y a-t-il des cambriolages?
ehs duh ot prehs-tah-syohN   *ee ah-teel day kahN-bree-oh-lahzh*

Is there time-sharing?   What is the rent?
Y a-t-il le partage du temps?   Quel est le loyer?
ee ah-teel luh pahr-tahzh dew tahN   *kehl eh luh lwah-yay*

How much is the maintenance of the apartment (house)?
Ça coûte combien l'entretien de l'appartement (de la maison)?
sah koot kohN-byaN lahNtr-tyan duh lah-pahr-tuh-mahN(duh lah meh-zohN)

Is... included?   the heat, the electricity
... est compris(e)?   le chauffage, l'électricité (f.)
...eh kohN-pree(z)   *luh sho-fahzh, lay-lehk-tree-see-tay*

the gas, the air conditioning   How much are the monthly payments?
le gaz, la climatisation   À combien sont les paiements mensuels?
luh gahz, lah klee-mah-tee-   *ah kohN-byaN sohN lay peh-mahN mahN-*
zah-syohN   *swehl*

Do I have to leave a deposit?   I'd like to take out a mortgage.
Dois-je payer une caution?   Je voudrais prendre une hypothèque.
dwahzh peh-yay ewn ko-syohN   *zhuh voo-dreh prahNdr ewn nee-poh-tehk.*

I'm going to the bank.
Je vais à la banque.
zhuh veh zah lah bahnk

Cracking the Code

Armed with a pencil and cup of coffee, you've decided to begin reading the real estate ads. Instantly, you frown and become exasperated at all the unfamiliar jargon. Table 24.3

will help you decode all the abbreviations so that you can determine what exactly is being offered.

1 *A Vendre*

Table 24.3 How to Read a Real Estate Ad

1. A vendre—for sale

2. maison de caractère—a house with character

3. 2 kms mer—2 kilometers from the sea

4. 8 kms Montpellier—8 kilometers from the city of Montpellier

5. 150m2 habitable—living space of 150.2 meters

6. 20m2 patio—a patio that measures 20.2 meters

7. grand séjour avec cheminée—a large living room with a fireplace

8. 4 chambres—4 bedrooms

9. mezannine—a landing between the ground and first floors

10. chauffage électrique—electric heat

11. the price of the house 850.000 francs—in new French currency

    85 million—in old French currency

    $140,000—in American dollars

12. 19 bis—This street has a #19 and then a second #19 called 19 bis. This is the equivalent of an address that would read 19, followed by a second address that would read 19A.

13. allée du bas Vaupereux Verrière le Buisson—the street on which the house is located

14. 91370—a regional code

15. Villeneuve-les-Maguelonne France—the city or village in which the house is located

16. tél—the phone number to call if you are interested

There's Hope for the Future

A person planning the buy or rent property in the future has to prepare for it financially. In French, the future may be expressed in one of the two following ways.

Aller + Infinitive

Since the verb *aller* means *to go*, it is understandable that it is used to express what the speaker is going to do. Since *to go* will be the first verb used, it will have to be conjugated. Refresh your memory:

> je vais, tu vas, il/elle/on va, nous allons, vous allez, ils/elles vont

The action that the speaker is going to perform will be expressed by the infinitive of the verb.

Je vais aller en ville.	Ils vont envoyer la lettre.
zhuh veh zah-lay ahN veel	*eel vohN tahN-vwah-yay lah lehtr*
I'm going to go into the city.	They are going to send the letter.

Today's Plans

Imagine that you are staying with a French family. Everyone is asleep and you want to go out and take care of some personal matters. Write a note in which you list five things you plan to do today.

The Future Tense

The future may also be expressed by changing the verb to the future tense. The future tense tells what the subject *will do* or what action *will* take place in future time. The future of regular verbs is formed by adding endings to the infinitive of the verb as shown in Table 24.4. You will notice that the endings for the future resemble the conjugation of the verb *avoir* (ai, as, a, avons, avez, ont), except for the *nous* and *vous* forms where the *av* (*nous avons, vous avez*) beginning is dropped.

Table 24.4 The Future

er Verbs	*ir* Verbs	*re* Verbs
travailler (to work)	choisir (to choose)	vendre (to sell)
will work	will choose	will sell
je travaillerai	je choisirai	je vendrai
zhuh tra-vahy-ray	*zhuh shwah-zee-ray*	*zhuh vahN-dray*
tu travailleras	tu choisiras	tu vendras
tew trah-vahy-rah	*tew shwah-zee-rah*	*tew vahN-drah*

er Verbs	*ir* Verbs	*re* Verbs
il, elle, on travaillera *eel (ehl, ohN) trah-vahy-rah*	il, elle, on choisira *eel (ehl, ohN) shwah-zee-rah*	il, elle, on vendra *eel (ehl, ohN) vahN-drah*
nous travaillerons *noo trah-vahy-rohN*	nous choisirons *noo shwah-zee-rohN*	nous vendrons *noo vahN-drohN*
vous travaillerez *voo trah-vahy-ray*	vous choisirez *voo shwah-zee-ray*	vous vendrez *vous vous vahN-dray*
ils, elles travailler*ont* *eel (ehl) trah-vahy-rohN*	ils, elles choisir*ont* *eel (ehl) shwah-zee-rohN*	ils, elles vendr*ont* *eel vahN-drohN*

The Future Tense of Shoe Verbs

Only certain shoe verbs use the changes within the shoe to form all forms of the future tense. All other shoe verbs follow the rules for future formation listed previously.

➤ Verbs ending in *yer* change *y* to *i* in all forms of the future. There is no more shoe since all verb forms are using *i* instead of *y*. Verbs ending in *ayer* may or may not change *y* to *i*. Both *je paierai* and *je payerai* are acceptable:

j'emplo*i*erai *zhahN-plwah-ray*	nous emplo*i*erons *noo zahN-plwah-rohN*
tu emplo*i*eras *tew ahN-plwah-rah*	vous emplo*i*erez *voo zahN-plwah-ray*
il, elle, on emplo*i*era *eel (ehl, ohN) ahN-plwah-rah*	ils, elles emplo*i*eront *eel (ehl) ahN-plwah-rohN*

➤ Verbs ending in *e* + *consonant* + *er* (but not *é* + *consonant* + *er*) change silent *e* to *è* in the future. Once again, there will be no more shoe, since changes are made in all forms:

j'achèterai *zhah-sheh-tray*	nous achèterons *noo zah-sheh-trohN*
tu achèteras *tew ah-sheh-trah*	vous achèterez *voo zah-sheh-tray*
il, elle, on achètera *eel (ehl0, (ohN) ah-sheht-rah*	ils, elles achèteront *eel (ehl) ah-sheh-trohN*

As a Rule
For *re* verbs, drop the final *e* from the infinitive before adding the appropriate ending.

Il m'attendra à midi.

He'll wait for me at noon.

As a Rule
Note that the *e* of the *er* infinitive remains silent in the future tense.

Je lui parlerai.

zhuh lwee pahrl-ray

I'll speak to him (her).

➤ The verbs *appeler* and *jeter*, double their consonants in the shoe in the present, and do the same in all forms of the future:

j'appellerai	nous appellerons
zhah-pehl-ray	*noo zah-pehl-rohN*
tu appelleras	vous appellerez
tew ah-pehl-rah	*voo zah-pehl-ray*
il, elle, on appellera	ils, elles appelleront
eel (ehl, ohN) ah-pehl-rah	*eel (ehl) ah-pehl-rohN*
je jetterai	nous jetterons
zhuh zheh-tray	*noo zheh-trohN*
tu jetteras	vous jetterez
tew zheh-trah	*voo zheh-tray*
il, elle, on jettera	ils, elles jetteront
eel (ehl, ohN) zheh-trah	*eel (ehl) zheh-trohN*

Verbs Irregular in the Future

The verbs in Table 24.5 have irregular stems in the future tense. Simply add the future endings to these stems to get the correct future form. Complete the chart with the correct form of the future tense:

Table 24.5   Verbs Irregular in the Future

Infinitive	Stem	
avoir (to have)	aur- (*ohr*)	tu
devoir (to have to)	devr- (*duhv*)	nous
envoyer (to send)	enverr- (*ahN-vuhr*)	il
être (to be)	ser- (*sehr*)	elles
faire (to make, do)	fer- (*fuhr*)	je
pouvoir (to be able to)	pourr- (*poor*)	vous
recevoir (to receive)	recevr- (*ruh-suhvr*)	nous
savoir (to know)	saur- (*sohr*)	ils
venir (to come)	viendr- (*vyaNdr*)	tu
voir (to see)	verr- (*vuhr*)	je
vouloir (to want)	voudr- (*voodr*)	elle

What Are the Conditions?

Would you like a big or small house? Would you like it furnished or unfurnished? How about a swimming pool? The conditional is a mood in French that expresses what the speaker *would* do or what *would* happen under certain cirumstances. The conditional of the verb *vouloir* or *aimer* is frequently used to express what the speaker *would like:*

> Je voudrais (J'aimerais) louer un appartement.
> *zhuh voo-dreh (zhehm-ray) loo-ay uhN nah-pahr-tuh-mahN*
> I would like to rent an apartment.

Formation of the Conditional

The conditional is formed with the same stem that was used to form the future, whether you are using a regular, irregular, or shoe verb. The endings for the conditional, however, are different. They are exactly the same as the endings for the imperfect. So, in other words, to form the conditional start with the future stem and add the imperfect endings shown in Table 24.6. For *re* verbs, drop the final *e* from the infinitive before adding the appropriate ending.

Table 24.6　The Conditional of Regular Verbs

er Verbs	*ir* Verbs	*re* Verbs
travailler (to work)	choisir (to choose)	vendre (to sell)
would work	would choose	would sell
je travaillerais *zhuh tra-vahy-reh*	je choisirais *zhuh shwah-zee-reh*	je vendrais *zhuh vahN-dreh*
tu travaillerais *tew trah-vahy-reh*	tu choisirais *tew shwah-zee-reh*	tu vendrais *tew vahN dreh*
il, elle, on travaillerait *eel, ehl, ohN trah-vahy-reh*	il, elle, on choisirait *eel, ehl, ohN shwah-zee-reh*	il, elle, on vendrait *eel, /ehl, ohN vahN-dreh*
nous travaillerions *trah-vahy-ryohN*	nous choisirions *noo shwah-zee-ryohN*	nous vendrions *noo vahN-dryohN*
vous travailleriez *voo trah-vahy-ryay*	vous choisiriez *voo shwah-zee-ryay*	vous vendriez *voo vahN-dryay*
ils, elles travailler*aient* *eel, ehl trah-vahy-reh*	ils, elles choisir*aient* *eel, ehl shwah-zee-reh*	ils, elles vendr*aient* *eel, ehl vahN-dreh*

The Conditional of Shoe Verbs

As a Rule
Note that the *e* of the *er* infinitive remains silent in the conditional tense.

Only certain shoe verbs use the changes within the shoe to form all forms of the conditional. All other shoe verbs follow the rules for conditional formation previously listed.

➤ Verbs ending in *yer* change *y* to *i* in all forms of the conditional. There is no more shoe since all verb forms are using *i* instead of *y*. Verbs ending in *ayer* may or may not change *y* to *i*. Both *je paierais* and *je payerais* are acceptable.

j'emplo*i*erais	nous emplo*i*erions
zhahN-plwah-reh	*noo zahN-plwah-ryohN*
tu emplo*i*erais	vous emplo*i*eriez
tew ahN-plwah-reh	*voo zahN-plwah-ryay*
il, elle, on emplo*i*erait	ils, elles emplo*i*eraient
eel (ehl, ohN) ahN-plwah-reh	*eel (ehl) ahN-plwah-reh*

➤ Verbs ending in *e + consonant + er* (but not (*é + consonant + er*)) change silent *e* to *è* in the conditional. Once again, there will be no more shoe, since changes are made in all forms.

As a Rule
The *e* had to be changed to *é* because the *e* in the *er* infinitive ending is silent in the conditional.

j'ach*è*terais	nous ach*è*terions
zhah-sheh-treh	*noo zah-sheht-ryohN*
tu ach*è*terais	vous ach*è*teriez
tew ah-sheh-treh	*voo zah-sheht-ryay*
il, elle, on ach*è*terait	ils, elles ach*è*teraient
eel (ehl, ohN) ah-sheh-treh	*eel (ehl) ah-sheh-treh*

➤ The verbs *appeler* and *jeter*, double their consonants in the shoe in the present, and do the same in all forms of the conditional:

j'appe*ll*erais	nous appe*ll*erions
zhah-pehl-reh	*noo zah-pehl-ryohN*
tu appe*ll*erais	vous appe*ll*eriez
tew ah-pehl-reh	*voo zah-pehl-ryay*
il, elle, on appe*ll*erait	ils, elles appe*ll*eraient
eel (ehl, ohN) ah-pehl-reh	*eel (ehl) ah-pehl-reh*

je jetterais	nous jetterions
zhuh zheh-treh	*noo zheht-ryohN*
tu jetterai	vous jetteriez
tew zheh-treh	*voo zheht-ryay*
il, elle, on jetterait	ils, elles jetteraient
eel (ehl, ohN) zheh-treh	*eel (ehl) zheh-treh*

Irregular Verbs in the Conditional

The verbs in Table 24.7 have irregular stems in the conditional. To complete the chart simply add the conditional endings to these stems to get the correct conditional form.

Table 24.7 The Conditional of Irregular Verbs

Infinitive	Stem	
avoir (to have)	aur- (*ohr*)	tu
devoir (to have to)	devr- (*duhv*)	nous
envoyer (to send)	enverr- (*ahN-vuhr*)	il
être (to be)	ser- (*sehr*)	elles
faire (to make, do)	fer- (*fuhr*)	je
pouvoir (to be able to)	pourr- (*poor*)	vous
recevoir (to receive)	recevr- (*ruh-suhvr*)	nous
savoir (to know)	saur- (*sohr*)	ils
venir (to come)	viendr- (*vyaNdr*)	tu
voir (to see)	verr- (*vuhr*)	je
vouloir (to want)	voudr- (*voodr*)	elle

What Would You Do?

Dreams are wonderful. Write a list of things you would do if you won the lottery tomorrow.

The Least You Need to Know

➤ The future is usually formed by adding appropriate endings to the infinitive

➤ The conditional is formed by using the future stem (usually the infinitive) and the imperfect endings.

Chapter 25

Money Matters

In This Chapter

➤ Banking terms

➤ Stock market terms

➤ The subjunctive

Chapter 24 prepared you for an extended stay in a French-speaking country. You learned the words and phrases you would need if you wanted to rent an apartment or condominium or even buy a house. You know how to describe the features you need to live comfortably whether it includes a gourmet kitchen with a breakfast nook or a living room with cathedral ceilings.

This final chapter is for anyone who must make a trip to the bank: a tourist who wants to change money, a business person with financial obligations, an investor with monetary concerns, or someone who is interested in purchasing real estate or a business. You will also learn how to express your specific, personal needs by using the subjunctive.

Get Me to the Bank

There are many reasons for a person in a foreign country to stop in a bank. The most common one is to exchange money (banks do give a very favorable rate of exhange). But perhaps you have greater goals; maybe you want to purchase real estate, set up a business, make investments, dabble in the stock market, or stay a while and open a savings and checking account. If so, then you will need to familiarize yourself with some, or all of the phrases provided in the mini-dictionary of banking terms in Table 25.1.

Cultural Tidbits

French banks can open anywhere between 8 a.m. and 9 a. m. and close between 3 p.m. and 5 p.m. Some banks close during the lunch break, which can last as long as two hours.

Table 25.1 Mini-Dictionary of Banking Terms

automatic teller machine	un distributeur automatique de billets, un guichet automatique de banque	*uhN dee-stree-bew-tuhr o-to-mah-teek duh bee-yeh, uhN gee-sheh o-to-mah-teek duh bahNk*
balance	le solde	*luh sohld*
bank	la banque, la caisse d'épargne	*lah bahNk, lah kehs day-pahr-nyuh*
bank book	le livret d'épargne	*luh lee-vreh day-pahr-nyuh*
bill	le billet, la coupure	*luh bee-yeh, lah koo-pewr*
borrow	emprunter	*ahN-pruhN-tay*
branch	la succursale	*lah sew-kewr-sahl*
cash	l'argent liquide (m.)	*lahr-zhahN lee-keed*
to cash	toucher, encaisser	*too-shay, ahN-keh-say*
cash flow	la marge brute	*lah mahrzh brewt*
cashier	la caisse	*lah kehs*
change (transaction)	le change	*luh shahnzh*
change (coins)	la monnaie	*lah moh-neh*
check	le chèque	*luh shehk*

324

checkbook	le carnet de chèques, le chéquier	*luh kahr-neh duh shehk luh shay-kyay*
checking account	le compte-chèques, le compte-courant	*luh kohNt shehk, luh kohNt koo-rahN*
credit	le crédit	*luh kray-dee*
currency	la monnaie	*lah moh-neh*
customer	le (la) client(e)	*luh (lah) klee-yahN(t)*
debt	la dette	*lah deht*
deposit	le dépôt, le versement	*luh day-po, luh vehrs-mahN*
to deposit	déposer, verser	*day-po-zay, vehr-say*
down payment	l'acompte (m.), les arrhes (f.)	*lah-kohNt, lay zahr*
employee	l'employé(e)	*lahN-plwah-yay*
endorse	endosser	*ahN-doh-say*
exchange rate	le cours du change	*luh koor dew shahNzh*
final payment	le versement de libération, le versement final	*luh vehrs-mahN duh lee-bay-rah-syohN, luh vehrs-mahN fee-nahl*
guarantee	la caution	*lah ko-syohN*
holder	le titulaire	*luh tee-tew-lehr*
installment payment	le versement échelonné	*luh verhs-mahN aysh-loh-nay*
interest	l'intérêt (m.)	*laN-tay-reh*
compound	composé	*kohN-po-zay*
interest rate	le taux d'intérêt	*luh to daN-tay-reh*
invest	placer	*plah-say*
investment	le placement	*luh plahs-mahN*
loan	l'emprunt (m.), le prêt	*lahN-pruhN, luh preh*
take out a loan	faire un emprunt	*fehr uhN nahN-pruhN*
long term	à long terme	*ah lohN tehrm*
manage	gérer	*zhay-ray*
money exchange bureau	le bureau de change	*luh bew-ro duh shahNzh*
monthly statement	le relevé mensuel	*luh ruh-lvay mahN-swehl*

continues

Table 25.1 Continued

mortgage	l'hypothèque (f.)	*lee-poh-tehk*
open account	le compte courant	*luh kohNt koo-rahN*
overdraft	le découvert	*luh day-koo-vehr*
overdrawn check	le chèque sans provision	*luh shehk sahN proh-vee-zyohN*
pay cash	payer comptant	*peh-yay kohN-tahN*
payment	le versement, le paiement	*luh vehrs-mahN, luh peh-mahN*
percentage	le pourcentage	*luh poor-sahN-tahzh*
promissory note	le billet à ordre	*luh bee-yeh ah ohrdr*
purchase	l'achat (m.)	*lah-shah*
quarter	le trimestre	*luh tree-mehstr*
receipt	le reçu, la quittance	*luh ruh-sew, lah kee-tahNs*
revenue	le revenu	*luh ruhv-new*
safe	le coffre-fort	*luh kohfr-fohr*
sale	la vente	*lah vahNt*
save	économiser, épargner	*ay-koh-noh-mee-zay, ay-pahr-nyay*
savings account	le compte d'épargne	*luh kohNt day-pahr-nyuh*
short term	à court terme	*ah koor tehrm*
to sign	signer	*see-nyay*
signature	la signatue	*lah see-nyah-tewr*
sum	la somme	*lah sohm*
teller	le caisser, la caissière	*luh keh-syay, lah keh-syehr*
total	le montant	*luh mohN-tahN*
transfer	le virement	*luh veer-mahN*
traveler's check	le chèque de voyage	*luh shehk duh vwah-yahzh*
void	annulé	*ah-new-lay*
window	le guichet	*luh gee-sheh*
withdraw	retirer	*ruh-tee-ray*

Money can also be exchanged at *un bureau de change*. These money exchanges can be found all over the streets of Paris and in other countries as well. Some offer excellent rates while others charge exorbitant commissions. It is always wise to investigate a few first.

You will notice that this receipt, from the airport where rates are not very good, shows a 15FF commission (about $2.50) for an exchange of $45. The worst exchange rates are given by hotels, so avoid them whenever possible.

```
        C C F CHANGE
           08/04/90

                        08:42 VG

Siege Social 39 Rue Bassano
Paris 8    47 23 43 99
AEROPORT PARIS ORLY


       OPERATION DE CHANGE No 004080096
       SUR CAISSE No 004

ACHAT DEVISES BILLETS

    45.00 USD
X    5.4500 /          1 =  245.30 FRF

COMMISSION FIXE           — 15.00 FRF
                          _____
                       =  230.30 FRF
```

Transactions I Need to Make

If you're planning on a trip to the bank, these phrases will be most helpful in common, everyday banking situations: making deposits and withdrawals, opening a checking account, or taking out a loan:

Quelles sont les heures d'ouverture et de fermeture?
kehl sohN lay zuhr doo-vehr-tewr ay duh fehr-muh-tewr
What are the banking hours?

Je voudrais…	faire un dépôt (un versement).
zhuh voo-dreh	*fehr un day-po (uhN vehrs-mahN)*
I would like…	make a deposit.
faire un retrait.	faire un paiement (un versement).
fehr uhN ruh-treh	*fehr un peh-mahN (uhN vehrs-mahN)*
make a withdrawal.	make a payment.
faire un emprunt.	toucher un chèque.
fehr uhN nahN-pruhN	*too-shay uhN shehk*
take out a loan.	cash a check.

ouvrir un compte.
oo-vreer uhN kohNt
open an account.

fermer un compte.
fehr-may uhN kohNt
close an account.

changer de l'argent.
shahN-zhay duh lahr-zhahN
change some money.

Est-ce que je recevrai un relevé mensuel?
ehs-kuh zhuh ruh-sehv-ray uhN ruh-lvay mahN-swehl?
Will I get a monthly statement?

Quel est le cours du change aujourd'hui?
kehl eh luh koor dew shahNzh o-zhoor-dwee
What is today's exchange rate?

Avez-vous un distributeur (guichet) automatique de billets?
ah-vay voo uhN dee-stree-bew-tuhr (gee-sheh) o-to-mah-teek duh bee-yeh
Do you have an automatic teller machine?

Comment s'en sert-on?
kohN-mahN sahN sehr-tohN
How does one use it?

Je voudrais prendre un emprunt personnel.
zhuh voo-dreh prahNdr uhN nahN-pruhN pehr-soh-nehl
I'd like to make a personal loan.

Je voudrais prendre une hypothèque.
zhuh voo-dreh prahNdr ewn nee-poh-tehk
I'd like to take out a mortgage.

Quelle est la période d'amortissement?
kehl eh lah pay-ryohd dah-mohr-tees-mahN
What is the time period of the loan?

À combien sont les paiements mensuels?
ah kohN-byaN sohN lay peh-mahN mahN-swehl
How much are the monthly payments?

Quel est le taux d'intérêt?
kehl eh luh to daN-tay-reh
What is the interest rate?

Quand faut-il commencer à faire des paiements?
kahN fo-teel koh-mahN-say ah fehr day peh-mahN
When is it necessary to start making payments?

Cultural Tidbits

One hundred centimes make up the French franc. The following denominations are currently used:

5, 10, 20—copper-colored *centime* coins

50 *centime* coin (1/2 franc), 1, 2, 5—silver-colored *franc* coins

10 *franc*—copper-colored coin

20, 50, 100, 500 *franc* bills (which are very colorful and depict historic people and monuments)

I Need More Money

Everyone needs more money. It seems that the more you have the more you want. In Chapter 20 we have seen that the verb *devoir* followed by the infinitive can be used to express need. Another way of expressing that someone *needs to* or *must* do something is to use the expression *il faut que...* (eel fo kuh)—*it is necessary that. Il faut que* and other expressions showing necessity are followed by a special verb form called the subjunctive.

The subjunctive is a mood, not a tense, and expresses wishing, wanting, emotion, and doubt. It is used after many expressions showing uncertainty and certain conjunctions, as well. Those applications will not be treated in this book.

Since the subjunctive is not a tense (a verb form indicating time), the present subjunctive can be used to refer to actions in the present or the future. The past subjunctive will not be treated in this book, since its use is limited.

In order to use the subjunctive there must be certain conditions:

➤ Two different clauses must exist with two different subjects.

➤ The two clauses must be joined by *que*.

➤ One of the clauses must show need, necessity, emotion, or doubt.

Il faut que je travaille dur.
eel fo kuh zhuh trah-vahy dewr
I (I'll) have to work hard.

Il faut que nous téléphonions à notre agent.
eel fo kuh noo tay-lay-fohn-yohN ah nohtr ah-zhahN
We (We'll) have to call our agent.

329

Il faut qu'ils se reposent.
eel fo keel suh ruh-poz
They (They'll) have to rest.

Formation of the Present Subjunctive

To form the present subjunctive of regular verbs, and some irregular verbs, as shown in Table 25.2, drop the *ent* ending from the *ils (elles)* form of the present and add these endings:

je	e	nous	ions
tu	es	vous	iez
il, elle, on	e	ils, elles	ent

Table 25.2   The Present Subjunctive of Regular Verbs

er Verbs	*ir* Verbs	*re* Verbs
parler	finir	attendre
ils parl**ent**	ils finiss**ent**	ils attend**ent**
...que je parle *kuh zhuh pahrl*	...que je finisse *kuh zhuh fee-nees*	...que j'attende *kuh zhah-tahNd*
...que tu parles *kuh tew pahrl*	...que tu finisses *kuh tew fee-nees*	...que tu attendes *que tew ah-tahNd*
...qu'il parle *keel pahrl*	...qu'il finisse *keel fee-nees*	...qu'il attende *keel ah-tahNd*
...que nous parlions *kuh noo pahr-lyohN*	...que nous finissions *kuh noo fee-nee-syohN*	...que nous attendions *kuh noo zah-tahN-dyohN*
...que vous parliez *kuh voo pahr-lyay*	...que vous finissiez *kuh voo fee-nee-syay*	...que vous attendiez *kuh voo zah-tahN-dyay*
...qu'ils parlent *keel pahrl*	...qu'ils finissent *keel fee-nees*	...qu'ils attendent *keel zah-tahNd*

As a Rule
If you look closely, you will notice that *er* verbs do not change in the subjunctive.

Shoe Verbs

Shoe verbs and verbs that are conjugated like shoe verbs follow the shoe rule when forming the subjunctive:

Boire	**ils boiv<u>ent</u>**
…que je boive	**…que nous buvions**
…que tu boives	**…que vous buviez**
…qu'il boive	…qu'ils boivent

Prendre	**ils prenn<u>ent</u>**
…que je prenne	**…que nous prenions**
…que tu prennes	**…que vous preniez**
…qu'il prenne	…qu'ils prennent

Manger	**ils man<u>gent</u>**
…que je mange	**…que nous mangions**
…que tu manges	…que vous mangiez
…qu'il mange	…qu'ils mangent

Envoyer	**ils envoi<u>ent</u>**
…que je envoie	**…que nous envoyions**
…que tu envoies	**…que vous envoyiez**
…qu'il envoie	…qu'ils envoient

Acheter	**ils achèt<u>ent</u>**
…que je achète	**…que nous achetions**
…que tu achètes	**…que vous achetiez**
…qu'il achète	…qu'ils achètent

Préférer	**ils préfèr<u>ent</u>**
…que je préfère	**…que nous préférions**
…que tu préfères	**…que vous préfériez**
…qu'il préfère	…qu'ils préfèrent

Appeler	**ils appell<u>ent</u>**
…que j'appelle	**…que nous appelions**
…que tu appelles	**…que vous appeliez**
…qu'il appelle	…qu'ils appellent

As a Rule

There are no changes to -*cer* shoe verbs in the subjunctive because *c* followed by *e* or *i* always produces a soft sound.

…que je commen*c*e

…que nous commen*c*ions

Verbs Irregular in the Subjunctive

Some verbs follow no rules and must be memorized. The ones that will prove to be most useful are:

Aller

...que j'aille (*ahy*)	**...que nous allions** (*ah-lyohN*)
...que tu ailles (*ahy*)	**...que vous alliez** (*ah-lyay*)
...qu'il aille (*ahy*)	...qu'ils aillent (*ahy*)

Vouloir

...que je veuille (*vuhy*)	**...que nous voulions** (*voo-lyohN*)
...que tu veuilles (*vuhy*)	**...que vous vouliez** (*voo-lyay*)
...qu'il veuille (*vuhy*)	...qu'ils veuillent (*vuhy*)

Faire

...que je fasse (*fahs*)	...que nous fassions (*fah-syohN*)
...que tu fasses (*fahs*)	...que vous fassiez (*fah-syay*)
...qu'il fasse (*fahs*)	...qu'ils fassent (*fahs*)

Pouvoir

...que je puisse (*pwees*)	...que nous puissions (*pwee-syohN*)
...que tu puisses (*pwees*)	...que vous puissiez (*pwee-syay*)
...qu'il puisse (*pwees*)	...qu'ils puissent (*pwees*)

Savoir

...que je sache (*sahsh*)	...que nous sachions (*sah-shyohN*)
...que tu saches (*sahsh*)	...que vous sachiez (*sah-shyay*)
...qu'il sache (*sahsh*)	...qu'ils sachent (*sahsh*)

Avoir

...que j'aie (*ay*)	...que nous ayons (*ay-yohN*)
...que tu aies (*ay*)	...que vous ayez (*ay-yay*)
...qu'il ait (*ay*)	...qu'ils aient (*ay*)

Etre	
...que je sois (*swah*)	...que nous soyons (*swah-yohN*)
...que tu sois (*swah*)	...que vous soyez (*swah-yay*)
...qu'il soit (*swah*)	...qu'ils soient (*swah*)

What Do You Have to Do?

Do you have a million things to do this afternoon? Me too. There's no escaping the necessary hassles and chores of our daily routine. Express what these people have to do using *il faut que + subjunctive:*

Example: il/travailler	Il faut qu'il travaille.
nous/préparer le dîner	je/se lever de bonne heure
elle/finir son travail	il/aller à la banque
ils/attendre un coup de téléphone	vous/être en ville à midi
je/téléphone à mon bureau	tu/acheter un cadeau
vous/accomplir beaucoup	elles/prendre un taxi
tu/descendre en ville	nous/faire les courses

Other Expressions of Need Taking the Subjunctive

Il faut que is a very common expression used with the subjunctive. There are, however, many expressions that you might use that will require the subjunctive. In order to speak properly, you should familiarize yourself with them:

It is imperative that...	Il est impératif que...	*eel eh taN-pay-rah-teef kuh*
It is important that...	Il est important que...	*eel eh taN-pohr-tahn kuh*
It is necessary that...	Il est nécessaire que...	*eel eh nay-seh-sehr kuh*
It is preferable that...	Il est préférable que...	*eel eh pray-fay-rahbl kuh*
It is urgent that...	Il est urgent que...	*eel eh tewr-zhahN kuh*
It is better that...	Il vaut mieux que...	*eel vo myuh kuh*

The Least You Need to Know

➤ French banks are modern, efficient, and provide the same services as ours.

➤ The subjunctive is used to express need.

Part 6
Answer Key

Chapter 2

Practice Makes Perfect

1. ay-reek luh pahrk
2. koh-leht lah-pyehr
3. mee-shehl luh-shyaN
4. ah-laN luh-shah
5. ah-nyehs luh-loo
6. roh-lahN lah-moosh
7. pah-treek luh-buhf
8. soh-lahNzh lah-foh-reh
9. fee-leep luh-behk
10. floh-rahNs lah-vee-nyuh
11. moh-neek luh pohN
12. doh-mee-neek lah-fohN-tehn
13. dah-nyehl la toor
14. zhahN lah vahsh
15. zhahn lah-ree-vyehr
16. ew-behr lah fluhr

Chapter 3

How Much Do You Understand Already?

1. The blouse is orange.
2. The service is horrible.
3. The excursion is impossible.
4. The guide is capable.
5. The client (customer) is certain (sure).

This Is Easy

1. The waiter helps the tourist.
2. Mom prepares soup and salad.
3. The mechanic repairs the motor.
4. The baby watches television.
5. The tourist reserves the room.
6. The guide recommends the café.
7. The employee sells the merchandise.
8. The child adores modern music.
9. The actor prefers Italian opera.
10. The family wants the comfortable hotel.

Give Your Opinions

1. Le jardin splendide.
2. La fontaine est superbe.
3. L'artiste est populaire.
4. La musique est splendide.
5. Le restaurant est élégant.
6. Le théâtre est ancien.
7. La cathédrale est magnifique.
8. L'acteur est fatigué.
9. L'hôtel est élégant.
10. L'opéra est amusant.

Are You Well Read?

1. The Savage
2. The Human Comedy
3. Artificial Paradise
4. The Stranger
5. The Infernal Machine
6. Terrible Children
7. The Vagabond
8. The Sentimental Education
9. The Pastoral Symphony
10. The Miserable People
11. Dangerous Affairs
12. The Human Condition
13. The Hypochondriac
14. Spectacle (Show)
15. Confessions
16. Nausea
17. Philosophical Letters
18. The Joy of Living

Chapter 4

Putting Your Idioms to Use I (Sample responses)

1. en voiture
2. en voiture
3. en taxi
4. en voiture
5. en avion
6. à pied
7. en bateau
8. en bateau
9. en bus
10. à pied

Putting Your Idioms to Use II

1. au revoir
2. tout de suite
3. en retard
4. de bonne heure
5. tout à l'heure
6. de temps en temps (de temps à autre)
7. du matin au soir
8. à demain

Putting Your Idioms to Use III

Restaurant	Musée		Cinéma

Le boulevard Victor Hugo

Café	Théâtre	la pâtisserie	Pharmacie

Putting Your Idioms to Use IV (Sample responses)

Bien sûr   Jamais de la vie

Bien entendu   Tant pis

D'accord   Au contraire

Putting Your Idioms to Use V

1. j'ai sommeil   3. j'ai faim   5. j'ai tort   7. j'ai raison

2. j'ai chaud   4. j'ai soif   6. j'ai trente ans 8. j'ai froid

Putting Your Idioms to Use VI (Sample responses)

1. mauvais   4. mauvais

2. du soleil   5. frais

3. beau

Chapter 5

A Proper Workout with Your Dictionary

1. feu   3. lumière   5. puits

2. renvoyer, congédier 4. allumer   6. bien

Chapter 6

He Is/She Is

1. avocate
2. dentiste
3. coiffeuse
4. facteur
5. bouchère
6. étudiant
7. chef
8. électricienne
9. infirmière
10. pompier
11. patron
12. mannequin
13. pâtissier
14. médecin
15. ouvrier

Now There's More Than One

Je vois les boutiques.

Je vois les croix.

Je vois les restaurants.

Je vois les palais.

Je vois les automobiles.

Je vois les tapis.

Je vois les magazines.

Je vois les autobuss.

Practice Those Plurals

1. les châteaux
2. les lunettes
3. les gens
4. les journaux
5. les colis
6. les palais
7. les ciseaux
8. les joujoux

What Have You Learned about Gender?

1. female
2. female/male
3. female

Chapter 7

Tu versus Vous

doctor	vous
cousin	tu
friend	tu
salesman	vous
woman	vous
two friends	vous
policeman	vous
friends	vous

Il, Ils, Elle, Elles

Charles	il
Lucie et Sylvie	elles
Berthe	elle
Pierre	il
Luc et Henri	ils
Robert et Suzette	ils
Janine, Charlotte, Michèle et Roger	ils
Paul, Roland et Annick	ils
La fête	ils
Le bal costumé	il
La musique et le décor	ils
es vêtements	ils
Le travail et le coût	ils
La cuisine et la nourriture	elles
L'ambiance	elle
L'hôte et l'hôtesse	ils

Conjugation 101

1. traverse
2. demandent
3. cherchons
4. accompagne
5. louez
6. présentent

Conjugation 102

1. finissons
2. réfléchit
3. jouissent
4. applaudis
5. réussit
6. choisis
7. agissez
8. remplissent

Conjugation 103

1. attends
2. descendent
3. perdons
4. répondez
5. entend
6. rends

Ask Me if You Can

1. Nous parlons trop?
   Nous parlons trop, n'est-ce pas?
   Est-ce que nous parlons trop?
   Parlons-nous trop?

2. Il descend souvent en ville?
   Il descend souvent en ville, n'est-ce pas?
   Est-ce qu'il descend souvent en ville?
   Descend-il souvent en ville?

3. Vous accomplissez beaucoup?
   Vous accomplissez beaucoup, n'est-ce pas?
   Est-ce que vous accomplissez beaucoup?
   Accomplissez-vous beaucoup?

4. Marie téléphone toujours à sa famille?
   Marie téléphone toujours à sa famille, n'est-ce pas?
   Est-ce que Marie téléphone toujours à sa famille?
   Marie téléphone-t-elle toujours à sa famille?

5. Tu attends toujours les autres?
   Tu attends toujours les autres, n'est-ce pas?
   Est-ce que tu attends toujours les autres?
   Attends-tu toujours les autres?

6. Les garçons jouent au tennis?
   Les garçons jouent au tennis, n'est-ce pas?
   Est-ce que les garçons jouent au tennis?
   Les garçons jouent-ils au tennis?

7. Elles écoutent le guide.
   Elles écoutent le guide, n'est-ce pas?
   Est-ce qu'elles écoutent le guide?
   Écoutent-elles le guide?

8. Luc et Anne semblent heureux?
   Luc et Anne semblent heureux, n'est-ce pas?
   Est-ce que Luc et Anne semblent heureux?
   Luc et Anne semblent-ils heureux?

Chapter 8

Ask Away (Sample responses)

1. Robert est d'où? Il voyage avec qui? Il voyage où? Comment est-ce qu'il voyage? Ils passent combien de mois en France? Où est-ce qu'ils passent deux mois? Qu'est-ce qu'ils désirent visiter? Quand retournent-ils à Pittsburgh?

2. Tu t'appelles comment? Tu es d'où? Qu'est-ce que tu cherches? Pourquoi? Tu désires pratiquer quoi? Quand parles-tu anglais? Qu'est-ce que tu adores? Comment es-tu?

Chapter 9

Express These Relationships

1. La mère de Michael

2. Le père d'André et de Marie

3. Les grands-parents des jeunes filles

4. L'oncle du garçon

5. Le grand-père de la famille

6. Le frère de l'enfant.

State Your Preference (Sample responses)

1. Mes actrices favorites sont...

2. Ma chanson favorite est...

3. Mes restaurants favoris sont...

4. Mon sport favori est...

5. Ma couleur favorite est...

6. Mon film favori est...

Can You (Sample responses)

1. Permettez-moi de me présenter. Je m'appelle...

2. Vous connaissez mon (ma)...?

3. Je vous présente mon (ma)...

4. Je suis enchanté(e).

5. Moi de même.

Using Avoir

1. as le temps
2. a l'habitude de
3. avez de la chance
4. ont l'occasion de
5. ai l'intention de
6. a lieu

Complete the Descriptions (Sample responses)

1. grande, magnfique
2. bons, intéressants
3. jeune, intelligent
4. belles, extraordinaires
5. grand, superbe

Personal Ads

1. A 25-year old French man who has charm and is romantic and cultured seeks a young French girl who likes to go out.

2. A tall, 26-year old seductive, sincere, intelligent, American male in a good financial position seeks a French girl who speaks English.

3. Francine, a 35-year old simple, calm, devoted, charming technician, who is a divorced mother, seeks a stable, courteous man who likes children, nature, and a quiet life.

4. A single, 27-year old nice, dynamic, sentimental blonde dentist seeks a young, tender girl who want a long-lasting, serious relationship.

5. Alexis, a 30-year old, elegant, charming, sincere, courteous, generous engineer seeks a single, simple, natural young woman for a lasting relationship.

6. A distinguished, refined, generous, easy-going, good-looking, 30-year old business-man who loves the finer things in life seeks to give a gratifying, envied lifestyle to a 20-25-year old woman.

Chapter 10

Airline Advice

1. Take only one carry-on into the cabin. Any dangerous articles will be removed from it at the security check.

2. Choose sturdy bags that lock. Place identification on the outside and inside of all bags. Don't put anything of value in your bags that will be placed in the hold. Carry on anything important.

Signs Everywhere

1. c   3. a   5. b

2. e   4. f   6. d

Using Commands

VERB	TU	VOUS	MEANING
aller	Va!	Allez!	Go!
continuer	Continue!	Continuez!	Continue!
descendre	Descends!	Descendez!	Go down!
marcher	Marche!	Marchez!	Walk!
monter	Monte!	Montez!	Go Up
passer	Passe!	Passez!	Pass
prendre (ch.11)	Prends!	Prenez!	Take!
tourner	Tourne!	Tournez!	Turn!
traverser	Traverse!	Traversez!	Cross!

Get There!

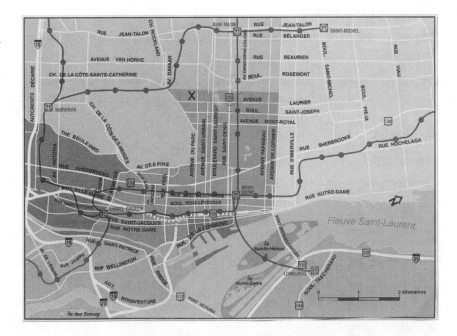

Chapter 11

Using quel

1. Quel train?
2. Quelle couleur?
3. Quelles blouses?
4. Quels journaux?
5. Quelle voiture?
6. Quelles cassettes?
7. Quel match?
8. Quels plats?

What's Your Number?

1. quarante-cinq, soixante-sept, quatre-vingt-neuf, soixante-dix-sept
2. quarante-huit, vingt et un, quinze, cinquante et un
3. quarante-six, seize, quatre-vingt-dix-huit, treize
4. quarante-trois, onze, soixante-douze, quatre-vingt-quatorze
5. quarante et un, trente-quatre, quatre-vingts, soixante et un
6. quarante-deux, quatre-vingt-cinq, cinquante-neuf, deux

Chapter 12

Just in Case

What to do in case of a fire:

If you can't control the fire you should close the door to your room and go to the exit by following the floor lights. Tell reception.

If a fire alarm sounds do the same as above. If the corridor or stairs are impassible due to smoke: stay in your room, show your presence at a window, and wait for the firefighters.

Using cer Verbs

1. commence
2. renonçons
3. remplaces
4. avance
5. annoncent

Using ger Verbs

1. range
2. déranges
3. partageons
4. nagez
5. arrangent

Using yer Verbs

1. paies (payes)
2. emploie
3. ennuyez
4. nettoie
5. essaie (essaye)

Using e+Consonant+er Verbs

1. promène
2. appelez
3. enlève
4. jette
5. amenons

Using é+Consonant+er Verbs

1. célèbre
2. Répétez
3. protégeons
4. espèrent
5. posséde

Chapter 13

The Forecast

Lille—Il fait froid. Le ciel est clair. Il fait un.

Reims—Il fait du vent. Il fait froid. Il fait trois.

Strasbourg—Il fait froid, mais beau. Il fait moins un.

Paris—Il y a des nuages. Il fait froid. Il fait du vent. Il fait cinq.

Tours—Il fait frais. Il y a des nuages. Il fait huit.

Nice—Le temps est variable et il fait du vent. Il fait quinze.

What's the Date?

1. le cinq août
2. le huit août
3. le quatorze août

4. le six août
5. le vingt et un août
6. le trente et un juillet

Using faire

1. font un voyage
2. faites la queue
3. fais venir
4. faisons une promenade

5. fait la connaissance de
6. fais des achats (emplettes)
7. fait attention
8. font une partie de

Chapter 14

Je vois un défilé

Je vois une fontaine

Je vois des animaux

Je vois des vitraux

Je vois un jardin

Je vois des fleurs

Making Suggestions (Sample responses)

1. On fait un pique-nique? Faisons un pique-nique.
2. On marche sur les quais? Marchons sur les quais.
3. On regarde les expositions? Regardons les expositions.
4. On fait une croisière? Faisons une croisière.
5. On va au jardin? Allons au jardin.

Where Are You Going?

1. Je vais en Espagne.
2. Je vais en Chine.
3. Je vais au Mexique.
4. Je vais en Russie.
5. Je vais en Italie.

6. Je vais en Angleterre.
7. Je vais en Égypte.
8. Je vais en France.
9. Je vais aux États-Unis.

Using y (Sample responses)

1. J'y vais.
2. J'y reste.
3. Je n'y passe pas mes vacances.
4. Je vais y descendre.
5. Je vais y dîner.
6. Je ne vais pas y penser.

Make a Suggestion

1. Voyageons-y. N'y voyageons pas.
2. Allons-y. N'y allons pas.
3. Restons-y. N'y restons pas.
4. Passons-y la journée. N'y passons pas la journée.
5. Assistons-y. N'y assistons pas.

Chapter 15

What Do You Put On? (Sample responses)

Work—Je mets une robe, des bas, des chaussures, un bracelet, une montre, une bague et un collier.

Beach—Je mets un bikini et des sandales.

Dinner party—Je mets une robe du soir, des bas, des chaussures et des bijoux.

Friend's house—Je mets un jean, une chemise, des chaussettes, des tennis et une montre.

Skiing—Je mets un pantalon, un pull, des chaussettes, des chaussures, un manteau, un chapeau et des gants.

Using Direct Object Pronouns (Sample responses)

1. Je l'aime.
2. Je ne les prends pas.
3. Je la choisis.
4. Je les regarde.
5. Je ne l'achète pas.
6. Je ne l'adore pas.

Using Indirect Object Pronouns

1. Offre-lui une montre.
2. Offre-leur un tableau.
3. Offre leur des cravates.
4. Offre leur des robes.
5. Offre-lui un bracelet.
6. Offre lui un pull.

Chapter 16

Where are you going?

Je vais à l'épicerie.

Je vais à la pâtisserie.

Je vais à la boucherie.

Je vais à la fruiterie.

Je vais à la poissonerie.

Je vais àu magaxin de vins.

Je vais à la confiserie.

Je vais à la crémerie.

Getting What You Want

Pourriez-vous me donner...s'il vous plaît.

1. cinq cents grammes de jambon

2. un litre de soda

3. une tablette de chocolat

4. une boîte de biscuits

5. un sac de bonbons

6. deux cent cinquante grammes de dinde

It's a Puzzle to Me

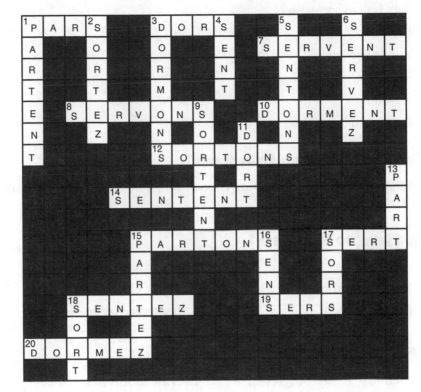

Chapter 17

Which Restaurant?

1. fine traditional cooking
2. French cooking and Lebanese specialties
3. seafood
4. Italian specialties
5. English food
6. American food, music every evening
7. French food
8. Lebanese and French specialties
9. Vietnamese and Chinese specialties
10. Vietnamese and Chinese specialities

11. Hot and cold buffet, ice cream, and pastries

12. fish, Italian specialties

13. Italian specialties

14. drinks and music

15. ice cream

16. seafood

17. businessman's special

We're Eating Out (Sample response)

Je voudrais réserver une table pour vendredi soir, à neuf heures, pour six personnes, à la terrasse, s'il vous plaît.

Using en (Sample responses)

1. J'en mange.

2. Je n'en prends pas.

3. J'en parle.

4. Je désire en manger un.

5. J'aime en préparer.

6. Je ne vais pas en essayer.

Should I or Shouldn't I?

1. N'en mange pas. Manges-en.

2. Prépares-en. N'en prépare pas.

3. Prends-en. N'en prends pas.

4. N'en choisis pas. Choisis-en.

5. Achètes-en. N'en achète pas.

How Was It? (Sample responses)

Quelles soupes délicieuses!   Quelle salade excellente!

Quel bifteck formidable!   Quels bons fromages!

Quel vin extraordinaire!   Quelle mousse magnifique!

Chapter 18

Extend an Invitation (Sample responses)

1. Tu veux aller à la montagne?

2. Vous voulez aller à la piste de ski?

3. On va au sentier?

4. Allons à la patinoire.

5. Allons à la montagne.

6. Ça te dit d'aller à l'océan?

Do You Accept or Refuse? (Sample responses)

C'est chouette.

Ça dépend.

Je n'ai pas envie.

Je regrette.

C'est une bonne idée.

Ce que tu préfères.

I Think... (Sample responses)

C'est émouvant.

C'est un bon film.

Je déteste.

C'est amusant.

C'est bidon.

C'est toujours la même chose.

How Well Do You Do (Sample responses)

1. Je parle français courrament.
2. Je joue mal du piano.
3. Je joue bien au golf.
4. Je cuisine parfaitement bien.
5. Je pense sérieusement.
6. Je travaille dur.
7. Je voyage souvent.
8. Je chante beaucoup.
9. Je danse assez bien.
10. Je nage peu.

Chapter 19

I Need These Shoes

He picks up and then delivers repaired shoes.

I Need Them Now

It promises to have your glasses ready in an hour and to sell special, high correction lenses that don't deform your face.

It's My Watch (Sample response)

Ma montre ne marche plus. Vendez-vous des piles?

I Need a New Camera

It buys (at the highest rate), sells (at the lowest rate), trades, and repairs the most famous brand cameras.

Relieve My Stress

1. nous
2. lui moi
3. toi
4. elle
5. eux
6. vous

Make a Comparison (Sample response)

Ma soeur est plus grande que moi.

Ma mère est plus vieille que moi.

Moi, je suis plus jeune qu'elle.

Mon mari, lui, il est plus patient que moi.

Chapter 20

I Don't Feel So Hot (Sample responses)

1. Je tousse. J'éternue. J'ai des frissons. J'ai de la fièvre.
2. J'éternue. J'ai une migraine.
3. J'ai mal à la cheville. J'ai de la douleur.
4. J'ai mal à la tête. J'ai du mal à dormir. J'ai de la douleur.

I'm Suffering

1. Je tousse depuis deux semaines. Ça fait deux semaines que je tousse. Il y a deux semaines que je tousse. Voilà deux semaines que je tousse.
2. J'ai mal à la tête depuis trois jours. Ça fait trois jours que j'ai mal à la tête. Il y a trois jours que j'ai mal à la tête. Voilà trois jours que j'ai mal à la tête.
3. J'ai mal au ventre depuis un mois. Ça fait un mois que j'ai mal au ventre. Il y a un mois que j'ai mal au ventre. Voilà un mois que j'ai mal au ventre.

Using Reflexive Verbs (Sample response)

1. Je me réveille. Je me lève. Je me déshabille. Je me lave. Je me baigne. Je m'habille. Je me coiffe. Je me maquille (Je me rase). Je me regarde dans la glace. Je me prépare.
2. Je vais me déshabiller. Je vais me laver. Je vais m'habiller. Je vais me coucher. Je vais m'endormir.

Commanding Reflexively

1. Baigne-toi. Ne te baigne pas. Baignez-vous. Ne vous baignez pas.

2. Dépêche-toi. Ne te dépêche pas. Dépêchez-vous. Ne vous dépêchez pas.

3. Rase-toi. Ne te rase pas. Rasez-vous. Ne vous rasez pas.

4. Habille-toi. Ne t'habille pas. Habillez-vous. Ne vous habillez pas.

5. Brosse-toi les dents. Ne te brosse pas les dents. Brossez-vous les dents. Ne vous brossez pas les dents.

6. Amuse-toi. Ne t'amuse pas. Amusez-vous. Ne vous amusez pas.

Chapter 21

Have It on Hand (Sample responses)

Il me faut des aspirines et des gouttes nasales.

Il me faut des aspirines.

Il me faut un rasor, des lames de rasoir et de la crème à raser.

Il me faut du maquillage, du fard, du rouge à lèvres et du mascara.

Il me faut du lait de magnésie.

Il me faut de la laque, du gel moussant, un peigne et une brosse.

Il me faut un antiseptique, et des pansements adjésifs.

Did You or Didn't You?

1. J'ai rempli... Je n'ai pas rempli...

2. Tu as répondu... Tu n'as pas répondu...

3. Tu as obéi... Tu n'as pas obéi...

4. Nous avons acheté... Nous n'avons pas acheté...

5. Elle a cherché... Elle n'a pas cherché...

6. Ils ont attendu... Ils n'ont pas attendu...

Ask Questions

1. Avons-nous travaillé...?   N'avons-nous pas travaillé...?
2. A-t-elle ovéi...?   N'a-t-elle ovéi...?
3. Ont-ils perdu...?   N'ont-ils perdu...?
4. Avez-vous trop maigri...?   N'avez-vous trop maigri...?
5. As-tu trop mangé...?   N'as-tu trop mangé...?
6. A-t-il attendu...?   N'a-t-il attendu...?

What Did They Do?

1. Il a fait...
2. Nous avons ête...
3. Tu as vu...
4. J'ai pu...
5. Elles ont pris...
6. Vous avez lu...
7. Ils ont eu...
8. Elle a fait...
9. Je suis arrivée...
10. Nous sommes revenus...
11. Ils sont restés...
12. Tu es partie...
13. Vous êtes allés...
14. Elle est sortie...
15. Ils sont descendus...
16. Elles sont rentrées...

What Didn't You Do Today? (Sample response)

Je ne suis pas allé(e) en ville.   Je n'ai pas regardé la télévision.

Je n'ai pas préparé le dîner.   Je n'ai pas écouté la radio.

Je ne suis pas resté(e) à la maison.   Je ne suis pas tombé(e).

Chapter 22

Phone Home

Automatically—Lift the receiver, when you get a dial tone, dial 19, you'll get another tone, give the area code for the country you are calling, give the area code of the zone you are calling, then dial the number.

With the help of a France Télécom agent—Lift the receiver, when you get a dial tone, dial 19, you'll get another dial tone, then dial 33 followed by the code for the country you are calling, a French operator will then pick up.

I Can't Talk Now

1. Elle doit réparer…
2. Nous devons aller…
3. Tu dois sortir…
4. Vous devez faire…
5. Ils doivent travailler.
6. Je dois partir…

Excuses

1. Je me suis cassé le bras.
2. Elle s'est réveillée tard.
3. Nous nous sommes occupés d'autre chose.
4. Ils se sont mis à travailler.
5. Vous vous êtes levées à midi.
6. Tu t'es couchée tôt.

Chapter 23

At the Post Office

A commemorative stamp celebrating the first anniversary of the Chunnel. It will be available May 3.

Savoir or Connaître?

1. savent
2. sais
3. connaissez
4. savons
5. connais
6. connaît
7. savez
8. connaissons

Formation of the Imperfect

avoir (to have)	nous avons	elle avait
boire (to drink)	nous buvons	je buvais
connaître (to be acquainted with)	nous connaissons	vous connaissiez
devoir (to have to)	nous devons	tu devais
dire (to say, tell)	nous disons	ils disaient
dormir (to sleep)	nous dormons	nous dormions
écrire (to write)	nous écrivons	elles écrivaient

faire (to make, do)	nous faisons	vous faisiez
lire (to read)	nous lisons	je lisais
mettre (to put [on])	nous mettons	nous mettions
partir (to leave)	nous partons	tu partais
pouvoir (to be able to)	nous pouvons	elle pouvait
prendre (to take)	nous prenons	ils prenaient
recevoir (to receive)	nous recevons	vous receviez
savoir (to know)	nous savons	elles savaient
sentir (to feel, smell)	nous sentons	il sentait
servir (to serve)	nous servons	elle servait
sortir (to go out)	nous sortons	tu sortais
voir (to see)	nous voyons	elles voyaient
vouloir (to want)	nous voulons	je voulais

Passé Composé or Imparfait?

1. était
2. était
3. chantaient
4. faisais
5. a sonné
6. était
7. a demandé
8. voulais
9. ai dit
10. suis parti(e)
11. sommes allé(e)s
12. nous sommes arrêté(e)s
13. sommes arrivé(e)s
14. brillait
15. faisait
16. avons trouvé
17. commencions
18. a attaqué
19. a crié
20. s'est échappée
21. avons passé
22. était

Chapter 24

Let's Buy Furniture

Your furniture will be guaranteed for five years and recovering for two years, should there be any problem with the manufacturing.

They will give free decorating consultation and will come to give free estimates and take measurements.

You will be given a guarantee against all risks for one year.

Your old furniture will be removed.

All guarantees are free throughout continental France.

Today's Plans (Sample responses)

1. Je vais aller en ville.
2. Je vais faire le ménage.
3. Je vais travailler.
4. Je vais étudier le français.
5. Je vais gagner beaucoup d'argent.

Verbs Irregular in the Future

INFINITIVE	STEM	
avoir (to have)	aur-	tu auras
devoir (to have to)	devr-	nous devrons
envoyer (to send)	enverr-	il enverra
être (to be)	ser-	elles seront
faire (to make, do)	fer-	je ferai
pouvoir (to be able to)	pourr-	vous pourrez
recevoir (to receive)	recevr-	nous recevrons
savoir (to know)	saur-	ils sauront
venir (to come)	viendr-	tu viendras
voir (to see)	verr-	je verrai
vouloir (to want)	voudr-	elle voudra

The Conditional of Irregular Verbs

INFINITIVE	STEM	
avoir (to have)	aur-	tu aurais
devoir (to have to)	devr-	nous devrions
envoyer (to send)	enverr-	il enverrait
être (to be)	ser-	elles seraient
faire (to make, do)	fer-	je ferais
pouvoir (to be able to)	pourr-	vous pourriez
recevoir (to receive)	recevr-	nous recevrions
savoir (to know)	saur-	ils sauraient

INFINITIVE	STEM	
venir (to come)	viendr-	tu viendrais
voir (to see)	verr- (*vuhr*)	je verrais
vouloir (to want)	voudr- (*voodr*)	elle voudrait

What Would You Do? (Sample responses)

J'irais en Europe.

Je voyagerais à travers le monde.

Je m'achèterais une grande voiture de sport.

Je louerais une villa en France.

J'aiderais les pauvres.

Chapter 25

What Do You Have to Do?

Il faut que:

1. nous préparions…
2. elle finisse…
3. ils attendent…
4. je téléphone…
5. vous accomplissiez…
6. tu descendes…
7. je me lève…
8. il aille…
9. vous soyez…
10. tu achètes…
11. elles prennent…
12. nous fassions…

Index

Symbols

C

E

G

W

X-Y-X

When You're Smart Enough to Know That You Don't Know It All

For all the ups and downs you're sure to encounter in life, The Complete Idiot's Guides give you down-to-earth answers and practical solutions.

The Complete Idiot's Guide to Learning French on Your Own
ISBN: 0-02-861043-1 ▪ $16.95

The Complete Idiot's Guide to Dating
ISBN: 0-02-861052-0 ▪ $14.95

The Complete Idiot's Guide to Hiking and Camping
ISBN: 0-02-861100-4 ▪ $16.95

The Complete Idiot's Guide to Cooking Basics
ISBN: 1-56761-523-6 ▪ $16.99

The Complete Idiot's Guide to Learning Spanish on Your Own
ISBN: 0-02-861040-7 ▪ $16.95

The Complete Idiot's Guide to Gambling Like a Pro
ISBN: 0-02-861102-0 ▪ $16.95

The Complete Idiot's Guide to Choosing, Training, and Raising a Dog
ISBN: 0-02-861098-9 ▪ $16.95

The Complete Idiot's Guide to Trouble-Free Car Care
ISBN: 0-02-861041-5 ▪ $16.95

The Complete Idiot's Guide to the Perfect Wedding
ISBN: 1-56761-532-5 ▪ $16.99

The Complete Idiot's Guide to Getting and Keeping Your Perfect Body
ISBN: 0-286105122 ▪ $16.99

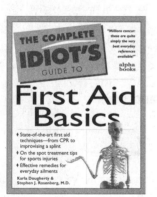

The Complete Idiot's Guide to First Aid Basics
ISBN: 0-02-861099-7 ▪ $16.95

The Complete Idiot's Guide to the Perfect Vacation
ISBN: 1-56761-531-7 ▪ $14.99

The Complete Idiot's Guide to Trouble-Free Home Repair
ISBN: 0-02-861042-3 ▪ $16.95

The Complete Idiot's Guide to Getting into College
ISBN: 1-56761-508-2 ▪ $14.95

You can handle it!